Sharp

Sharp

A Memoir

DAVID FITZPATRICK

WILLIAM MORROW

An Imprint of HarperCollinsPublishers

Small portions of this memoir were published in *New Haven Review*, *Better Health*, and *The Barely South Review*.

SHARP. Copyright © 2012 by David Fitzpatrick. All rights reserved. Printed in the United States of America. No part of this book may be used or reproduced in any manner whatsoever without written permission except in the case of brief quotations embodied in critical articles and reviews. For information address HarperCollins Publishers, 10 East 53rd Street, New York, NY 10022.

HarperCollins books may be purchased for educational, business, or sales promotional use. For information please write: Special Markets Department, HarperCollins Publishers, 10 East 53rd Street, New York, NY 10022.

FIRST EDITION

Designed by Jamie Lynn Kerner

Library of Congress Cataloging-in-Publication Data has been applied for.

ISBN 978-0-06-206402-8

12 13 14 15 16 OV/RRD 10 9 8 7 6 5 4 3 2 1

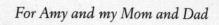

For Amy and my Mom and Dad

AUTHOR'S NOTE

This is a work of nonfiction. The events and experiences I have detailed herein are all true and have been faithfully rendered as I remember them. In some places, I've changed the names, identities, and other specifics of individuals who have played a role in my life in order to protect their privacy and integrity, and especially to protect other patients I encountered over the years, who have a right to tell their own stories if they so choose.

The conversations I re-create come from my clear recollections of them, though they are not written to represent word-for-word documentations. Instead, I've retold them in a way that evokes the real feeling and meaning of what was said, in keeping with the true essence, mood, and spirit of the exchanges.

CONTENTS

Sharp

PROLOGUE

WHEN I TRY TO FIND AN EXACT POINT WHEN LIFE WAS STEADY, blessed, and good, I always land in the summer when I was twenty years old, on Martha's Vineyard. This was three years before mental illness began to eviscerate me and left me for dead. It was before I started to slash my own body with razor blades in a fury that at times seemed otherworldly. It was before my college roommates became monsters and before recreational drugs played such a prominent role in my life. In the simplest sense, it was a golden time with high school buddies and a semiperfect girl who strolled into my viewfinder with ease and a lightness that disarmed me and made me laugh out loud.

Really, a time to soar.

That summer makes me ache with its mixture of portent and joy. What on earth would I tell my twenty-year-old self today? I know I'd want to explain the horrid facts; I'd want to protect him and warn him of the tsunami bearing down on his skull, but I'd also start with the basics. I'd begin with the positive and tell him to squeeze his shining lady tight, to taste her until his jaw ached, to go hard, strong, and brave and suck the dew out of the remaining dawns. I'd tell him to play, write, whistle, dance, and screw with abandon; to inhale the tanning oils on every luscious shoulder; to guzzle a few Rolling Rocks at dusk with friends on the Circuit Avenue porch; to gorge on watermelon and swallow the seeds; and to feel the ocean stinging his eyes and dive right back under. To bodysurf on South Beach until his fingers and toes are pruned and blue, until his chest aches. And then to count the different varieties of butterscotch reflecting off the Gay Head cliffs at sunset. Oh, to know it would soon crumble and slip through his hands—what would that do to his capacity for joy? How precious do the clear head, tight belly, and pumping thighs become during the three-mile morning jogs? Oh, how succulent is the rain pounding the steaming blacktop!

I'd tell the younger me to hang on and not give up. I'd tell him so much more, of course. I'd sit him down and ease his mind. I'd give him details, to keep him from falling into the well, into the snake pit, but there are things I don't think he'd be able to take in. Who is ready to hear that he won't be capable of articulating malaise—or that he'll carve himself up brutally and after half a decade spent bleeding, the illness, the hospitalizations, and the inertia will become addictive and almost rote? Nor could he comprehend that his overly sedated, bloated, and numbed body would morph into that of a professional mental patient, just another circuit rider jumping from one institution to the next?

When the obliterating wave finally released me in 2006, what remained was a forty-one-year-old man who was fragmented, extremely timid, and certain of only a few things, one of which was how to describe my experience of illness. I've read that Winston Churchill called it a black dog, others an enveloping fog or an avalanche of anguish, but I'd be a lot more vague and general about it and say it was an inhuman darker force that felt worse than death.

I'd call it the terror.

1

Family History

M<small>Y MOTHER ONCE TOLD ME ABOUT THE FIRST TIME HER OWN</small> mother was carried away by aides in white uniforms. "I was six when they grabbed Nannie at the top of the stairs in Somerville," she said. "As she left in the ambulance, she was screaming, 'My throat is burning, it's on fire, my throat is on fire!' "

"I'll never forget it," my mother said. She also told me about her older sister and how she, too, was institutionalized and had a couple of breakdowns while she was growing up. My mother, a young teen then, took a trolley car from Somerville to the Brighton mental ward to visit her sister. The hospital was set way back behind huge bushes and inside, up long, winding stairs. She found her sister on the eighth floor studying the traffic and trees from her barred window.

"She was dressed up in a black hat and gray veil and was wearing these delicate white gloves, as if she'd be going shopping at any moment." My mother stopped in her telling then and took a breath. "She was ranting, lost," she said. "The only thing I could do was sit with her, hold her hand. And so that's what I did—that's what I had to offer."

My mother is the only one of her siblings not to have been hospitalized.

My family tree is spiked with mental illness. It's loaded with souls who've done their institutional time—aunts, uncles, grand-mother, etc. Our clan is an unusually close group of faces—loving, supportive, truly good people. And we've taken our psychic bruises. Emotional struggle wasn't discussed much—I know that's not unusual for Irish Catholics—but we kept things especially hushed. Once in a while we picked up whispered facts involving several nervous breakdowns and institutionalizations. A grandmother's history of electric shock and numerous hos-pitalizations, one uncle running away from the pack and never wanting contact again, another who was bipolar and was treated with electric shock, and a great-great-grandfather who lived up on a hill away from his kids and wife in Ireland. His loyal wife brought meals to him each day.

My dad lost his sister to postpartum suicide when I was in sixth grade. (The child was born safely and was healthy, but my aunt died of an overdose of medication.) I remember sleeping over at her boyfriend's apartment on the Lexington Green. This was in 1976, a few years before she married. Our whole clan had gathered to celebrate the Bicentennial. I ended up wetting the boyfriend's pull-out couch, and I was so ashamed. But my aunt came over to me with a big grin that morning, her cheeks flushed and dimples blazing. She said, "Don't you worry, mister, I won't breathe a word of it to any newspaper. In a few years," she said, kissing me on the nose, "the girls in Guilford will be lining up to take you anyway—they won't care if you breathe fire, they'll just want to gobble up your smile."

She looked so beautiful that morning, that whole day, really. I couldn't ever imagine her with tears; it just didn't fit into my young brain. I assumed my aunt would zoom her way through life with rosy cheeks and marvelous dimples.

Depression also hit my father, a rock of rocks throughout my life. He struggled with it in his thirties, though he never spoke of it until later. The only example of sadness I remember from my dad is the morning after my brother Ted died, one day after he was born. I was seven, and my father rushed into our kitchen with tears and a fatigued, unshaven face. "I pray you'll never learn what it's like to lose a child," he wept, slamming cabinets. That glimpse of anguish was the first time I'd seen my father as vulnerable, and it shocked and frightened me. I obsessed about my father's expression and his words and worried that one day I, too, would fragment in the same way.

Richard Henry Fitzpatrick Jr., was six feet tall and handsome. He graduated from Boston College with a business degree and put in his time with the army at Fort Knox, Kentucky, and in Munich before getting his MBA from Michigan and joining the Ford Motor Company. He worked long hours at Ford in Missouri, Michigan, and New Jersey before purchasing Crest Lincoln Mercury in New Haven at the age of thirty-eight. Despite his long hours on the job, my dad was a near constant at my Little

League games, and I loved to hear his shouts of encouragement from the sidelines.

"Way to hang on to that ball, Fitzy," his voice ricocheted across a baseball diamond or football field. I loved having him watch me—taking jump shots or jogging beside him or even chucking the pigskin around in our front yard. My fondest memory of him is at the Cape, where he'd come up on long weekends and for two weeks in August. We had a tiny cottage there on Wild Hunter Road in Dennis, impressive in name only, I assure you. It was a periwinkle-blue shuttered saltbox we'd been coming to since I was four years old. When my father arrived after his long drives, he woke me with a kiss, and his rough sideburns chafed my cheek. His stale breath caused me to turn away slightly, but then seven hours later, the smell of thick maple bacon and blueberry pancakes sucked me downstairs. I'd see him standing in the kitchen, grinning, dazed, and exhausted, but apparently content, with a broken black spatula in hand. Those scents carry a wave of unavoidable scrumptious nostalgia for me.

MY MOTHER AND I CLICKED FROM DAY ONE. ELAINE MCNALLY Fitzpatrick sometimes looked to me like an Indian princess with long black ponytailed hair and then, a few years later, like a darker Jackie O in a yellow canvas beach chair at the Cape. She was brought up Irish Catholic and, after raising five children, she announced that she wanted to "marry and bury people," so she attended Yale Divinity School and became a United Church of Christ minister. Her early anger at the exclusion of women as priests in Catholicism later caused me to examine my own thoughts on the gender of God. My mother is an enormously warm and kind person, and it's a thrill to observe her still preaching on Sundays. She recently told me I was her favorite child—a baby who rarely cried and who slept through the nights. A handsome, popular, athletic boy who could woo almost everyone. "A child whose name means 'beloved' in Hebrew," she said.

It's no surprise that my earliest memories involve her. In a sort of dreamscape, I see her rushing into a bathroom to wipe my backside. I was three years old, I think, maybe a little older. Her colors that day were fluttering, a blurry mix of lemon and fuchsia, and she moved into the bathroom with just a hint of annoyance, reached out her arm and with two swishes of her wrist, scrubbed away the foul-smelling poo. I bent my head down to my knees, and we played peekaboo through my legs for a moment. Her flyaway onyx hair spilled down over her face briefly and then zip—everything became clean and fun and we were right side up again. She waved her finger at me and said, "You've got to start doing this for yourself, son. You're too old for Mommy to be wiping you. You're a big boy."

This saddened me—I adored this process with my mother, the frank intimacy in the bathroom. Though it wasn't so much her colors or her cascading hair that bedeviled me, it was the scent of her perfume mixed with the lingering odor of my waste. She smelled clean, subtle, nothing too heavy or obnoxious. Just fresh and very alive.

When I look back like this, I don't just envision my life, or hear the music or the voices of the time, I smell them. I breathe them in—both the sour and the florid, from the mundane to the divine. Things like buttered popcorn, begonias, sweat-drenched basketball uniforms, burnt rubber, baked apples with cinnamon, chlorine-filled pools, wet dogs, Body on Tap shampoo, my father's Borkum Riff pipe tobacco, incense at Mass, Ivory soap, Love's Baby Soft, Brut, gasoline, crispy marshmallows, fertilizer, barbecues, fear, and late spring rains. All of it.

I'M THE MIDDLE CHILD OF FIVE—THREE BOYS AND TWO GIRLS. Growing up, Laura, the eldest, was the sweet, outgoing sister who was always doing the right thing and looking out for the rest of us. Andy was a year behind Laura and unusually combative and angry with me, though friendly with the others. He was handsome and athletic, but his teeth seemed to be perpetually clenched; he was an aggressive soul, ready to pounce. I was two and a half years younger than him, more naïve than most kids my age, and utterly perplexed by his rage. Dennis was three and a half years my junior and was a bright spot in my life, a charming, gregarious soul who loved every type of music except the polka. Dennis has blue eyes like you wouldn't believe—brilliant and warm. They are not an ice blue, or a gray blue, but more of a dazzling, luminous sky blue. A ferociously optimistic hue—kind of an I'm-going-to-make-you-laugh-in-spite-of-yourself blue. Dennis was born with Williams syndrome, a genetic disease that affects intelligence; he possesses two traits common to that disease: he is genuinely upbeat and he is also very musical. Baby sister Julie didn't come around until Laura was a junior in high school and so, in many ways, she had a separate childhood from the rest of us. Dennis and I got to enjoy Julie's early years more than did Andy and Laura, who were already exploring the world. Ted, who died in 1972, lived for only a single day.

One malodorous constant of my youth was urine. Piss was the language of truth among the three brothers in the family—

each of us was a flagrant offender. And the hovering constant odor, especially during the summer heat upstairs in our unfinished second floor at the Cape, bound us together in shame for years. For a while there in the seventies and eighties, it seemed like most of my cousins who stayed over also wet the bed. As if we had some extra yellow gene tucked into our chromosomes. Even my paternal grandmother, a dynamite force of Irishness who made it to the age of ninety-eight, always ended our Thanksgiving or Christmas gatherings with the bathroom credo: "Tank out, everyone must tank out!"

Urine is anxiety, nervousness, to me, and in the extreme, it represents mental illness.

OLDER BROTHER ANDY WAS A FIRST-CLASS GOON TO ME GROWING up, a consistently angry, dogged, and harsh soul who struck and mocked with impunity. He was just a badgering, punching machine who almost always did his deeds far from the eyes of my folks and Laura. It went on for years—about thirteen of them. I know that part of my life isn't horrible or unusual. I was an upper-middle-class white boy who was contented for part of the time. But my brother's tenacity in punishing and mocking was harrowing. I was known to him by typical nicknames—one day it was "pathetic-weakest-baby-scab fag" or "you tragically deprived little fucker." Then, as he grew and matured, "vile and malodorous excrement" became a favorite, particularly when it was delivered with just the right dollop of wit.

His pursuit of me didn't cease unless there was someone else in the room. And though he never broke a bone in my body, never stabbed me or did anything too life threatening, the relentless hunt terrified me. My panic with Andy was kept in a special buried compartment of my psyche—and I didn't access it much. Surrounding that locked box were wonderful facts: an exciting new town of Guilford, Connecticut, where we moved when I was eleven years old; Little League baseball and football; new friends; and a neighborhood girl who looked like an angel when we wrestled out in front of our houses.

Even so, Andy's presence sapped a substantial part of my spirit. I told some elementary school classmates about his treatment of me, and one felt it was just normal brother stuff. I was worried, though; it seemed extra bizarre, with a laserlike focus. I wasn't sure what to call it exactly.

An older kid, a sixth grader, overheard the conversation and said, "Perhaps what your brother desires is fratricide."

"Huh?" I said, ashamed that I didn't know the word.

"It means he'll kill you," he said. "Perhaps he truly wishes to end your life."

The summer after that conversation, on Andy's twelfth birthday, we were at our cottage on Cape Cod. It was August 5 and high tide on Bay View Beach. All of a sudden, Andy jumped on me, wrestling me into the sea and shoving my head underneath the surface. I remember thinking, "This bastard's going to kill me on his freaking birthday!" He kept me there, scraping his nails into my neck as I struggled and kicked underwater. He wouldn't let me up until an older neighborhood teenager leapt on top of him and tore him off me.

"What are you doing to your brother?" he yelled. "You're going to kill him, Andy."

"Nonsense," my brother smiled, pinching the back of my neck. "Just having fun with my little scab, David."

He seemed to have an early fetish for using the terms "scab"

and "vile" together in the same sentence. Like when I was playing catch with my Uncle Chuck at the Cape. Andy picked up a
rock and threw it at me. It clunked off my chest, and my uncle
looked at him, aghast. "What the hell was that?" he said. "You
attacked your brother—he wasn't doing a thing to you."

"He's vile, Chuck," he said, shrugging. "When will you
learn—he's vile and scabby."

"You can't do that to a person, especially your brother," he said.

"Hmm," he said, walking away. "That's interesting because I
thought I just did."

ONCE I WAS HIDING FROM HIM IN THE BASEMENT ON CHIMNEY
Corner Circle, a charming but drafty house on Long Island
Sound that we rented when we first moved to Connecticut from
New Jersey. I was in fifth grade and Andy in eighth; Laura was
in high school and Dennis was in special ed at Cox Elemen-
tary. Julie was in utero at the time. My parents had moved us to
Guilford so Dad could start his car dealership in New Haven.
Our gray triple-decker had unsteady windows that rattled like
teacups when the gusts came in off the water.

I gazed out at the surf from the basement windows, watching
it rush into and over the seawall, making the wet rocks shine the
color of bone, the color of flesh, until, as the sun disappeared,
they turned pewter and, finally, black. The spray from the sea hit
our faces straight on when we stepped into the backyard. Downstairs, in between the washer and the dryer, I had found a simple
nook, a secret spot safe from Andy. I liked to go there and listen
to myself breathe where no one could watch me, where I could
sit in the corner and study the ocean, the light.

I imagined wondrous, fantastical things waiting beyond the wet stone. Perhaps cartwheeling, giggling nymphs or teams of naked girls yearning to dance and frolic with me and only me. They'd tickle my belly with their toes, and their long chestnut hair would tumble to the ground and spread into the earth, where candied tulips would sprout up high and deliver me over rough waters to a safe, strong fort far from my brother.

It was early March, one particular blustery, gray day, when Andy discovered me. He had heard me use the bathroom or something. He ran down the stairs and rushed me, grabbing my neck and throwing me into a door that led to the backyard. I should have run, gone to find Laura or my brother Dennis, but after more of his pushes and curses, I was fed up. I turned and threw a punch at him, striking him in the Adam's apple. His response was a cackle.

"Oh, you're approaching sixth grade now, and you still think you can fight me, Mrs. Vile Excrement?" he said, laughing. "You're a silly bitch." He kicked my ass then, punching me repeatedly. Not too much, though—he was forever stealthy about the physical hurting, the harassing. He knew he'd be in trouble if he laid into me too much, if he left too many marks. Each of the battles I had with my older brother was brief and intense; I put up the best I could, but he was larger, and he hit harder. But I always fought back—I wasn't going to allow him to walk over me.

That day in the basement, though, was different. It was during that skirmish that I decided to accept the punches for the first time. Change the strategy. I remember glaring at him and thinking, *Don't fight back, David, let it come, let the shit have his fun.* I went limp and gazed at him like some modern-day St. Sebastian as he clocked me a little more. Then he hovered over me and held his fist up in the air as if he was about to strike again, allowing spittle to drop down near my face and then sucking it back into his mouth.

On that day, I retreated fully and completely inside myself and waited. The more Andy watched me, the more comfortable I became with this change. I found a kind of strength by doing nothing. It was the first time I saw . . . a confused look, possibly defeat, pass across Andy's brown eyes. I had him on that March day in the basement. *I beat him.* He got his jollies only if I pushed back, only if I struggled and tried to defend myself. It made it easier for him when I grew combative, angry. What fun is it to mock and punch someone if they don't struggle with you, if they just sit there like some piece of vile, malodorous excrement? What the hell is the purpose?

This passivity eventually stopped him more than any of my punches. No defense became my best offense and, eventually, a pattern developed in our back-and-forth. He hit and I endured. But he didn't tear into me with that same ferocity. He did it for a while then made a frustrated face and walked away.

One evening after I pulled the St. Sebastian defense on him, I awoke in the middle of the night, and I have a vivid memory of him standing above me on my bed. He was wearing his underwear, and he waved a miniature flashlight in my eyes. He'd begun using three words—scabby, vile shit—to describe me, and I'm sure I heard them that night.

"Go to bed, Andy," I said. "Get back to your room or I'll tell."

"You think they care?" he said, nudging my belly with his toes. "You think anybody cares?"

"Screw you," I said.

That night, and so many others, is a swirl of Andy's insults and degradations. He was very creative in his ways of putting me down.

"Stop it," I said, kicking at him.

"Oh, poor, forgotten baby," he said.

"Leave me alone, ass-face," I said.

"Ooh," he said, chuckling and stepping down from the bed. "A curse word from David— stop the presses."

I yelled out and eventually my father stumbled wearily into my room. "Go to your room, for God's sake, Andy, and stop teasing—leave your brother alone."

"Of course, Dad," he said. "Goodnight. Sleep well."

The next day I looked up his two favorite words in the dictionary. Vile was "morally despicable or abhorrent," according to the Webster's pocket edition. And scab was "a crust of blood and serum over a wound" or "a detestable person."

Strangely, there were times when Andy and I got along and shared fun moments, especially in neighborhood team sports. We played tackle football or Wiffle ball with friends, and we laughed and things seemed decent, almost normal. One time when we were living in Missouri, he won a Burger King contest to be the batboy for the St. Louis Cardinals, and he let me tag along in the dugout. It felt special, sweet. Each of the players signed baseballs and bats for us, and they announced Andy's name over the loudspeaker. His face beamed that night. But when we were alone with no one around, it was another story entirely.

My school life in Guilford was fun, bright, and filled with eager young faces besides mine: they affirmed me, laughed at my jokes, played sports, and rode bikes with me around the neighborhood, our knuckles freezing in the autumn chill. Then I'd come home, and Andy would be there, lurking. There was a schizoid quality to my existence—on one side was enjoyment, laughter, friends, and the rest of my family—and on the other side was Andy, who really screwed with my brain. It was unnerving and awful, but I wouldn't stop to ponder it—I couldn't. That would only mean thinking bad thoughts. Mean and hateful thoughts about him. I didn't want to do that because people liked me; they loved me because I was gentle and good. My mother told me I had gifts to give the world, so many. I couldn't betray the folks who expected goodness, couldn't deal with that. My catechism classes had taught me well: turn the other cheek. Just turn it, again and again, and God will hold a special place for David in his heart. Right inside that huge and welcoming heart.

THE MOST REFRESHING AND DELIGHTFUL THING ABOUT LIVING IN the first Guilford neighborhood was Tina Lodge, a sly, willowy girl in my grade who had the longest blond hair I'd ever seen and lived two houses down from us. She had these four enormous black Newfoundlands that slobbered over both of us when we rolled around with each other in the grassy circle between our homes. It was an early crush—we were both eleven, I think, maybe twelve. And I felt so free with her out near the sea, the dogs like huge black bears wagging their tails, spittle everywhere. I felt alive with her, warm and funny inside. At times, I closed my eyes, embraced her, nuzzled her neck, and smelled her hair, and she said things like, "You are such a flirty, silly boy," and then, "How come your brother hates you so?"

I was shocked—I thought his rage was visible only to family. It embarrassed me—that other folks saw my secret. "He says I'm a vile scab," I said to her.

She thought for a few seconds as I wrapped my arms around her and we wrestled to the ground. Then we both giggled and rolled onto our backs, looking up at the sky, our bodies beside each other. "That's very specific," she said in a professorial voice. "That he felt the need to call you a *vile* scab, beyond just a regular scab—that's intense."

"Yeah," I said, reaching out my hand and patting her cheek gently, absentmindedly. We watched the sky quietly for a moment, one chubby cloud splitting into triplets above us. "That's Andy in a nutshell."

2

RELATIVE INNOCENCE

I LOVED MY NEW TOWN OF GUILFORD WITH A TRUE FERVOR.
Making friends came easily, and there seemed to be an unend-
ing supply of them. This was especially true in middle school,
where they gave me an award in eighth grade for simply being
a good guy, a decent soul. Those early teen years felt touched
with a type of innocence. I dated several girls in middle and high
school, but no one compared to my first Cape Cod love, Molly.
The two of us fooled around with other faces during the long
school year—she in Massachusetts and I in Connecticut—but
once we hit the Cape, we were glued to each other. Then, during
my first year and a half of high school, I made the mistake of
following in Andy's footsteps and attending Notre Dame in West

Haven, an all-boys Catholic school. I quickly grew tired of their discipline and dogma but mostly just missed my friends back home. When I eventually returned to Guilford High as a midsemester sophomore, I felt exuberant and relieved.

Andy's onslaught against me grew much less severe as he approached adulthood. He didn't quit the scorn or mockery, but the St. Sebastian defense definitely squelched his attempts to belittle me and left him subdued. When he got his license and a girlfriend, he pulled back from pursuing me like some lion rethinking his meal on a zebra at midbite. I don't know if he had some sort of religious epiphany in an open field or just grew sick of the sibling hatred. But one Friday night when I was a freshman, I was watching television in the family room with Julie and Dennis when Andy rushed up the stairs and invited me out with his friends.

"You're inviting me . . . out?" I said.

"Yeah, it's just a couple guys in Hamden," he said, "they told me to maybe bring . . . someone along."

I looked at him, waiting for the punch line. "And you thought of me, your brother?"

"Yeah," he said, scuffing his Docksiders on the floor. "It's no big deal—just thought you might like to come."

"Go with your brother, David," my mother called from downstairs. "It sounds like a good time."

"Okay, then," I said and soon found myself sitting in a theater watching shapely teenage girls remove their blouses on a giant screen in Hamden. Beside me was Andy giggling with his high school friends.

"So what do you think of those?" he said, nudging me as the camera zoomed in on a breast.

I felt the world spinning out of control at that moment,

whooshing right past. This truce had happened so abruptly, so suddenly, and then it was as if that's the way things had always been. It really threw me at first: one day, enemies, next day—nothing bad had ever taken place between us. There was never any mention of it—*our past does not exist.*

Our truce, combined with his leaving home, made my last two years of high school stress-free and fun. I felt so damn comfortable with my parents and Dennis and Julie. It was my own personal renaissance, if you will, a time when I felt wide awake and safe from harm and had the best friends in the world at Guilford.

I played high school basketball and baseball and even joined a relatively secular Catholic retreat group from Guilford. As older students, we counseled younger kids on how to deal with peer pressure, listened to Cat Stevens and James Taylor records, and went to weekends at Enders Island off Mystic, Connecticut. One of the things I remember about this island is playing coed hoops and all of us guys trying to bump against as many breasts as possible on the court. It was a great time to be silly, harmless, decent, and free. Like an epitaph of what was, the yearbook described me as "Nicest Smile and Friendliest."

On St. Patrick's Day during my senior year, my friends and I serenaded the student body with "Danny Boy" and "Too Ra Loo Ra Loo Ra." All the kids laughed, but the secretaries in the office grew teary with nostalgia. Life was rolling along solidly, and I felt so alive that whenever I saw kids who seemed depressed, I instinctively wanted to yell out, "Come on, it'll get better—just read a little Salinger, listen to James Taylor, and life will be superb. We're young and strong, we can take on anything that comes our way."

◆

IN THE SUMMERS, MY FAMILY HAD BEEN GOING TO OUR COTTAGE on the Cape in Dennis since I was a young child, so it was a surprise to them when I asked about spending the season on the island of Martha's Vineyard with my high school buddies. After some serious salesmanship by me, my parents agreed to let me go, and my dad loaned me a 1983 Buick for several months. At the end of May, I picked up my friends Kevin, Rich, Eric, and Tim and headed to Woods Hole to catch the ferry. My summer girl, Molly, and I had decided to take the summer off from dating. Everything about that time seemed to be about new beginnings, fresh starts.

And so I return to the brief, quixotic summer, the charmed time on the island, where I lived in a leaky-roofed, skunks-below-the-porch alley apartment on Circuit Avenue In Oak Bluffs, Massachusetts. My friends and I played Frisbee across the colorful, throbbing avenue in front of our apartment, and one afternoon we nearly clocked Carly Simon on her head. She just ducked and waved at us and slipped into a record store a few doors down. We worshipped at the altars of James Taylor, Paul Simon, R.E.M., Steve Winwood, and Peter Gabriel, dancing, spastic, and goofy, our arms swinging jubilantly on our porch. We swirled around, entertained one another with a combination of grotesque versions of the Samba, the Charleston, and the Hustle all in one. A few times we woke up at 3:00 a.m. with large buckets of rain spilling down through the gaps in the ceiling. We just shook it off, dried ourselves off, and slept downstairs.

In the morning we went for long runs to Vineyard Haven and back. With Eric, Kevin, and Rich busy with their summer jobs pumping gas and landscaping, Tim and I had the best deal, working at a hotel on South Beach. I was an inefficient chamber-maid with a great bunch of girls, and Tim was the maintenance man who struggled with hammering nails. Several times, the five of us guys skipped work and went to Chappaquiddick, where we invented a game with nothing but an old tennis ball, a waiting ocean, and perhaps a little too much enthusiasm.

We shared our ratty place with three sweet women from the University of Massachusetts, including a vibrant Portuguese girl from Fall River named Maria (her smile was gleaming and per-fectly aligned). My friend Kevin and I used to walk down the street, through the T-shirt and knickknack shops, singing her praises, "Ave, Ave, Maria . . ."

But there was one girl who topped even Maria in my eyes. I met her at a party on the other side of the gingerbread houses in Oak Bluffs in early June. My Emily was living there with five friends, other girls from Mount Holyoke and Bucknell who also worked at the inn at South Beach in Edgartown.

Emily was a Mount Holyoke girl, and I immediately noticed her slender, fluid neck, the sad eyes with spectacles, and the smiling, slightly rounded face as she stood with a drink in her hand. She was an art history major, though to me she looked more like a sculptor with her high-top Chuck Taylors caked in brown and navy spits of clay and paint. She had a precise, thin nose and smelled faintly of brand-new books. Close-cropped ebony hair. To me, who had begun reading some of the confes-sional poets at the time, she looked a little like Anne Sexton. It was hard to imagine beating something like that.

She was thin but that was just her disguise. To a passerby she even looked vaguely asexual but when she spoke, when her narrow lips opened, she sounded a little throaty and self-deprecating . . .

oh, man. She often displayed her sharp and intelligent wit, and when I stood beside her for the first time, I breathed in that clean, bookish scent. I knew it was never cool for men to swoon—that, in fact, gentlemen should stick with serious crushes—but at that moment, in the living room on Martha's Vineyard, I was a goner. Perhaps it was someone else standing beside me or maybe a candle burning in the kitchen, but I was overcome with the scent of vanilla. It was pleasant, nuanced, not that in-your-face Yankee Candle crap at Stop & Shop, but a hint of it, just a trace.

I was studying her as she answered a relatively pompous question about being trapped in a castle forever and being allowed to have only three pieces of art to hold on to for eternity. "I'd take the debut album by the Violent Femmes, Matisse's *The Dance*, and perhaps *To the Lighthouse* by Virginia Woolf," she said.

"I'd go with James Taylor, Mark Rothko, and some Hemingway," I said and she giggled.

"How do you put James Taylor and Mark Rothko together in the same sentence?" she asked.

Flustered, I blurted out something about Rothko, how my professor at school said he wept the first time he stood in front of one of his canvases at the Met. When I said my author selections were Updike and Salinger, she made a face.

"Pretty predictable," she said. "Maybe you're a budding misogynist, my friend?"

"Oh, please," I said. "Show mercy."

She smiled. "I've heard about you from my cousin Eric. It's David, right?"

My heart jumped. "Yes—and you're infamous Emily?"

She grinned. "Very good," she said, signaling to the two tanned girlfriends around her. "Are you seriously going to carry on a conversation about art with us when you've been described by your friends as a huge Wham fan?"

"Years from now their genius will be recognized," I said and blushed.

My first two years at Skidmore College hadn't produced any chats like this. The spark was immediate—I wanted to kiss her belly, then her kneecaps. Within two minutes of walking into the party, I felt pretty much in love with the skinny girl. I was twenty and felt as if I'd discovered my very own long-necked princess. And with her frequent taps on my elbow and the light in her shifting brown eyes, I'd spotted a familiar longing. An invitation to play, to pursue.

One night, ten days after we first met, Emily and I walked to the Oak Bluffs harbor when we grew tired of the crowd in her apartment. I wanted to nibble her long neck, the elliptical slope of her calves, but I stayed relatively cool and calm and we latched fingers and sat down on the edge of a dock and let our feet dangle over the blackish night sea. Behind us were some kids eating at a fried clam shack, and the scent of that food and the salt air, mixed with Emily's touch of vanilla behind her ear, made for a wonderful moment for a first kiss.

With the children whispering behind us, I laid one on her and nearly leapt into the air. As we wrestled with each other in the shadow of the clam shack, confessions were made, and she admitted she liked Salinger, too, and that she even had JT's *Mud Slide Slim* in her record collection. I felt thirteen years old with her—nervous and giddy. My breath was short, my skin tight and covered in goose bumps. My tongue felt thick and hairy, my hearing overly sensitive, and each scent in the universe flew up my nostrils like smelling salts and shook me, shocked me. Staggered me around as if I'd been dosed with a secret hallucinogenic cocktail. Plus, I was hard as a rock. Then we retreated to where we would do most of our fooling around—in an open space with a wooden covered stage and seats for about three hundred in the middle of the gingerbread houses. It was called the Pavilion. We giggled then and made fun of ourselves, told secrets, exaggerated everything, and later went to Mad Martha's where we ordered an ice cream sundae and devoured it on the beach under an orange moon.

The days and nights just took off from there, sped up, with Emily and me working together at the inn at South Beach in Edgartown in the daytime and fooling around whenever possible. We went skinny-dipping and ate at a funky restaurant with Dixie cups, wine, and steamers. We ripped apart lobsters, picked blueberries in Chilmark, and rode that damn carousel way too frequently. I even brought her off the island to visit my folks in Dennis. On Independence Day, we watched the fireworks explode beyond us over the Oak Bluffs green. That evening, I blew raspberries on her thighs and passed a small note to her in pale blue crayon that read, "I Love You." She wrote back the same in goldenrod.

OUR LOVE FELT SUBSTANTIAL, DIFFERENT, AND UNIQUE TO ME. Emily was sweet and kind, generous—just like Molly—but she had a seasoned, artsy feel about her that charmed me. I was proud to have her beside me, looking so cosmopolitan and hip. She discussed art with me, even corrected a perception I had about writing.

"So though you profess worship of Hemingway and Updike—

they aren't truly artists?" she said, her eyes squinting. "What do you call it then?"

"All I know is I adore soaring colors and sculpture," I said. "Like Kandinsky, Gauguin, Picasso—that seems more intensely artistic than simple words."

"God, you are an English major," she said. "You're supposed to defend well-written words to your death." Then she stopped and kissed my cheek. "How are we ever supposed to have a heated debate?"

"I could fake it," I said.

"Doesn't it take art to describe colors, to make them real and alive to the world?" she said.

"Of course."

"Maybe," she said, taking her glasses off and nibbling on them. "If I could analyze you for a moment, you don't respect writing because it comes easily to you—you're good at it." She held her finger up dramatically and said, "In closing, may I say you don't respect yourself enough."

"That must be it," I said, watching her closely. Her eyes were huge, darting. "But then, what are you down deep, beneath all the polish but an insecure, trembling wanton?"

"Wanton?" she said with a grin. "I'm not as naïve as you," she continued, and then, "outside of sex, that is. I am most definitely a lady about this town."

"Who will you choose to make you less innocent?"

She laughed. "I don't know—there's this one cute Irish lad, but he expresses rather base tastes."

"Like?"

"Well," she said, "he enjoys the music of George Michael and Andy Ridgeley and couldn't tell the difference between Bach and Brahms if his life were on the line."

"Ah," I said. "I'd say it's a mark of the purest mediocrity—drop him while you still can."

She smiled slightly. "We'll see."

I WAS TOO NERVOUS TO BUY CONDOMS—I WAS FAR FROM A CASA-nova and had never used them with my other partners. We had always just been very lucky. I guess I thought every sexual relationship would be as smooth and memorable as my first.

Emily had told me she was inexperienced and, though I found that thrilling and touching, it also scared the crap out of me.

So I went to the pharmacy right down the street from our apartment with my gallant friend Tim, who volunteered for this undercover assignment. I pretended to look at the magazines while Tim went up to the pharmacist to get the contraband. I heard Tim speak to the pharmacist in his most charming and professional voice, "Sir, would you have a family planning section here at this establishment?"

"You mean counseling help for families?" the pharmacist said. "That would be in Vineyard Haven."

Tim cleared his throat and said, "More like something to keep family growth steady and under control?"

"I'm not really sure . . ."

"Prophylactics, sir," he said finally. "Do you have them in your store—I can't seem to find them."

Eventually, Tim grabbed a discounted pack of twelve Excita Brand Condoms. "For your pleasure and hers," the package read.

Now that we had the goods, Emily and I were almost set. We just needed a good spot to have sex. She didn't want to do it at the Pavilion or on a beach so we waited to use her bedroom, which she shared with a Mount Holyoke friend. Finally, one night while we were a little tipsy, we snuck into the girls' bedroom, and I did my best with some assistance from Emily. The friend was sleeping five feet away in the next bed, which added both pressure and allure. And, just like that, the condom tore. We tried another, but from then on, nothing worked for me. Nothing. I was ravenous for her, but then when the moment rolled around, I overanalyzed and obsessed. I told myself, *This is so easy, it's natural, why isn't it fucking working? Why the hell can't I get hard with a condom near? Is there something lacking in me? Am I weird?* Try as I might, I couldn't do it for the remainder of the summer.

ON THE OUTSIDE, I APPEARED IN GRAND SHAPE THAT SEASON. I was young and in love with a fabulous girl, hanging out at a beautiful, hip spot with true friends. But inside things were fraying and beginning to fragment. A seed of unrest lay behind my smile. A few days after Emily and I abandoned our first attempts at making love, I was struck by a harried dream.

It featured a fat man I'd spotted bagging groceries at the local A&P. He had beady, glacial-blue eyes, and in the dream, he floated high in the air, soaring like some dirigible, checking out the evening lights around the island. Then a hard rain started, the wind picked up, and lightning struck, ripping into the man and piercing him. He came tumbling down, screaming, and smashed through my bedroom window. He was bleeding like crazy with shards of glass poking out of him. As I watched from my bed, he sat up, grasped the glass pieces on the floor and stabbed them into his belly, face, and wrists with a furious glee.

I yelled at him to stop, to please cease or he would die. He giggled when he realized my limbs were somehow Krazy-glued to the mattress and I was unable to help him. His laughter was part manic heckle and part desperation. He continued to stab himself and groan while the blood was pouring off him. That's when I woke with a scream. The next day I wrote down the dream in a quick few hours and realized it was the best writing I'd ever done. It gave me an odd sort of hope. The story was macabre and melodramatic, of course, but I felt psyched. Getting that story down on paper galvanized me.

During the next week when I spotted that huge fellow at the A&P, his eyes bore through me as I looked at him; he appeared incredibly anguished and broken. He scared the hell out of me and made me think, *Thank God, I'll never have to feel what he feels.* After that, I did my best to stay away from the A&P.

The fat man's beady blues reminded me of an old codger at the Cape who used to pay me to clean up his yard as he watched from his porch with a Scottish terrier. Leo was in his late seventies, a bald artist with stretched, leathery skin, and I was sixteen, a busboy at Marsh Side Restaurant in East Dennis. He painted on an easel out front all day, sipping whiskey; then sometimes he put down his palette and brushes and just studied me. When I finished work once, he called me up onto the porch. "I like to watch you," he said. "Do you mind? Does that disturb you?"

"I'm not sure," I said as he counted out the forty dollars.

He hesitated for a moment. "Would you mind taking off your shirt next time?" he said. "When you do the lawn? I'll pay an extra thirty."

"What do you paint?" I said, ignoring the question and walking over to one of his canvases. It was a watercolor of me in my green trunks and royal-blue T-shirt, a mishmash of color, but I could find a fuzzy, warped version of myself in it. I liked it, and I told him. It seemed like an oozing dreamscape. As I walked toward my mother's canary-yellow Mercury Lynx, I heard him clear his throat.

"So next Tuesday you'll mow the lawn without a shirt?" he said.

"Absolutely," I said. "But that's it—and you have to give me one of your paintings by the end of the summer."

"It's a deal," he said.

As he turned to go inside, I yelled from the driveway, "Leo, what is it that you want to capture?"

"How about everything?" he said. "Youth, hope, desire, frustration, sex, taut muscles, perhaps some heavy melancholy. All that and more."

"Heavy melancholy?" I said.

He waved his hand. "What do I know? I'm an old man with a loyal dog that paints and makes guesses about young men."

"Like a fortune-teller?"

"Yeah," he said. "Something like that. I think my colors pick up emotions—the brushes lay them down for me to see the truth in people."

"The truth?"

"It may not be," he said, spreading his palms out. "But I'm just an old fogey—passing the time with brushes and whiskey."

ONE TIME, EMILY AND I WRESTLED AND ROLLED EACH OTHER ON a just-made-up bed on the second floor of the inn on South Beach. Just as I started to escape her and dust a windowsill, she started nibbling on my ear. I stood at the window then and surveyed the dunes and watched some children throwing a violet Frisbee beyond one of the cottages. It appeared to hover in the air forever, just a simple bright disc that spun and whirled beyond their fingers and then eventually dropped into the grass. I thought, *This is memorable, perfect; take the picture. Zoom in, focus and click and store for later.* For years, I tried to hold on to that moment—it was so clear, so precise. I had noticed myself doing that a lot more since my last year of high school—my eye became a constant video feed. I had a hyperawareness of watching and being watched. I had to be ready for everything. Cameras seemed to be everywhere, not in a schizoid, paranoid way, but in an appreciation of the infinite things to absorb. Nothing should be missed. It all had to be soaked up, taken in, and figured out so it could be stored forever. It was important to be always ready, always on.

"I THINK WHAT I FIND INTRIGUING IN YOU," EMILY SAID TOWARD the end of the summer, "is the social ease and precociousness you have. Sometimes you're funny as hell and the next you come out with something almost too touching and beyond naïve."

"Yeah?" I said. "Good grooming and extra sit-ups paid off."

She smiled slightly and squeezed my hand. "Really," she said. "It makes me wonder what's inside, down deep, what's waiting there for me?"

The truth was I didn't know much about myself and tended to steer clear of any introspection. I was twenty, and there was a familiar churn of anxiety in my gut, a constant worry about being left alone, especially with older males, but that was just some bad luck with Andy. I knew the world was observing me like a movie—not staring, not some microchip broadcasting my every move to aliens, but like a film had begun and I was in it.

Later, just before we all left the island, I had a strange moment with a palm reader in Oak Bluffs that seemed silly at the time. She refused to read me. I stopped in on a lark, said hello, and gave her the fee. I forget how much, maybe five dollars or something. Then she sat down and closed a saffron-colored curtain while I stretched out my sweaty palm. She fit the part with a nose ring and scarf.

"I think it's too complicated," she said, almost immediately. "Your life looks complex and bumpy."

"Is bumpy a term you'd care to expand on?" I said, smiling uncomfortably.

"No," she said. "I don't wish to. I won't—it's out of my hands."

"Jesus, lady," I said. "Lighten up." I hesitated a minute and said, "It's not too bumpy, is it?"

"It's out of my hands," she said, returning the money and closing the curtain. Later, I thought she reacted that way because I was jumpy or, perhaps, appeared overly revved. But I can't say that it didn't haunt me, that it didn't hover in the back of my mind like a prescient mosquito, popping up every now and again to warn, "Something's on its way."

On one of my final nights in Oak Bluffs, I stumbled back from Emily's to the apartment at 1:00 a.m. feeling tipsy and spent. I passed by the silent, sleepy gingerbread houses, their pink-, lime-, and mustard-colored ornate touches barely visible in the moonless night. The only sound I could hear was some music flowing from Circuit Avenue, which was otherwise quiet. Half-way down the street, I passed an apartment above an army-navy surplus store and discovered where the music was coming from. A single light was on, and the curtains fluttered gently in the night breeze. Peter Gabriel and Kate Bush were singing, imploring each other not to give up.

A rush of sadness, something bittersweet, nearly knocked me over, and I stood beneath the window on the edge of tears. Their voices boomed and pierced me, the volume seemed to grow as I stood there, looking up at the sky. The collection of stars dripped with fragmented, interstitial light. I wanted to jump up there and wrestle one of them down for my new girl, Emily, for my buddies, for everyone I'd ever met. I wanted to take that star on a ferry across Nantucket Sound and show it to my speckle-eyed Molly, to my family. I would paint it with orange, indigo, and emerald stripes and then use it to play catch with my brother Dennis on Bay View Beach. I yearned to kick it back and forth, to spin it on my fingers, balance it on my head, roll it over the dunes, and then responsibly, carefully, return it to its place in the sky before the next evening. It was the least I could do for all the good souls I had met on that island.

3

BEING WATCHED

WHEN I WAS SEVENTEEN, A MAN APPROACHED ME AS I WAS shooting baskets outside the Dennis-Yarmouth High School on the Cape. It was midsummer and hot, and my family and I were staying at our cottage over in Dennis, about five miles away. I wanted to be in great shape and was even toying with the idea of starting on the Guilford basketball team the next season. Or maybe I could get to play every now and then. *I was always on that fucking bench!*

As I was dribbling around, I could feel the stare and could tell I was being observed. But I couldn't figure out who was doing it. I glanced around and then walked over to my car, my mother's car, that same canary-yellow Mercury Lynx wagon I'd driven the summer before. I didn't see anything so I walked back to the court and shot some more baskets. That's when I turned again and watched a large man bike past about a hundred yards away. He eventually stopped in front of me.

I took a few steps back and put on my T-shirt. He looked to be in his fifties, very portly, and was wheezing. The bicycle was too small for him and had a little emerald basket that held a ruby T-shirt. He wore a tight, shiny blue wrestling uniform with one of the straps off his arms. His face was flushed, and beads of sweat collected on the blacktop at his feet. I couldn't see what color his eyes were, but I thought, *What the hell is this?*

"How we doing today—shooting some hoops, huh?" he said.

"Yes, but I'm tired, going to be getting on my way," I said.

He cleared his throat, tugged at his crotch, and dismounted from the bike. "You don't know wrestlers around, do you? People who might be interested in getting pinned and grappling with me?"

I shook my head and picked up the basketball at my feet. "No—I'm not from around here," I said. "Just a summer person."

"What about yourself, son?" he said. "It seems like you might be a pretty good wrestler."

"Good-bye," I said. "I'm going to head home now, sir."

"Where's home?" he said. "Son, just stop a moment, won't you? Would you wrestle with me? Don't be so rude—wouldn't you like to do it now?"

I hopped in my car and took off as quickly as I could. When I came to the main road, I looked in the rearview. He was waving at me from his bike. *You must do your best to never be by yourself,* I scolded myself as I drove away. *Bad things follow you around when you are.*

◆

THIS WAS NOT THE FIRST TIME I'D EXPERIENCED SOMETHING LIKE this. I had a history of being watched and pursued. At age twelve, I had a bad encounter along Route One in Guilford with a lanky drunken man who grabbed me and kissed me. It was December 21, 1977, and my sister, Julie, was born that night in New Haven. This ugly lazy-eyed fuck embraced me, pressed his damp and puffy down jacket against my body. I still remember the smell of alcohol on his breath, along with the funny odor of tobacco hovering around him and his damn tongue maneuvering, twisting around my teeth and mouth. His arms were so solid and he gripped me and wouldn't let go.

I had been walking quickly, nearly running over to a friend's house up by Bishop's Orchard when he seized me and pulled me back from the main road about ten feet. He immediately started kissing me and whispered something I couldn't understand. Then he relaxed a little and said "Don't run, kid. Hey, kid—wait." I sprinted through the rain, clammy and cold, with the smell of fear around me. I tried to stop crying on the front porch of my friend's house.

"You're so full of crap," his older brother said when I stepped into the house and told them what had happened. I repeated the story, and my friend and his brother shook their heads.

"Truly," I said, dumbfounded. "Why would I make up that story?"

"You are definitely smoking something strong to come up with that stuff," the brother said. "Now come on and eat—my mother's got some steak for you."

"You've had a long day," the mother said, coming into the kitchen with the meal. "Let this take your mind off the silly things, okay?"

The next day I got off the bus at our new Dromara Road house, and five workers were gathered around an olive Ford pickup, their tool belts slung low on their hips, taking a break. My eyes scanned their faces and stopped when I saw the same fucking man from the night before. He took a big sip of something, maybe beer or soda, and spat it out in front of me. The other carpenters laughed, and I looked up at him and he glared at me for four long seconds and then smirked and walked away. He knew I'd never tell.

For most of my teenage years, I had recurring nightmares about a faded pair of Levi Strauss jeans that would unzip, revealing zillions of penises flopping out at me. In the dream, I quickly sliced them off with a Ginsu knife and dove into this narrow, slick vagina that had orangey day-glow smiley faces attached along the wall. There was an ocean of sorts down there, and I swam and did handstands, held my breath and blew bubbles, and freestyled from one end of what I guessed was the Fallopian tubes to the other. Sometimes dolphins with the face of my beloved second-grade teacher, Mrs. Barkowski, nuzzled my crotch. It was so bizarre, erotic, and goofy.

Each time when I woke up, I tried to figure out whose private parts I'd been inside of. Was it lovely Miranda Hess from seventh grade? Was it that new, cute girl I'd seen at the Cape with the cat eyes named Molly? Or was it Mrs. Barkowski herself? I felt semirelaxed for part of the dream, and then ZAP— the whole vision repeated itself quickly. Unzip. Flop. Slice, dive, swim! Again and again—one image after the next. This occurred nightly maybe ten thousand times throughout my teens. In my relatively twisted, guilty Catholic gourd I was sinning big-time, swimming inside women's personal areas, dreaming of penises attacking me, flopping away like hooked eels on a boat. These were definitely mortal sins, and so I blocked the dreams out of my mind as best I could.

I heard certain words whispered every day by guys in the locker rooms. Back home, Andy once used those words to describe me. He whispered, *"faggotpussypussyfaggot,"* and I wasn't sure what they meant. I knew one was bad and the other quite good, but his use of them made both seem extra horrible. My mind raced: *Am I some sort of pervert? Do the dreams mean I'm gay?*

At my parents' and Andy's suggestion, I went for a week to a cross-country camp after my freshman year at Notre Dame High in West Haven. The coach ran us ragged for a couple days, and then we had to go through an initiation night for the newbies. The six of us tried to experience the hazing with a "positive attitude." They brought us down to the end of the dorm hallway, and we stripped to our jocks. They gave each of us two peach pits and told us to manipulate one pit between our buttocks and crab-walk fifty yards down the hall, drop off the pit and pick up the other one (with our cheeks, of course) and return in crab style. During the action, the Doors blasted out of someone's stereo, "Break on through to the other side . . ."

"You guys are great," the captain said as the races went on. Some of the onlookers jeered, others cheered. The coach had closed his door and wasn't available for the night. After the crab-walk experience, they brought us down to the showers and lined us up against the wall. Upperclassmen came in with peanut butter, Vaseline, jelly, and Marshmallow Fluff and wiped it over our hair, our faces, chests, bellies, and legs. The Doors' music was pounding away, and the upperclassmen's eyes were glassy; they looked stoned or drunk though I know they weren't. They smiled or sneered and caked it on, giggling. I felt like I was on some bizarre game show.

"These boys are getting away easy," someone said. "The newbie football players in the next dorm across the way have to stick those 45 records up their asses and crab-walk." Later, we showered up and ate pizza and drank soda with the team. An upperclassman kept telling us we could do exactly the same to next year's newbies.

I transferred back to Guilford High School a few months later.

IT WAS AT A SIMPLE DANCE DURING SENIOR YEAR AT GUILFORD High when I felt myself break through a small door of awareness about the world. I found an understanding, or at least a realization, of the vast expanse beyond Guilford and within myself. Nothing dramatic precipitated it—no tabs of LSD or mushrooms or even a beer buzz that set me off. Our high school gymnasium was being torn down, so they moved the soiree to the middle school. A few minutes before, my friends had taken off in a station wagon without telling me, and I was alone and bothered, surrounded by classmates who were loud, sullen, or drunk. I couldn't stay in that claustrophobic, sweaty school any longer. It was late autumn, and the roads were damp even though it wasn't raining right then. There was a thrilling snap in the air that rushed up my nose. I left the dance and jogged two hundred yards up the drive to the school's entrance, where I saw students smoking cigarettes and couples kissing and waiting to be picked up by friends and parents. I turned onto Long Hill Road and started running home. I was overcome by the feeling that I had to see my parents alive and smiling, breathing.

It was maybe three miles back to where I'd parked my car at a friend's house. I was afraid of skunks and of those dark shapes in my peripheral vision—were lanky men waiting to grab me, to kiss me or kill me like before? Were they real or ghosts or a little of both? I kept running, exhaling in short spurts, listening to the sound of my breath and watching it form in front of me like bursts of pollen. I had been in a minute, compacted shell of relative limitedness for most of my young life, a place where there were no real-life fears like hunger, love, sex, death, or pain. Now I felt all that burst open as I rushed on through the night. There was a slight disturbance ticking in my head that kept me sprinting, my feet pounding the pavement. Periodically, I walked to catch my breath but then dashed off again. There were no streetlights for a good half mile or so, and I flew along the side of the road, not stopping.

I thought of the Cape where I played Wiffle ball with a buddy who became a perfect older brother to me. Ed was funny and silly and took me under his wing—we played golf three times a week, and I recalled the ripe, fecund smell of the pine forest rough and the fertilizer rising up off the fairways as the sunshine grew stronger each day. Ed and I went bowling, played touch football, and sometimes he told me about his girlfriend in East Providence who gave him blow jobs at a drive-in movie theater and how she swallowed. *SWALLOWED! Did girls really do that? That's fucking incredible!*

I wanted to be Ed. He was kind and didn't taunt me like my older brother; he was funny and cool and enjoyed my company. So I followed everything he did, listened to his rhythmic tunes, and went with him and a whole group of kids to a teen disco in Hyannis called Reflections. I learned the latest moves there, had them memorized so that when I returned to Guilford at the end of the summer, I'd offer something unique. *I must always offer and entertain with something fresh,* I believed then.

I understood that it was important not to turn people off with inappropriate obtuse comments, despairing moods, or any problems of my own. Keep the show going, for Christ's sake; keep the witticisms and the shorthand ready for any possibility. If I didn't, people would exit the scene, and I needed people around—God, I definitely needed people around.

As I was running in Guilford, I thought of sprinting down my favorite summer street, Wild Hunter Road at the Cape. There were no streetlights, and it was completely black each night. This was going to be like closing my eyes and stepping into a sealed closet with nothing but crickets. I took on my fears, I guess, or maybe I just didn't have a ride home and needed to get there as quickly as possible. So I dashed through that five-hundred-yard shadow and believed that if I landed one foot in front of the other, it would carry me along the road as it changed from macadam to dirt, and I'd feel my ankles buckle a bit when my feet landed on the stones and mud. This would set the neighbor's German shepherd, Beefy, barking ferociously behind his kennel. Then, suddenly I'd be at our cottage, the Sandy Fitz. We had a little blue sign hanging beside the front door with a cute yellow lantern that drove the kamikaze moths crazy in August.

Inside, my mother was asleep in a mildewed orange-and-white-patterned chair with some poetry on her lap, and things were just fine. She woke up for a moment and asked, "How was your night, darling?" and I said that it was great, so great. Once again, the world felt like it was bursting upward and out of me. And for another night, just one more night, things were going to be okay. That night the sky wouldn't be crumbling on any of us.

As I ran to my friend's house in Guilford, I let the memories of the Cape float away into the darkness. A Volvo approached with people yelling, calling out to me. I stopped, and my friends said, "Come on, Fitz, what are you doing out here in the dark? We're going back to the dance." But I told them I felt like running, and I was a little out of it, and they said, "We'll take you back to your car," and I shrugged them off, said no, and sprinted again, pumping my legs, feeling my calves and thighs burn a little as my sneakers kissed the pavement. I had been running on the cross-country team for a season so I was in good shape, and I felt the chilly breeze touching the sides of my ears and my lips, chapping them a little. I heard the Volvo's engine idling behind me and then it drove off with a beep. When I was halfway there, I took a shortcut into a more residential section, and I felt myself shifting down, gliding some as the slight panic slowed.

Lights were on and people were watching television or pissing in their bathrooms or sitting down and having a snack of Wise Potato Chips and Dr Pepper. I walked a little, taking huge breaths, and recalled that basket of chips and soda from a party the week before on the same street. I forget the girl's name, but her parents were away, and she was drunk and we gave her a six-pack, and she came up to me in the kitchen and let her hand run down my belly to my crotch and grabbed me. Just seized me out of the blue. It was such an overt sexual move that it thrilled me and sent me into a panic. Suddenly the party shifted, and a bunch of classmates were all in that girl's den watching MTV, drinking Dr Pepper and rum. I believe Nik Kershaw was singing, "Wouldn't it be good to be in your shoes, grass is always greener over there . . ." Then April—her name was April—looked over at me and I thought, *Wow—she feels desire, she really wants to touch me.* Is that possible, you ask, that at eighteen I still didn't know that girls were sexual? I'd slept with Molly by then and I guess I thought it was just her, maybe, that she was so special that she wanted to be with me because I was the one, true thing. She was my first, so I thought she was unique in her desires.

I kept running through the residential section, passed the house with the girl who had grabbed me that week, and came to a long stretch of darkness without streetlights. I felt so alive, and an intense rush of awareness filled me. It was the first time I started snapping photos in my head, turning and clicking, and saving them for a later time. Not that I hadn't had crystal-lized memories before, but this was the feeling that my brain was working as a rapid-fire Polaroid, turning, measuring, and shooting.

I felt such clarity, such precision in my head then, and I took full-color shadowy shots of everything. There was an empty crushed gallon of skim milk in the weeds, a vandalized stop sign that had "Making Sense" underneath it in orange spray paint, a slightly torn Harlequin romance paperback spilling out of a trash can at the end of a driveway, two purple socks, and a pile of fragmenting, yellowing T-shirts. I quickly rounded a corner onto Route 77, and a rust-colored Ford Mustang beeped at me and voices yelled and cursed and hung with me for a moment and then disappeared into a grove of stripped-bare maples and elms.

Two hundred yards ahead was the blinking yellow light and the right turn that became Step Stone Hill. I took that corner and started to calm down, to return to the world, to breathe slower. I was just a half mile away, but then a car pulled up behind me, and it was the class secretary, Betty Stewart, and her girlfriend in her sky-blue Chrysler K-Car. I didn't want to look weird so I accepted the ride. I sat in back and the radio was on quietly. It was Kool and the Gang, and I was breathing hard and sweating and they said, "Are you okay, David?" I thought, *Well, I'm okay but it's a different type of okay.* I stayed silent until I thanked them for the lift and then got out at my friend's house.

I was in my car soon, heading home and, Jesus Christ, it felt comfortable, but the headlights couldn't precisely take photo after photo, soaking up each thing. Roadway signs, fences, a dead raccoon, somebody's belt, or was that a snake? The interior lights had a green glow, and when I looked into the rearview mirror, all I saw was my teeth.

Then I shut the lights off and drove down that long straight-away of Route 146, and the marsh reeds were spooky tall, like pictures I'd seen of yellow-brown cornfields in Iowa or Kansas. They whipped past as I accelerated to seventy-five and felt the corner of the road flying at me, eating at the tires, so I flipped the headlights back on, and then, suddenly, I was pulling the car into the gravel lot. I rushed in to find my folks having some wine in the kitchen. They smiled, and I kissed them both and held them, hugged them tighter than usual. It felt almost like checking to see if they were fully formed. I soaked up their faces with my mind and then stayed up late and watched *Friday Night Videos* and then David Letterman.

I believe this was the first night I felt a better grasp of exactly what life could consist of. Like I broke through or kicked off something important. That I shed some silly, protective, fried-ice-cream-like coating that kept secrets far away, which allowed me to view my world as it might be. These moments occurred during a period I referred to as my renaissance—that time after my brother left and there was no sadistic presence in the home. I was disappointed, though, that this new freedom of psychic possibility included rushes of melancholia, along with an ache tapping at the corner of my skull. I wanted to say something to my conscience, something terse and wry like, "Wait just a second—this is my time, so back the hell away, sadness. Don't you dare come looking for me now!"

4

THE FOUR PRICKS OF
THE APOCALYPSE

After I returned from my summer on Martha's Vineyard with Emily and my high school friends, I drove to Saratoga Springs for my junior year at Skidmore College and moved in with four roommates. We'd become decent buddies during freshman and sophomore years, and we'd played intramural basketball together in previous semesters. Our friendship was based on sarcasm and an ironic kind of humor that festers in lost college students. Jasper had been an early pal, and he was always peppering me about my sexual experiences.

"Are you sure you're not a virgin, Fitz?" he'd ask repeatedly.

He seemed unusually fascinated with my life and my take on things, as if I were a unique timepiece that had to be dismantled so he could see how it worked. We lived in campus apartments, set back away from the school.

The roommates were big partiers, always intent on getting shitfaced and stoned whenever possible. I had tried pot once in high school and maybe two other times as a freshman and sophomore. But I'd never had cocaine or LSD. This motley quartet consisted of Curtis, a portly philosophy and marketing double major from Montreal, who was the sometimes brutal/sometimes sickly sweet instigator of activities; Jasper, the bowlegged Maryland baseball catcher with curly red hair; Bobby, a short stocky wrestler with a shaved head from Poughkeepsie, New York; and Sy, a California surfer freak who always found a way to use the words "cock ring" in his sentences. Sy didn't move in with us until the final year.

Everything they did was about inhaling, swallowing, and smoking as many drugs as possible. Once I joined the crew, we used large quantities, mostly pot and some cocaine and a small amount of acid. And I was complicit in most of it—once coaxing the others to gather around the house bong on a Thursday evening, "Do it for America, for all the good kids watching."

I hadn't clicked with many friends during my first two years at Skidmore. I think other students looked at me as an anomaly— just a sheltered, naïve Catholic kid from southern Connecticut who had a good turnaround jump shot in the intramural basketball league. Skidmore was not a Catholic bastion—there was a sizable percentage of Jewish students, and the college was stridently secular. I think my naïveté was what attracted the roommates. They were like a pack of roving wolves and I was a weaker calf.

I was a test case for them, less sophisticated, maybe, and they liked joking around. They got a kick out of me—I made them chuckle. The anxiety had been building in me since the end of the summer, and one late afternoon in early September we gathered around the TV to watch football and porn. Their behavior pushed me further into a panic, an anxiety about life and where exactly I fit into it. It was more than a young man's nerves about impending graduation. This unnamed panic consisted of massive doubt that I belonged anywhere at all, along with a sense that my base, my wholeness, was fracturing.

IT WAS A PITCHER OF SKIM MILK, A DISCOUNTED BLUE PLASTIC container from Price Chopper, but it started the domino effect of pouring incidents. Jasper dumped some on me after the house bong had been passed around while the New York Giants played on CBS. Curtis loved that team, and especially their tight end, Mark Bavaro. "That man is the best in the world—I want to marry him," he'd shout after several bong hits. "I think I may actually want to suck his cock!"

This first time I was covered in ice cold milk, and I remember feeling it soak my hair and drip down my cheeks. I also recall thinking, *Wow, they're really giggling*, and how disorienting that was. I liked laughter—when it came from something I said or from a shared joke with another person maybe—but this felt different. They were collapsing around me on the floor, nearly pissing their pants while I looked at them. I was confused. *Should I flee or kick them?*

I didn't run right off. I think I said, "Oh, give me a break," and walked into the kitchen, shaken by the intensity of their laughter and its tone. I licked the milk off my lips and kept listening to their voices.

"We're sorry, Fitzy," Jasper called from the other room. "Come back, come back—it won't happen again."

There was a childish lift to his voice, kind of like when kids talk about something they're excited about. A discovery. The voice changes—you can't hide the joy, can't fake it. So I filled up a pitcher of water in the kitchen and came back around the bend and threw it at Jasper. Then the boys—Curtis and Bobby— yelled, "Oh, not—not a smart move on Fitzy's part. Not a wise move." The water had splattered on the wall, a small part of it landed near the TV screen.

"You nearly hit the TV, asshole!" Jasper said. "And that calls for serious payback, big-time retribution. Give me the container, Bobby. Let's fill it to the top and give this fellow a lesson."

Jasper and Curtis wouldn't stop after that. They taunted and pursued me with the milk pitcher for a second, third, and fourth time. I figured it might have been my reaction, the way I didn't scream, the way I didn't move, and just kind of shrugged it off and gazed back at them as they rolled around. "Oh, Jesus, Oh, Jesus," Bobby gasped and then poured Grand Union iced tea and some ketchup on me. Everyone giggled and coaxed each other to do more.

I later wondered what would have happened if I'd struck back, maybe punched Jasper during the first spill. Would everything after that have been different? Perhaps that would have kept the drama away.

But in the following months and semesters a familiar sound around the apartment was Curtis barking threats like, "You're giving us that look and we have no choice!" His voice would crack as he stood over me, gazing down with his eyes shining. He'd hold the container above me and say, "Watch it, now, sonny boy." Then one of them would dump the water or squeeze the mustard, and the laughter would ricochet everywhere. That's when I would watch the four roommates doubled over, convulsing.

Initially, at least, I smiled through the haze of marijuana, trying terribly hard to be part of the joke, to get it. I grabbed my towel and took a shower upstairs, washing everything off, rinsing away the mess. Several times they waited until I had toweled off and gotten dressed and then did it all over again.

This lasted for four semesters, and I never put my hand up to block it, to keep the water, mustard, milk, or Grand Union lemonade away. For the first year and a half, it happened only when we were stoned, laughing and sated after ordering two large pies from Domino's. Maybe we had just watched some porn or had mushrooms. Then more came over my head, and soon it happened three or four times a week with Curtis and some cheap beer and a pitcher of watermelon Kool-Aid. There were many smiles around me, so many grins. I know it sounds silly, but there was so much warm laughter.

"What are you doing?" I said.

"We're holding a baptism," Curtis said. "And I'm saving that very shameful Catholic soul." He was wide with a thick neck, handsome face, and large belly. He was built like a fire hydrant, close to the ground.

"Why are you doing this, Curtis?" I asked with a frankness I never recaptured.

"Don't ask why," he said. "Try why not? It makes it more fun." Then splash, down came more Kool-Aid as the others exploded with laughter, jeering, clapping.

◆

I SPOKE WITH EMILY IN THE EVENINGS, AND WHEN SHE ASKED about the commotion and raucous laughter in the apartment, I didn't know what to say. I was ashamed that this humiliation had developed around me, involved me, and centered on me. *How had it unraveled so rapidly?*

"David, is everything okay?" Emily asked from what seemed like the other end of the earth.

I laughed and said, "Oh, it's nothing, Em—just learning about the very real danger of condiments in upper New York State." From then on I started to have chats with myself up in the bathroom mirror. I dubbed them "The Triweekly Lavatory Lecture Series," and the proliferation of liquids as weapons was the first night's topic.

After the drugs and dousing started increasing, I'd leave the laughter and come upstairs to the larger bathroom with the wide sink and mirror. I'd lock the door and then have interviews with various sides of me, different aspects of David. I preferred the distance of my sardonic, stoned interviews—it kept me from fully understanding what was happening—from *truly, completely* feeling it and owning it. I peered into the bathroom mirror, refusing to blink, and watched my face change, evolve, blur in my head, as if I were stepping into another universe. I interviewed myself and pretended I was Bob Costas. I said things like, "I'm quite disappointed in your performance lately, Fitzy—you're slipping, buddy. All that pot and the refrigerated perishables in today's game are scary, ruthless. You never know when you're in peril. And more is coming your way, so please watch your ass."

I had first done that type of thing—staring at my own reflection until it blurred—at my folks' house when I was home from Martha's Vineyard. From that point on, whenever I was in Guilford for winter or spring break, it continued. I sat at my word processor in

Andy's old room and looked out into the backyard as I wrote part of a passionate but horrible first novel. I tapped out a few pages a night and then peered into the double-paned glass and watched my face contort—it both intrigued and frightened me. I watched my eyes dissolve and new faces rush in behind them like wispy, clever ghouls. It was almost like practice for hallucinations or something. I didn't need any drugs when I was home because I had the windows waiting for me. Calling me. I thought *Who is that second face in the reflection—which was the original? Is this what the palm reader on the Vineyard was warning me about—is this the start of my very bumpy ride? Why does that both petrify and thrill me?*

Gazing into the reflecting windows scared me, but I wouldn't look away. It was as if I were venturing into a pliable city of mystery, darkness, and partial madness directly behind my eyes. I imagined that the faces in the panes had personalities and voices; they seemed to tease me. Sometimes I whispered things in a Dr. Seuss–like tone so softly that I didn't know if it was my voice or not: *Do you want to play with us or be alone and sulk with your bone? Lift off and shoot and do loop de loops, there's nothing to be fearful of, dear king of the kooks! It's all pretend and filled with wow, so won't you come out and soar with us now?!*

THERE WERE TIMES, AFTER I'D SMOKED TOO MUCH POT, WATCHED porn with the roommates, and been dumped on with juice that I'd shiver and hustle upstairs. I headed to my bedroom at the end of the hall, locked the door, and lay down on the bed, my heart stomping through my chest. I took some deep breaths, so relieved to be alone, far away from them. Eventually, one of the guys, usually Jasper, ended up knocking on the door.

"Oh, holy Fitz," cooed Jasper, a Catholic himself. "It's been decades since my last confession. You know we think you're the tops—we'd never intentionally offend you. Tell me you forgive me for my sins. Have mercy on me so I may rest easy and have sweaty, enjoyable intercourse with my wench tonight."

I was annoyed, but eventually I sighed and caved in and said something like, "Go in peace, boy—I forgive you for your rawness."

The voice laughed then and knocked good-bye on the door. "Oh, come on, it wasn't that bad, was it?" he said. "It was good fun and no one supports you more than we do, man. You are the holy one, Father Fitz, the best in the galaxy."

"Go to bed," I said.

"Bless you and keep you," he said.

SENIOR YEAR THE INCIDENTS HAPPENED WITH MORE FREQUENCY, a few times without the hazy assistance of drugs. The other roommates began to join Curtis and Jasper, and it was similar to a fire burning, charring and sucking me up like dry kindling. Every weekend if I wasn't down at the Cape with Emily, I was doused with liquids. Once they broke down my door and pulled me out of bed so they wouldn't soil my mattress. When I limped out of the place in May with my diploma, the rug looked and smelled ripe.

Years later, I wrote a story about this experience and called it "Lord of the Pricks." In that version there was more fight in me; at the climax, I dangled one of them off a roof of the building, waited for him to crap his pants, and then pulled him back up over the railing, kicked him in the throat, and left him on the roof to rot.

"Why did you go along with it?" one student nurse at the hospital, annoyed with my passivity, asked me a few years later. "How could you have possibly thought they were your friends?"

"I got used to it like a puppy," I said. "The next morning they came in sober and smiling and said, 'You're the best, buddy. We never let anyone mess with you—you know that.'"

"How is that possible for you to believe them?" a fellow patient queried in a group. "Why didn't you tell anyone, your family, a professor? Why didn't you fight back?"

"I don't know," I said. "I'm embarrassed that I don't have a better answer. I guess somehow the haze of drugs made it so fuzzy, so far away, and it became protocol."

"You should have tried, man," the patient said. "You should have pushed through and yelled for help."

"No one would have believed it," I said. "It sounds pathetic, but they were all I had in the friends department."

At times, I ran and did a type of interval training, sprinting for a few hundred yards and then walking and then starting up again. I went each day and pushed hard to give my body mental rest, to exhaust myself utterly, to work on the act of forgetting. I usually ran past a chalet-shaped ski shop called something like Tip Top and maroon ranch houses and a few mobile homes. Stretching beyond them for another mile or so were cinnamon and ginger marshlands.

Sometimes, I pushed myself and sprinted up a slight hill beyond that to the stables where the school had their polo horses, which were extravagantly huge, muscular, and lithe. I rested inside the expansive barn and nodded to students I didn't know.

They were caring for the horses, washing them down, cooling them with giant sponges the size of Wonder Bread. Some of the girls talked softly, cooing to the great equines as they fed them. One time I held out my hand with three Halls lemon cough drops, and an older woman looked at me and shook her head, frowning.

On an insipid dare, I once took LSD with Jasper, Sy, and Bobby, and we strolled back near the stables in the moonlight. That plump white rock was hovering so close in the sky— it looked edible and scrumptious and I wanted to suck on it. I wanted to swallow it whole. I wanted to crunch the crevices in the surface and feel them erupt inside of me, to devour them. The woods back there were creepy but fun, the way branches and dead leaves snapped and crinkled beneath my sneakers.

I heard children's voices calling out. Maybe they were playing tag in the darkness. Maybe kick-the-can or hide-and-seek. I heard students, too—girls laughing or screaming, guys growling and bragging. Maybe they were drunk or maybe they were just pleased and relieved to have another Friday evening free for copulation. We crept around the stables but couldn't find an open door, so we barked at the moon. Silly, stupid college stuff. We were so pleased with ourselves. Look at us, world, we can be ironic with scrumptious hallucinogens in our system! What a talented group of young men! Take us in—cherish us!

Later, I remember being stoned and stunned, temporarily mute, covered in Mott's applesauce and Gulden's mustard on my bedroom floor. I saw the faces of my roommates howling, their teeth glistening with something close to delight. I recall a girl-friend of one of the pricks crying out, sobbing and struggling in another room, having a bad trip. There were loud, grinding guitars and a thick bass line was spilling from stereo speakers on the floor somewhere. I found myself breathless, frozen. That moment was broken by a beer being poured over my head, and then another girl said, "Come on, guys, leave him alone."

"Sorry about that, buddy, but you asked for it," a deep voice giggled. "Good night."

Then it was dark and wet at three in the morning, and I moved my body and exhaled. I rose and walked to the bathroom, studying my hair, chest, and face in the mirror. Pale and still tripping hours later, I washed the mess away and tasted the sweetness and the mustard. I fell into bed, my heart pulsing, bouncing through my chest. The pillow breathed.

THE ST. SEBASTIAN STYLE OF BATTLE HAD WORKED WELL AGAINST Andy, but it backfired with the Skidmore Pricks; they saw my submissiveness and their eyes grew wider, hungrier. I was hyperaware at times as the semesters wore on, paranoia blazing away in my skull with the pot and cocaine scurrying through my veins. A rush of silence and fear hovered around me when the sun fell and the bongs came out.

Today, when I think about how my older brother treated me—then about the cross-country camp experience and then the roommates—I think of a weird synchronicity, a pattern that seemed to find me somehow. Did the years of subjugation to my brother make it easier for me to fall into the stuff that happened with the Skidmore Pricks? Was there some way I called for it? Too passive, too willy-nilly, too milquetoast for the masses? Is that just paranoia or really bad luck?

THERE WAS A FIFTH ROOMMATE WHO DIDN'T PARTAKE IN THESE activities. Maxwell had jet-black hair and stayed in his room downstairs with his girlfriend for what seemed like eighteen hours a day. He had unusually tanned, almost wind-chapped skin, and owned a Fender guitar he rarely used. He was rumored to be taking antipsychotic medication during his last semester.

I smile at that now, wondering which medication he was on. Maybe he could have recommended something for me. Sometimes late at night, in the midst of it all, I looked up and saw Max passing through on his way to the bathroom. I used to wonder what he thought about me and if he ever worried they might be coming for him next.

The Pricks didn't approve of Emily. They thought she was snooty and cocky, and they told me not to get so sold on a Mount Holyoke girl.

"Don't get pussy-whipped, David," Curtis sad. "It's kind of pathetic to see."

Jasper, who became a popular baseball player in his last year of school, started out as the guy who was sleeping with three girls simultaneously after his first week. I could never quite figure out his appeal—he wasn't incredibly handsome, and he treated his first girlfriend at school like crap. But the talk, the rap, my God, he could charm a corpse back to life. He had curly red hair and felt it was his right to screw most anything. What I remember most was how poorly he treated his girlfriend. Curtis once described Jasper as the only one in the apartment without a soul. When we moved down to the campus apartments for junior and senior years, Jasper felt it was his time to strut his stuff big-time. "I remember as a freshman, looking up to the studs of this school," he said one night, rambling away on a coke high. "Now it's my gig—I am the man, and the girls look to me. I bring the party."

I admired his brashness, though, and confided in him for a while. I told him that I loved Emily after returning from the island; I told him she and I joked about marriage, that we were deeply in love and that I was thrilled with her. "Well," he said one night after sharing a few more lines with me, "it may feel like thrilling love, but there's only one way to see if it's truly love."

"What's that?" I said.

"If you fart in front of each other—now, that's love," he said.

"That's it?" I said.

"I know it sounds silly," he said, "but there's a whole bunch of real, honest communication in farting with the girl you really admire."

"Serious?" I said, studying him.

"They also must let you screw them in the ass," he said. "That's a really important part of any long-term relationship as well. It's crucial."

"Jasper," I said, "that may be the most ridiculous thing you've ever said."

He held up his hand and licked off the last bit of white powder on the mirror. "Joke if you will, mock me until you're blue in the face. But I challenge anyone to defy those facts." He took his finger and crossed his heart. "Okay, granted, I'm pretty fucking wired at this point, and maybe in the old days that never occurred as much. Maybe not for your perfectly sweet and dear parents, but for today's couple, I say get the tape recorder out. A successful modern love consists of mostly flatulence and anal sex."

I felt light and airy, my brain spinning. "Can I quote you on that?"

"Absolutely."

5

A Reprieve of Sorts

During my junior year, Emily and I traveled to my parents' cottage at the Cape once or twice a month and had a ball. It was great to get away and forget what was occurring at school, though I still couldn't say exactly what it was. I had become aware recently that I was feeling an intense, increased anxiety in every aspect of my life. This wasn't helped by all those damn drugs and those fucking nights with the roommates! Crazy stuff, if you really thought about it. But I didn't think about it—I couldn't mentally allow myself to. The only thing that felt good was Emily. When it was time to leave for a long weekend with my girl, I hopped on the highway and then the Mass Pike and threw some James Taylor, Jackson Browne, or George Winston cassettes on the car stereo. I picked her up at the bus station in Boston, and we drove laughing over the Cape's Sagamore Bridge, counting the exits to the cottage in Dennis an hour and a half later.

We both felt a solid love, serious and true and fun as hell. I was always taking photographs because I believed our relationship needed to be memorialized in more than just passionate letters back and forth. Emily sprawled out in an ancient cemetery off 6A with a shredded red blanket from my childhood and a plastic picnic basket I found in a closet. Or one of her leaning against a lifeguard chair on an abandoned beach in November with a black cape thrown around her shoulders, doing a *French Lieutenant's Woman* look better than Meryl ever did. I took a photo of her playing and rolling in the sand like a puppy, blowing a seductive kiss my way. "Hey," she cooed. "Can we head back now and have some wine and socialize with each other?"

The winter beach was freezing, but the sunsets were alive with purple, blue, and tangerine streaks—perfect for a quick shot. Or two. So many of those damn photos; I was determined to capture the moment, almost as if it didn't exist for me if I didn't see the results from a lab later. Life was an MTV premiere in my skull; watching and observing. Just like that fat man at the A&P with the beady eyes or the old artist observing from his porch at the Cape.

I STARTED WRITING MORE ON MY OWN INSTEAD OF TAKING CREative writing courses because they always made you share your personal stuff. Opening up, speaking. I was terrified of revealing myself and speaking in front of people; it scared the crap out of me. I was fine outside the classroom, chatting with professors, but inside—I couldn't do it. And so I wrote at the apartment. First I produced a weak novella that I showed to a kind Shakespeare teacher who was gentle but honest. "This doesn't quite make it, son—it needs a lot of work," he said. It was about a distempered editorial cartoonist at a tiny newspaper with big dreams and horrible luck in love. Very disappointing stuff.

I took this professor's criticism very hard. At the time, I had a warped view of writing. I felt revision was a sin for a true writer, absolutely the worst thing an author could do. If I couldn't get it down smoothly and near-perfect on the first try, why go back? Even when I heard writers discuss their styles, revising their work twenty-five times, I just figured they hadn't yet seen the best way to do things. The pure, honest, and best way like mine. I told myself that writing it in one sitting—that was the mark of real talent. It was a silly way of looking at writing, but after that moment with the professor, I gave up on stories for several months and just concentrated on Emily.

She had a queer laugh, a quiet chuckle that always tickled me. It was the kind of laugh you had to earn—she wasn't going to give it up easily. I admired that. I was just the opposite, always willing to laugh if someone made the effort at a joke, even when it wasn't funny. I recall Emily's slight laugh in my ear once during a winter weekend at the Cape. We were going to have a go of it in the dunes, but it was just too cold and sandy, so we headed back to the cottage and did it there. I wrote her one line of poetry: "Emily, my love, I explode with you in my heart." She simply placed it into her pants pocket with a smile. I was convinced that we had something rare. "Our love will shine on forever," I said.

We took the soapiest baths and showers, and I loved scrubbing her body, getting every inch of her, rinsing and fixing her up until she looked stunning, shimmery. I wanted to dive into her body, swim around, live inside her. I wrote a short story about climbing into her eyes and taking a seat up there, an infinitesimal mini-me, of course, and watching life fly at her. I figured I could go to class with her and sleep and take part in her dreams. Maybe in the bathroom in the mornings, I could see some of her friends naked. Maybe defend her if anything got too scary in that anxious head of hers. I explained to her that this plan wouldn't be for an extended period, just a year or so. When I told Emily this idea, she grimaced and said, "No thanks, David—I don't think that's going to fly."

My parents were worried about my going away to the Cape on weekends. "I don't want you turning our beloved cottage into a motel for lovers," my mother said. "You're supposed to enjoy your time at school in Saratoga."

"It's just true love," I told them. "Don't worry, it's the real thing. I'm going full blast with my heart."

We did love each other for a time—me longer than her, I know. She started discussing the future more—said she might want to work at a magazine or be a designer after graduation. When she asked me about the future, I joked and made excuses. Truth was, I was terrified and had no idea. I felt the rising panic of someone headed into senior year with no clue. And I had no wish to get a job.

"Yeah," she said, "but everyone gets a job eventually, right?"

"Why do I have to do anything when all I want to do is write?" I said.

"Maybe you could do magazine work?" she said. "Or work for a newspaper?"

"That's not creative to me," I said. "It's just the bare bones—I don't derive pleasure from the bones."

Her face grew flushed, and she said, "Fine—I get that about

you. But isn't there a point where you have to head out there into the brave new world and play their game until you find your niche?"

"Why?" I said, looking down at my feet. "Why do I have to play their game?"

"Jesus," she said. "Why are you so obstinate sometimes about obvious truths?"

"Whose obvious truths, Emily?" I said, staring back at her. "Where is it written?"

"Mostly in my student loans," she said gently, grabbing my hand and patting it. "Maybe if you had any sense of financial obligations."

"Oh, great," I said. "Insult me for that."

"Look, my love," she said. "At some point, you're going to have . . . to do things you don't wish to. People do. I do. Everyone does, right? I mean, eventually don't you have to?"

"I guess," I said.

Right after the argument, feeling slimy and pissed off, I dropped Emily off at the Boston bus station and drove straight to Molly's college in New Hampshire, where I found a phone book and got her number. Molly picked up right away and told me she was living off campus. I headed over to see her, and we slept together that night. I felt enraged at Emily for not seeing life my way—and so I reacted in the cruelest fashion I knew. Sex was so simple with Molly; we knew each other so well—we had known each other since we were kids—and we merged together like perfectly grooved parts.When I left the next morning, she asked me, "Do you truly love this girl more than me?"

What could I say? In one way I did, but in the other way, the way of first love, first kiss, rolling around and giggling as teenagers, she was my girl forever. Any time I crossed the Sagamore Bridge onto Cape Cod, it was Molly territory. She owned most of my ghosts of the mainland, and Emily owned the ghosts of the Vineyard. And yet I felt guilty for what I'd done. I tried to explain the confusion to Molly. I felt love for both of them, but I knew that only made me sound like a horrible leech, so I didn't say much and never really answered her question.

I drove home crying because I was so ashamed. It was an impulsive reaction, one that would become familiar in the future and that would hurt people I cared for in the same way. Five days later, I sobbed and confessed to Emily over the phone, thinking it would be a great reducer of stress, that it would get my error off my chest and let me take some healthy deep breaths. "I hope this confession saves the relationship," I said, but she only wept briefly and then cut off any more venting.

"I don't want to hear the details—just don't do it anymore, okay?" she said.

Of course, telling her only made things worse. I felt her take several steps back from me, maybe taking stock of her life, understanding, perhaps, that I didn't have much of a future with her beyond this last year of school.

That summer, the break before our senior year, I spent a weekend with Emily and her family at Lake George, where they rented a cottage for two weeks. Her sister and her parents were down a slight hill at one point, eating a picnic lunch of hot dogs, apple juice, and beer, at most fifty yards away. Emily and I had the most indelicate sex of our young lives then—two lovers grunting and thrusting on top of a down quilt. She was half panicked, half thrilled, saying, "Jesus, oh, faster, faster!"

Later, we swam out seventy yards in the lake and climbed on a wooden raft. I lay down on the dock's warm surface, and Emily turned and rested her head on my belly. "How are you doing thinking about school?" she asked.

"I'm all right," I said. "Waiting for the year to begin, I guess. Always waiting—and you?"

"Yeah, this is it," she said. "We'll have my room all to ourselves, and you can come down on Thursday nights. We'll have tea, we'll go to a museum—we can steer clear of those arrogant roommates."

"Oh, come on," I said. "They're just kind of rowdy boys—mostly harmless pranks."

She was silent for a moment, choosing her words carefully. "I think toxic might be a better choice."

I swallowed and stroked her neck; God, what a neck. "They're what I have, Emily—they're my friends," I said.

"Sad but true," she said. "I love you, though."

"Yeah," I said. "Me, too."

Her younger sister took a Polaroid of us on the dock and showed it to us when we swam back to shore. It had me sitting up by then wearing an ugly purple sailor hat that Emily hated. My belly is ribbed with muscles, my legs are taut and tan. Beside me, Emily sits like an angular, perfectly designed model. Slight frame, tiny breasts. Sleek hair with Ray-Bans on and her hand resting on mine. Again, Anne Sexton without the haze of malaise.

Late in the summer, I came into Manhattan with Emily and her sisters to see a UB40 concert on the water. The music was alive and exciting, but the people in front of us smoked hash and passed it around. The insipid laughter that spilled out of them was like an elbow to the gut; it took my breath away, and I panicked. That sticky sweet smell was just a reminder that autumn was coming soon with brilliant color, books, sex, and love, but also with a pretty steady diet of drugs and humiliation. Though I refused to call it that. I thought the Pricks were merely excitable partiers, boys who seemed not to have a care in the world. "We'll always protect you no matter what," they said after a night of drugs and teasing. "Consider yourself safe with us, man."

THE SUMMER BEFORE MY SENIOR YEAR, I HAD STARTED SEEING A psychologist in New Haven, and he thought I needed considerable help. I'd been feeling lost, a little spacey in my day-to-day interactions with others, and my parents had picked up on it and suggested I meet with him as much as I needed. My father paid for the therapy.

"People may tell you that they respond to your charm and naïveté, and that's great," Dr. Grinder said, "but always feeling a need to please is dangerous for self-development. It's important for you to carve out a trail for yourself, to begin to separate from the pack and find a passion you can pursue."

The doctor was an affable fellow, a tall, thin man with salt-and-pepper hair. He gave me some general psychiatric tests and listened to me. Not that many people had really listened to me.

"I don't know why I'm here," I said on our first day. "Just some lingering melancholy."

"A tune-up?" He smiled.

"Yes."

Dr. Grinder frequently talked with me about books and how important they were. "You must contribute to the world you live in, son," he said. "And it sounds like a possible way for you to do so is through writing."

I never told him about the roommates; it wasn't that I was consciously ashamed, but that I still didn't see how it was affecting me. I hadn't even allowed myself to consider what they were doing.

"You have a growing depressive disorder," he said at some point. "You must address it or it will clean house and address you."

"What do I do?"

"I'm sure they have counselors somewhere near your school, David." Dr. Grinder smiled.

I shook my head. "Just let me get through school and then I'll address it, okay?"

"Why is it bad to seek help there? What do you fear?" he said.

"I don't know," I said. "I think it's best if I wait until I'm through."

DURING OUR SENIOR YEAR, I VISITED EMILY AND WENT TO SOME of the socials. We stayed up forever in her single room, just the two of us rolling around on two mattresses spread on the floor. I teased her about her record collection, which was too perfect, I thought, and she pointed to the Rothko poster she'd added to please me. The curtains were drawn, and the only light in the room was the glowing green dial of the stereo that was giving us Terence Trent D'Arby straining through "Wishing Well."

Those nights had longing, the romanticism of postcoital murmurs, and it felt safe, so very safe, for me. We discussed sex. Her and her friends' favorite fantasies were vague, indefinable. And me, I told her with a resigned and embarrassed sigh I was a born voyeur. I wanted to see her in different kinds of compromising positions with another who was more amorously gifted, more skilled. I imagined her delicately long neck stretched out, groaning . . . I escaped into my distant fantasies.

I recall when Emily rolled back and forth and then mewed in my ear. Jesus, I loved that sound. I enjoyed being open with her, feeling unencumbered and free when we held each other—that's when I felt most protected and alive. Some of the time Emily just touched me. It was a familiar but odd feeling, sitting in the darkness, feeling almost entirely by myself, except for that warm, thin hand. It was eerie, like a floating sensation. The room was pitch-black save for that glowing stereo in the corner of my vision, and I'd tense and relax and then tense again, drifting off into a fantasy with her warm whisper. "Yes? Yes."

Mount Holyoke is located in South Hadley, Massachusetts, and we spent a lot of time downtown, frequenting a bar or café. We visited there with her girlfriends and they tolerated me for a while. But after I got too drunk a few times at a party, they shut me out. Once you crossed their boundary, their taste-assessment litmus test, their walls went flying up, and no reentry was allowed. So Emily and I hit double features and drank beer with some of her friends' dates from Dartmouth or Wesleyan. Good guys mostly, pre-med or finance. The cocktail parties for the Manhattanites-in-training were filled with a cappella groups from Ivy's or a jazz trio playing in the corner of a room. Emily wanted me to be more social, to explore topics with people. I told her I didn't want to prepare for Manhattan, that it scared me, and she rolled her eyes.

I TOOK SINGING LESSONS WITH AN ANCIENT WOMAN NAMED OLIVE at school. I learned that it was the best way to get a couple of credits—Curtis had told me about this, and I thought if I was honest with the teacher, she might let me skip the recital that most students had to complete. I couldn't face the workload of another full course, so the voice lessons worked out perfectly. Olive had gray curls and was three inches below five feet; she had battled polio when she was younger, and her right leg swung out wide, like a little girl walking away from the beach with sand in her bathing suit. I convinced her that I was too timid to sing at the final recital, so I just stood erect in her little office and performed for her and another old lady a few times each week. With a piano accompanist and a view of a parking lot, I pretended I was James Taylor rehearsing for an upcoming tour. I closed my eyes and sang "Terra Nova" and "That Lonesome Road" with all the sincerity I had left.

My accompanist was a fifty-six-year-old Russian fellow named Rego who had gray hair and a pinched nose and drove a classic black Jag. He came to several of the roommates' parties, and I found myself chatting with him over beer and cocaine. Those parties were a combination frat house and poetic free-for-all. I rarely attended, as I spent most weekends with Emily. But when she canceled, I had an opportunity to witness the magical soirees the roommates spoke so highly of during the week. There was the requisite swallowing of goldfish and high fives handed out by boisterous baseball undergraduates.

The roommates had also strung white bedsheets from the ceiling throughout the first floor of our apartment. They handed out colored markers, and everyone was supposed to write out their favorite sexual dream, song lyric, or impressive non sequitur. Rego spoke with me about the passion of Muscovite women while he wrote Russian curses on the sheets. "Leningrad pussy is most pungent," and stuff like that.

I walked upstairs and went down to the end of the hall to my room, where I saw a blond sophomore snorting coke off my copy of *Franny and Zooey*. "You appear to be doing cocaine on my desk," I said to her, and she giggled.

"Would you like some?" the girl said, wiping her left nostril with her pinkie finger. She pointed to the book and said, "Great story, by the way."

"Oh, thank you," I said, crouching down and doing a line. When I started in on a second, she tapped my shoulder and smiled.

"Easy there, buddy," the girl said. "Your best friends gave it to me—not you."

"I'm pretty sure they're not my *best* friends," I said.

"Don't kill my buzz tonight, hon," she said, patting me on the shoulder. She left, closing the door behind her. I locked it and sat on my bed, looking around the room. There was an apricot quilt from my little sister Julie's room hanging on my wall. My grandmother had made it when Julie was a baby. I had brought it from Guilford as an ironic joke of some sort, though I don't recall what that was. It was pink and baby blue with teddy bears and orange bows and red scooters—in an odd way, it was my favorite keepsake. I had some sentimental James Taylor tickets around or a sweet card from Emily that held meaning, but that little blanket of my sister's, about four feet by four feet, gave me more comfort than anything else in the room. Sometimes I took it off the wall and let it drape over me while I slept.

Whenever I wore my little sister's blanket, I couldn't help but feel eased. Julie had the most squeezable cheeks back then—with a chipmunk look to her in the early years. We had fun together when she and my parents came up for family weekends. I'd run with her, gripping her hands and swinging her high into the air over benches and the stairs around the campus. She was five then, and she'd giggle and say something like, "We are most definitely soaring high today, David." I remember her in a maize-yellow jacket and lime boots as she traipsed through the mud puddles, splashing around. She'd hum or sing a new tune she was learning at school. Soft, touching, she was one sweet girl.

I could hear people crowding in the hallway, people looking for Jasper, who was busy entertaining and flirting away. I could hear his voice through the crowd. It slithered underneath my door, like some insidious airborne infection.

"It's a magical night for nostrils," he was saying. "Who wants to do a few lines?"

ALL THE LOVE AND INNOCENCE IN THE WORLD AT HOME COULDN'T stop the storm coming for me, slowly rising, swirling inside. It was as if fragments, grayish-black flickers of the anguish and the future struggle, would course through my mind's eye, hover for a few seconds, and then speed on. These pieces lived just behind the skin, and they moved through me like a steadily building pulse.

There were also good people at the school who gave up on me when they saw the drugs and the crowd of fools I lived with at the end of my time at Skidmore. One of the good guys was Bart, an art major from Seattle. He was a gangly fellow who liked to play tennis with me and show me bright abstract paintings over in the art building on the far end of campus. He liked to splash huge crisscrossing strokes of raspberry, melon, and vermilion with bright splotches of royal blue dotting these massive canvases.

He was surrounded in that department by long-necked lesbians in fringy boots and skinny fellows sheathed in ebony who favored tragic, haunted figures and crucifixion scenes. I didn't know a thing about art, but I thought Bart had the beginnings of something. He at least believed he had the balls to be a real artist, one who painted with something other than old reliable black or dung brown. Bart talked to me about this while we hit the tennis ball back and forth during a match one day.

And there was Celia from Idaho, who was extremely gentle with small hands and nails that were long and painted vivid grape. She was a dancer but preferred the modern stuff. I once saw her dance in a bronze hood as the grim reaper, rolling over the other dancers. She chased others around the stage, reaching for them, tackling a few, growling and laughing as the music thumped and rocked. I found that world riveting, something I had never considered. I had never met someone who had posters of Twyla Tharp on her walls.

One time Celia and I were downtown at a bar, and she was doing shots of tequila. It was not typical of her—she was usually quiet and rarely drank. Her pale face had a determined, set look to it, and her green eyes seemed a shade darker. She was very focused on the task of imbibing. She had her dirty blond hair swept back into a ponytail. She leaned over and patted my ass playfully and said, "What the hell are you doing here at this school, David?"

"I don't know," I said.

"Really—what sold you on Skidmore?"

I hesitated and then said, "Mostly the carpeted dorms and the way the library glittered in the November ice as my parents and I drove away after an interview."

"Really? No shit?" She smiled.

"Yes," I said. "I was thinking of St. Michael's in Vermont, but their dorms smelled bad, and there was no carpet. It felt too dank and a little bit like a high school."

"Where did your family go?"

"Most of them went to Boston College, and I thought it was too big for me," I said. "An abundance of Irish Catholics isn't always a good thing."

She rolled her eyes and said, "Sounds like some unusual research on these matters." She looked over at a friend walking through the door as the jukebox rattled and blasted an old song, "Smoke on the Water," I think.

"I feel horrible," I said, and she cupped her ear.

"What?" she said. "I didn't get all that."

"What do you think you'll do after graduation in a few years?" I asked.

"Twyla Tharp is going to hire me, and we'll put together many pieces." She smiled and downed another shot.

"I love that you dream so grandly," I said and gripped those tiny hands with the grape nails. That night we fooled around, and she made these intense growling, animal noises as I nibbled on her skin. For two weeks we wrestled together in her room, and then one night she walked me to the student center and squeezed my hand while a band played David Bowie's "Young Americans."

"I don't think I can save you," she said.

"From what?" I shouted, buzzed.

"You've fallen into some sort of well. I thought I might reach you and pull you out, you know?"

"I don't want to fall any further," I said, and she kissed my cheek and held my hand on her lap until the song ended. Then people were clapping, and she slipped through the crowd and waved back at me. I saw her periodically around campus but that brief relationship fell away. And with it those gorgeous grape nails.

ONCE WHILE I WAS STAYING WITH EMILY AT MOUNT HOLYOKE, and she was taking her December final exams, I went through her drawers and found a journal and flipped through it. I found a page that read, "David is arrogant about his writing," but the word "arrogant" had a line through it. I felt guilty but shocked—just how had I given the impression of arrogance? Was I too cocky, did I ask her too many times what she thought of my stories? Oh well, never again would I ask her!

Emily had seen how my roommates treated me: threatening me, standing over me with a gallon of water or milk or fruit juice. They didn't hold back much with her around anymore. "You can't give me that look, Fitz, and not anticipate damp treatment!" Curtis teased in front of Emily.

She grabbed me by the arm, and we went upstairs to my room at the end of the hall, and she told me to snap out of it, to witness what exactly the roommates were doing to me. I brushed her off, not capable of really hearing her, of grasping what that meant. I couldn't put the pieces together then—I didn't want to either. I was usually in a drugged, numbed haze by that point.

When she took the bus back down to Mount Holyoke, my stomach lurched, and the roommates whispered, "Fitz—she's not cool at all. She's got several horseflies up her ass."

"No, no," I said. "She's very cool. I love her."

Jasper sat me down in his room, where he and Sy were getting high. "It's like this—you know I wouldn't steer you wrong. I've known you for four years, now, right?"

"Yeah," I said.

"The woman has too much cockiness," he said, "and we don't like her. Why don't you let her go and start talking to the Marker girl you follow around on campus?"

"Yeah," said Sy, nodding his head. "I bet she'd love to warm your tender, vulnerable cockles."

They were cold, nauseatingly sardonic, but it was true about the girl, Marker—I'd become obsessed with her. It took place as Emily and I had begun to drift apart. Marker had a faraway look to her like the female figures in Edward Hopper's paintings. She had a distance, a melancholy posture that somehow comforted me. Her "mark" was a port-wine stain running down half her face and neck; sometimes I'd go to the campus center and stroll beside her, breathing in her fruity scent at the mailbox or in line at the cafeteria. I thought she was enticing; her fingers were petite and delicate, and her smile was crookedly perfect. I was growing sad and alienated, and I felt this girl understood me, that she had perhaps been teased about the stain on her face as a child. I thought we might help each other out or, more accurately, that she could assist me, and we could make love, and I could disappear into her body, and she could be strong for both of us.

Of course I never spoke with her directly, only bumped into her once as I was coming out of a building. In my fictional memory, that building was the chapel, and she signaled to me and led me inside, and we said some sort of incantation together, restoring my dissolving faith, and then we went on a long walk through the woods and fell in love. I imagined her with a muscular, toned Jesus dangling in her cleavage on a thin silver necklace. But, in reality, I think one time she simply offered me a smile as we passed on a sidewalk near the chapel. I turned and leered at her. She possessed gravity-defying breasts, the way only a nineteen-year-old can. I wanted to suck on them with all my might, to kiss her stain wherever it went on her body.

I wanted to share secrets. I thought she could heal me and maybe I could help her. I wanted to hold that pristine girl tight, to roll around on the ground and have furious sex. I'm so ashamed that I never learned her name, never even spoke with her. She was someone up on an altar for me, just another idol to worship from a distance. I kept her nameless in my fantasies. It was so much easier that way, you know?

I believed in my head, in my heart, that we'd eventually find each other. Our relationship was visceral, true, and absolute and would lead us into each other's embrace. It was our destiny.

Looking back, this felt like my first real taste of delusional thinking.

I FELT I NEEDED SOLACE AND COMFORT FROM THE GNAWING PANIC that fed on me when I attended lectures for school. I could just barely make it to classes at that point, couldn't trust myself to speak or chat with the others. I felt like a fraud, like a wasted blubbering blob of anxiety. I tried to ease the feeling by walking over to the theater and attending two or three student productions; I marveled at the braveness, the balls of those actors. *How do they let themselves be so naked out on the stage?* I wondered. Usually, I disappeared into the library to absorb as much as I could of Hemingway, Updike, and Kate Chopin.

My English professor, Dr. Whaler, was extra gentle to me during my last semester and rarely pushed me to speak in class. But one day in class he finally asked me what I thought of Thomas Pynchon's *The Crying of Lot 49,* and the only thing that came out of my mouth was "It was a lot different than most." Everyone laughed and my face flushed. As he moved on to someone else, I felt that I couldn't really breathe and had to excuse myself to get some water. When I came back, I avoided everyone around the table and sat on the floor behind them, doodling on my notebook, not caring, waiting for the class to finish.

A place that drew me was the chapel. It was a compact but

beautiful building with lots of open light. It was deserted and safe, and sometimes, especially in my last year there, I snuck in at off hours and said the Hail Mary. This was really the only time I prayed. I was embarrassed to be there somehow—afraid my roommates would see me there and would use it to verbally bludgeon me. But I was willing to risk it because there was such a great stillness in that chapel. I even went in a few times when I was stoned and sat admiring the windows and the colors. They danced marvelously at those moments, oozing from the stained glass, dripping and slipping from white to sky blue, emerald to a dappled vermilion and gold. The chapel was only a quarter mile from the student apartments, but it felt like a different world.

I got a similar feeling being in the art space in a corner of the student center. It was just a diminutive glass room filled with fluid and colorful paintings and sculpture by students. When I walked inside it, I was lifted from the noise of bickering, snickering faces, and I could take some deep breaths. An art student was always assigned to be there, and they were kind and sweet and told me about each work. Sometimes those were the only substantial conversations I had on campus.

By this point, I had become a recluse, a drugged, numb soul who was afraid of most everything. At the end of the final semester, just that whiff of pot or hash nearly doubled me over. Paranoia was pretty much unbearable when I spotted the bong on the floor or kitchen table—my abdomen would seize up and I'd stiffen, stumble, and shake as I hustled up the stairs to my bedroom. And though I was a willing doer for a great part of those semesters, the last month I wouldn't touch the stuff. There was a final evening in early April that broke my back, when I got stoned with the roommates and they dumped everything they had on me—milk, water, beer, pasta, and mustard—and I almost broke down. As I went up the stairs to shower and clean everything off, I heard them whispering. Sy, who'd only lived with us for two semesters, was giggling uncontrollably.

"I used to watch you guys do this to Fitz when I first moved in and I thought you were the cruelest bastards," he was telling them. "But now I finally get it—it's so fucking addictive!"

I sat in the shower for thirty minutes, resting on the edge of the tub, trying to take easy, slow breaths. There was repeated knocking on the door, but I just ignored them and shampooed my hair over and over. Eventually, the knocking stopped, and I stood and took my hands and placed them under the showerhead and pushed hard against the pea-green tiles as the hot water rushed onto my face and chest. It was nonsensical, this pushing, but I felt like I had to keep the walls from collapsing.

IMAGES OF EMILY DANCING ON A FELT TABLE IN A SNOWSTORM ARE seared into my memory. I see her feet shuffling as she grinned, swaying just a touch, one floppy yellow mitten rising defiantly in the air while the other gripped her wine. It was one of the last joyful moments we had together in the midst of a crumbling relationship and a crumbling life.

By winter break of senior year, we were struggling to hang on to anything resembling the relationship we'd had. My high school buddy Kevin came over one evening with his girlfriend and suggested the four of us hike up to Top Rock, a large outcropping of stone seventy-five yards up the street from my parents' house in Connecticut. From the garage we grabbed aluminum folding chairs, a blue felt table, plastic cups, and two bottles of white wine and started lumbering up the street. We cut through a neighbor's property and found a clear section of rock that over-looked the train tracks where my old pooch, Jiggs, had met his demise a decade earlier. We could look out a half mile beyond at Long Island Sound, glistening black.

There were already six inches of snow on the ground, and huge, fat flakes were falling from a moonless sky as we set up the table and chairs. We then toasted one another, growing drunk in the mini-blizzard. The snow was cold and wet on my face, and I couldn't stop kissing Emily's flushed cheeks. They were so delicious and shiny. We sang goofy songs, gulping the wine, and eventually Kevin convinced each of the girls to try and stand on the felt table. His girlfriend, Shelley, got up there first but fell off after trying and refused to climb back on. But it was Emily, all 119 pounds of her, who held on, clutching her cup of chablis, demure as ever, toasting the snow and the near-whiteout conditions and saying things like "You know the view from up here isn't half bad."

The three of us on the ground huddled around the table with our arms ready, waiting for it to collapse and for Emily to tumble. But she remained for a while, part rock star, part levitating snow goddess. The table never broke, and she stayed up for a good five minutes, had another glass of wine, pretended to do a little soft shoe in her narrow boots, giggling like a kid with the flaky, damp confetti swirling and drifting around her. It was one of the most alluring things I'd ever seen. Eventually she had enough and tried one of those "trust falls"—just floating backward. For a second, she was hovering in the night sky, a gigantic cloud in my vision and then she dropped into my arms. The four of us left then and hus-tled home, our bodies frozen, not even thinking of the furniture left behind. Kevin and Shelley headed back to his folks' house, and Emily and I made love in my parents' guest room, listening to the moisture as the air turned milder. The gentle, insistent sound against the window was a slight tip, tip, tip of sleet.

Emily's laughter while up on the table had sounded different from what I was used to hearing from her. This had been a real guffaw, not a restrained chuckle. She was the last woman in the world you'd expect to do that, dancing up there, even if we were in the middle of nowhere in a snowstorm and she had a great deal of chablis in her system. That moment is gone for me. There were no photos, and I know it's lost, and yet, as each year passes, it gains more detail just because that was my mythic moment with a sweet, pretty, and semiperfect girl. When we made love in the guest room later on, life felt fresh and dazzling again, like when I first kissed her on the Vineyard. Briefly, I felt at home—perhaps for the last time.

KEVIN AND I RETURNED TO TOP ROCK DURING SPRING BREAK. His girlfriend had left him by then, and Emily and I were barely together anymore. It was April, and Kevin and I marched up the street without speaking, following the same path, now muddy, through the woods. We found the tables and chairs just as we had left them three months earlier; and we each grabbed one and walked right to the edge of the cliff. Growling, we took in a big inhalation, bent over and threw those goddamn things into oblivion (or, at least, down fifty feet to the woods and rocks below). Every ounce of the frustration and broken feelings went hurtling to the ground. It was interesting to watch them crash into the stone, to see how they fractured on impact. I remember thinking, "That would have looked good on video."

No one in my family ever asked about the furniture.

◆

My last senior project for a sociology course was a five-minute video about angry gestures that transcend language and culture and that every person in the world expresses in a fit of rage. I had no one else to help film it other than the roommates so I had the four giving me the finger, grabbing their crotches, doing the chin flick and kissing their fingers and then slapping their asses.

I got a B- on the project, and then a day after graduation, I got in my car and drove home to Guilford. I put the tape into the VCR and watched it. The film opened with me introducing the segment. I had on my olive army jacket, khakis, and a plum shirt from the Vineyard and was standing in front of a brick wall near the music building. I remember how tired my face looked and how young the four Pricks were. Just kids, I thought. Kids with tons of drugs and nothing to hold them back, nothing to keep them in check. That's really what we were down there in the student apartments, amoral animals on the loose.

I watched the video while sitting in the den, absorbed those severe, innocent faces smirking, laughing, mouthing "fuck you" as they grabbed their dicks or flipped me the bird. I didn't get it at the time; I knew something weird had gone on, but I hadn't accepted that it was truly and completely cruel. I rewound the tape again and then it was gone—perhaps I had erased it accidentally, because it was too scary, too much. Too truthful. Maybe it would be too difficult to watch repeatedly, but whatever the case, the tape played back a single time and then it was white static. The nonsense was gone forever.

◆

FOR HER MOUNT HOLYOKE GRADUATION, I GAVE EMILY A SIMPLE white cotton dress and a Guess watch. I started telling her that I was feeling poorly, feeling broken, and she clearly didn't want to hear it. Two months later, on one of our final days together, we were at a megamall in New Jersey, and she was looking at shoes in a department store. I said, "Isn't it weird how people stumble, that you make their base unsteady, and they fall like a sand sculpture?"

She exhaled audibly and said, "Why would you think about something like that? What good does talking about that kind of stuff bring forth?"

"I truly love you," I said desperately, and she just shook her head and walked on.

Nothing I said was right anymore.

That night Emily and I didn't have much to say to each other; she was aware of the hovering malaise, the inertia that had swept over me starting back in January. Or maybe even before. We had sex one final time that night, and she wept.

"It felt like you were just raping me," she whispered, walking over to the bedroom window. And then, "You just . . . didn't turn out the way I thought you would."

God, how those words pierced my chest, chased after me for a substantial amount of time. They brought me to my knees. I wept for several minutes and then got my things.

THAT SUMMER AFTER GRADUATION, I WENT WITH MY FATHER TO the 1988 Seoul Olympics in South Korea. My dad was a car dealer, and he had sold the most Isuzu vehicles in the New England region. My mother had another obligation, so it was a chance for my father and me to grow closer, to have some fun. Unfortunately, we didn't connect, though we ate together, played tennis, and went to the Olympic competitions. But I look back on it now, and I know I was starting to drift. My mind was in a mini-fog. I looked up at my father and his business success with a combination of intimidation and pride. What could I ever do to equal the success he'd had in his life?

One day we took a bus up the infamous thirty-eighth parallel and spoke with a muscular, massive, square-jawed soldier from Bristol, Connecticut, who was standing watch there. "You have to be over six foot four to stand guard," he explained. The US Army wanted to intimidate the North Koreans and vice versa. The solider sat with my father and me in the mess tent and said, "Look at the inside of my hat here," revealing a photo of his girlfriend and the American flag. When I asked him what her name was, he winked and said, "Why you want to know that, hotshot?"

On the way back to Seoul, the trees and the hillside were hyper-green, lush. Huge leaves with tropical-colored flowers and bright, pastel-colored corrugated tin shacks built up along the slippery, muddy roads. A car dealer from Stonington, Connecticut, a Spanish man in his sixties, sat beside me on the bus and told me that he had once been a mortician and described "all the tricks of the trade." How they bunched up certain bodies to fit into the coffins, how they drained the fluids. When he asked my age, and I said twenty-two, he laughed. "My God, son, you act like you've still got that umbilical cord tied around your neck. It's time for you to start living!"

"So I hear," I said, and he looked away.

◆

AFTER FIVE DAYS IN KOREA, WE FLEW TO BANGKOK FOR THE NEXT leg of the trip. One night, another young dealer from the Midwest invited us out to the sex parlors with a few couples. My father declined, and I backed out just before they left in a taxi. The next morning at breakfast the people bragged so much about their night and described it in such detail that I've incorporated their night's experiences into my memory. It sits there, crystal and vivid as my high school graduation, even though I was actually on the hotel's patio watching the churning, muddy Chao Phraya River until midnight . . . But in my mind, I did go along with them, and we found an abnormally cool bar and had much terrible wine. We got drunk and watched the fleshy spectacle around us. So many naked bodies. I sat fascinated and turned on by the bouncing, topless waitresses who bounded by and said, "Wait until you see this next dancer."

Then a skinny, well-endowed Thai man climbed up on a wide bar and had intercourse with two bored-looking women who couldn't have been much over eighteen. There were thumping drums and terrible ringing music and even a strobe-light type of thing flickering across our dazed faces. I felt myself teetering toward something, some drop. I forgot about this teetering by imagining Emily's body up on the stage getting filled by this dancing elephant man in the disco lights.

At the next bar, we watched girls no older than my classmates opening beer bottles with their vaginas. Edward from Wichita kept on repeating the phrase, "Would you look at that—well, how about that?"

"Tell me how that's possible?" the wife beside me was yelling above the music. "Would someone please tell me?"

Dancing girls stumbled over to our table and kissed the men's

ears and stroked my arm hair and whispered, "You want cigarette, do you want cigarette?"

"Go ahead, man," Edward laughed. "Go ahead with them—
just take a cab back to the hotel."

"I don't think so," I said, shaking my head at the girls.

"We have a wimp at the table," Edward repeated a couple of
times until his wife said, "Honey, shush."

After a few hours watching that hungry river out back on the
hotel patio, I went up to our room and slept fitfully.

BACK IN GUILFORD, I DECIDED TO SHARE AN APARTMENT IN
Boston with a couple of the Skidmore Pricks. I had nowhere else
to go, and I wasn't thinking very clearly. Dr. Grinder gave me the
name of a therapist to look up in Belmont, though I doubted I'd
follow through. Emily was long gone by then, and I felt desperate, broken, and lonesome. The Pricks were familiar to me, they
knew me, and so I went. I hustled out for a final jog in Guilford
in late October just before I left for Boston. The leaves were
gone by then, and I raced up Moose Hill Road at dusk, finding it
peculiar that not a single soul or vehicle passed me for the whole
fifty-minute jog.

The sky was nearly dark, grayish blue, and it seemed hostile.
My breath grew short, and I wanted to yell out at the collection
of dirty sheep over a stone wall, to beg for something, anyone, to
assist me, to please speak to me. My mind raced as I sprinted:
*What if everyone in the world has been asphyxiated, and it was just
me, alone, sprinting on this road over and over? What would I do?
Where the hell would I go?* The stripped trees looked diseased,

dying as the branches lurched and drooped out over the street. I continued to rush home, down the sloped road, fearful that someone would grab me, hurt me, and suck me up into the sky like a razor-red demon.

OUR THIRD-FLOOR APARTMENT IN BOSTON WAS ABOUT A HALF mile from Fenway Park. Curtis was holding on the phone, waiting for Sweet Sandy to pick up. She was a phone sex girl he found in the back of the *Boston Phoenix*. He started telling her about his secret weapon and massaging himself through his jeans. He started calling out to me, "Hey, friend, Sweet Sandy from the land of delight wants to entice you. She gets soaked for depressive, bitter Irish lads."

I felt nauseous. I stayed in the kitchen and didn't say anything, angry or ashamed or both as I heard him giggle and unzip his pants. Bobby was visiting from New York and was beside me, stoned and grinning. He shook his head and said, "Oh, that freaking guy, man. You gotta love him."

Eventually, I walked out the door and started running. I wasn't dressed correctly—I had on shorts and a red-checkered flannel shirt and moccasins. It was early December and maybe thirty degrees. I went down around the homeless man in the garbage bins and the Star Market next door. There was a Salvation Army woman ringing her bell, her head covered with a purple scarf except for her squinting eyes. I sprinted past honking cars, my moccasins barely hanging on. The freezing air pierced my chest, and my legs were numb as I ran past year-round baseball fans with their bumper stickers and vanity license plates that read "Red Sox Rule." I ran past Fenway Park—it wasn't baseball season and the streets were empty along Yawkey Way, and the crowd wasn't roaring inside, but I imagined I could hear them. I ran farther away from the apartment, from the cheering, invisible crowd in the empty ballpark. I ran beyond them and left them as my heart continued to race.

When I couldn't run any farther, I stopped and found a half-empty diner, perhaps two miles from my apartment. I sat down, catching my breath, and ordered a hot chocolate and a slice of apple pie. My face felt numb, and my eyes and nose were runny. The waitress made a joke about my lack of warm attire, and I smiled. About an hour later, I took a cab back to the apartment. Bobby and Curtis had headed out to a bar and left a note with the address. It said something like "Join us for more fun."

I shut the lights off in the apartment, and climbed into bed.

With no one else to watch, Curtis pretty much ceased teasing me. Then in March he left to find himself, to follow some guru on a Caribbean houseboat. "This is about my time now," he said to me as I dropped him off at Logan Airport. And that left me alone to crumble with some dignity. At least I didn't have a breakdown in front of him—there was comfort in finally being alone.

THREE WEEKS BEFORE I STARTED COLLAPSING IN BOSTON, KEVIN and I drove into Manhattan to see Tim and Eric and also Emily. She had called and suggested that "we get used to seeing each other since we have mutual friends." Eric's new girlfriend and future wife, Tracy, was living with her right around the corner on the Lower East Side. I remember sitting in the passenger seat of Kevin's car and feeling the hole in my chest grow increasingly wide the closer we got to Manhattan.

I met her about three o'clock on a Friday afternoon at a small Italian restaurant half a block from where my friends lived. Emily was always punctual, and it was no different this time. She looked thinner, as cosmopolitan as ever with penny loafers, new jeans, a black turtleneck, and a funky fat indigo leather belt. Her hair was shorter than before, and that swan's neck was sleek as ever, with just a hint of tired shadow beneath her eyes. We embraced for a moment, and I felt my gut slam against its walls with something like nausea. I don't think I had fully realized that we were over. I know that sounds hard to believe, but I hadn't. And, of course, I knew it then before I asked the question. I knew it was futile, stupid, sad, and pathetic, but I had to ask and so I did. "Can we give it another chance?" I said, watching her eyes fall. "My new therapist in Boston said sometimes these things can be worked out."

I think she said she was sorry and stood to leave—had we even ordered anything by then? Her lips turned down just slightly, and I watched her be as nice as possible, showing grace or pity? Something sweet, I sensed. *She didn't want to have me lose it there in front of everyone, anyone. Were there other diners?* I know we spoke for probably four minutes after that, so no doubt she told me about her work at *Fortune* magazine, asked about Boston, my parents and family. We politely sipped our beers and then walked outside. I leaned against the brick façade of the restaurant. It was cool for early April, and she said she liked my windbreaker. "That's great that you're still writing, too," she said.

"The newspaper went out of business a month ago," I said, and she nodded.

"Okay, then," she said, and we embraced, and I inhaled all of her, and I believe it was a new scent. Good-bye to vanilla, I guess. Good-bye to nuance. Definitely more bold—new lover, huge city, more sophisticated scents, and boatloads of happiness. All that shit.

Then she walked away, and I watched the slim slope of her shoulders as she turned the corner. Gone. I remember a time a year earlier at Skidmore when we were parked in a student lot, basically hiding from the toxicity of my apartment. We listened silently to Bruce Springsteen groan about losing love.

I felt exhausted as I started back down the street to my friends' apartment. Traffic was rolling by on the avenue, and the sky was a grayish white. I noticed an older couple ahead of me, their fingers entwined, making their way down the sidewalk. I stopped to tie my shoes—I'd put on bluchers instead of sneakers to meet Emily. I thought that would be impressive to her, a sign of maturity, true growth. There was a squashed empty can of V8 near my feet and when I stood up, I kicked it into the street. Two pigeons scattered. I wandered through a convenience store for a few minutes, bought a strawberry Charleston Chew and, eventually, returned to my friends' place. I found them watching television in the living room. The three looked up at me. "How'd it go?" one said.

"Anyone up for leaping off the Empire State Building tonight?" I said.

6

DISINTEGRATING IN
BOSTON

I RETURNED TO BOSTON FEELING EXTREMELY AGITATED AND UN-
steady. I tried to go running a few times but couldn't get my
energy focused. I visited my grandmother in Somerville, and she
made a pork roast for me to bring back to the apartment. I sat
with Nannie and had tea and Lorna Doones and she tried to
make me grin.

"Emily was always too skinny anyway," she said. I loved
Nannie: her smile, her triple-decker home on Cambria Street, the
incredible kitchen scents, the mahogany banisters and moldings,
the memories of that house and our Christmases together. The

porch where she and my grandfather used to wave good-bye as we headed back home to Connecticut, New Jersey, Missouri— everywhere. My giggling cousins, sisters, and brothers opening presents, my parents, uncles, and great-aunts singing Irish tunes. Mourning another Red Sox season. Her grumpy, chubby cat Pennant shuffling around amid the laughter. There was always lots of laughter.

I wandered over to Copley Square each morning, forcing myself to get out and act as if I felt together, as if I didn't feel so far away from the universe. I bought a few novels at the bookstore, but my concentration was shot. A friend recommended I read a new Pulitzer Prize–winning nonfiction book on poverty, and I tried to explain that I couldn't read about reality. That it was overwhelming and that I stuck with make-believe. I repeated a line I'd heard, something like "Give me fiction or give me death," and we chuckled. I was hilarious. I started to wander through museums frequently, especially the Boston Museum of Fine Arts right around the corner. I had been coming for two weeks or so since the small newspaper I had been working for had collapsed, taking my obituary-writing career with it.

I spent mornings there trying to morph into paintings. I found that some of Edward Hopper's female characters looked so forlorn that it eased me some—I wanted to cheer them up, maybe have a chat in the diner or on their beds before the cityscapes. I noticed that Hopper's women had the same melancholic distance in their posture that I had spotted in the girl with the mark at Skidmore, and being with them made me feel less alone. I was most moved, though, by Gauguin—his canvases were mesmerizing. I wanted to taste them, to lick the colors, to gulp the ocean, crunch the mangoes with my incisors. His gargantuan piece *Where Do We Come From? What Are We? Where Are We*

Going? nearly made me faint. It took up an entire wall, and I studied it close up, waiting for everyone else to leave the room so I could inhale it through my nose.

One time when a crowd was gathered, I caught the mixture of a passing lady's Chanel No 5 combined with the clean, dry scent of a perfectly kept viewing space. I closed my eyes and imagined me and Mr. Gauguin in Tahiti, having tropical elixirs in the shade with his dark, wise women. The painting became liquid, and I believed that, if I got a running start and prayed and hoped and got worked up enough, I could dive into the somber blues and mustards, and all would be sweet. I reasoned that it could take me a while to blend in, but perhaps I could offer consolation to the characters—the anguished face crowded in the corner; the child eating fruit; or the old lady preparing to die.

Perhaps I could frolic with the beautiful young woman and find more fauvist colors in Gauguin's other works—maybe he'd even let me jump from one painting to the next. I convinced myself that if I could only enter his masterpiece before my mind caved, I'd be saved. I felt my mind crumbling, splintering, and I reasoned that I had better make my move soon. I was almost certain that Gauguin's characters would welcome me, and we'd go skinny-dipping or sneak away and have a bonfire beneath the palms.

One day a museum guard who had seen me standing too close to the Gauguin stopped me and said, "You doing okay, slugger? You look a little feverish, like you might tip over or something." Oscar was a nice fellow, a portly Latino with a wide, flat nose, and we had nodded hellos to each other almost every time I'd been in his area of the museum. But the minute he spoke to me like that, I knew he had pegged me as a canvas-jumper, and I knew my time at the museum was up. I ran back to the apartment and fell into a state that can only be called disintegration. I actually had nothing to do all day, all week, but still I felt rushed, panicked. Like I needed to sprint. Why was I always trying to escape, to get away?

I took my second shower of the morning and banged my head against the tile walls of the bathroom. I felt there was a film of disgust or scum on me and I had to wash it off, to remove it or bang it until it fell away. I felt that something harsh was bubbling up and growing inside me, and so I scrubbed myself vigorously, even jerked off to try and calm down. Whenever I closed my eyes, I saw variously sized vaginas, penises, breasts, and muscled buttocks pushing, straining into one another, as if they were clogging up the bath drain. They weren't connected to bodies but were separate muscles and appendages. It confused me terribly. I wondered, *Is that in my mind? Am I seeing visions or is it my imagination or is it racing, swirling thoughts? What the fuck is going on?*

After a while, I dressed and walked near Boston University to a sticky-floored, mostly deserted movie theater for a 1:30 matinee. I think it was a Tuesday in April, and the Spanish movie *Women on the Verge of a Nervous Breakdown* was playing. I sneered at the title. I thought, *How perfect, how absolutely perfect!* The actresses in the film seemed so loud to me, like sandpaper on my brain, but even so, the darkness felt safe and welcoming inside the theater and I was able to rest for ninety-five minutes.

Part of me wanted to call Dr. Shelly. He was a therapist in Belmont I had started seeing when I first came to Boston, the one Dr. Grinder had recommended. I saw him once a week, and he'd just started me on my first antidepressant, amitriptyline. "I'm concerned about you, son," he had said with an intense, furrowed look. I had wept during the last session, actually bringing Emily's five-month-old breakup letter to him and having him read it during our visit. I cried and said, "I've become out of fashion so rapidly."

"She says here she was unhappy for many months," he said.

I looked up at him. "Who cares right now?"

"Are you angry with me?" he said.

"No," I said. "I just feel depleted and fucking broken, and I don't want to appreciate her goddamn side of it today."

"Fair enough," he said. "How can I assist you?"

The thing I loved about Dr. Shelly was the grounding effect he usually had on me—I had never met anyone who appeared so comfortable in his own skin. He was balding and solid, a rugby player from years ago at Bowdoin. Very low to the ground, like an anteater or something. *My doctor is like a wise, tender, and benevolent anteater,* I wrote in my notebooks. I wanted to sleep with him or sleep beside him and have him watch over me. Not to have sex with him—but to cuddle within his presence, his aura. To stay on the couch beside his wife and him at night. I wanted to inhale his calm and feel it. But recently when I'd seen him, that calm—the cooling effect—didn't happen.

When I got out of the movie, it was overcast, and I walked over to buy two slices at a pizza café. It was next to a bookstore in Copley Square, and across the street I saw ballet dancers up on the second floor of a dance studio. They looked young, these girls, maybe twelve or thirteen, but so graceful and agile. I wondered what they were dancing to—I didn't know much classical music, but I imagined some score from a piano echoing around them, something lyrical and sweeping.

I had seen a number of performances at Skidmore; Jasper's gentle girlfriend Marissa was the most graceful and talented dancer in the school. I recall that no one leapt as high as her, and she was so petite that the effect was thrilling. Her calves were extraordinary, and sometimes I sat in the audience and watched her prance and fly in the air or, perhaps during a modern piece, roll around on the ground and shudder. Then she would rise quickly to leap once more. When I watched that stuff, it made me think, *At least the whole school isn't lost on me. At least I'm soaking up life; it's more than the hazing, isolation, drugs. At least I'm feeling juice in me when I watch the dancing. It's not just wasted cash.*

I waited for my two slices and watched the younger girls jump and soar like Marissa, but they just kept bending and twisting. I watched the dancers a little longer and then turned away. I felt my head pound where I'd banged it earlier in the shower. I noticed that a homeless man with sores and bruises on his mouth and cheeks was staring at me from across the street. He had a stained black-and-white-checked sleeping bag and was holding out a Red Sox hat as people walked by, his hand shaking visibly. A few people gave him change, and he appeared to scream at them anyway. I finished my slices and, feeling desperate to ease him, ordered a pie. I waited for what seemed like an hour to get a small pepperoni and then walked over and tried to give it to him. "Fucking forget it!" he said, nearly spitting at me. "You think this will take care of the crap inside of me?"

"So sorry," I said and hustled back to my apartment, leaving the pizza with the man.

When I was alone for dinner, I often made butternut squash with Smucker's raspberry preserves. That evening, the night it began, I was out of butternut squash. I didn't want to go back out into the night, into the world with people and their smirks and grimaces, but I hustled over to the Star Market and bought squash, Nilla Wafers, and four Bic disposable blades. When I returned, Michael Jordan was on the TV, with several seconds remaining to hit an amazing jump shot against the Cleveland Cavaliers.

I stopped unloading the groceries for a moment and concentrated on the game. Of course it was MJ, so the ball swished right through. I shrugged, fatigued by his near perfection in every area of basketball, and turned down the sound and flipped on the stereo. I left the groceries on the table and found an oldies station, Fats Domino singing "Blueberry Hill." I took out Emily's old letter and spat on it. I felt heavy, far away, and I began to rip open the razor container, the package crinkling as I tore into it. I tucked the letter underneath my arm and wedged a butter knife in between the double blades, pushed and felt the plastic break and the two small blades fly into the air for a millisecond before landing with a barely audible "ting, ting" on my Formica counter. (The music was on so I probably couldn't have heard that sound, but in my memory, the "ting, ting" is very distinct and clear.) Then I picked up the letter and walked over to my cheap, uncomfortable, peach Caldor's piece-of-shit couch and kicked it with everything I had. "Fuck!" I said and watched it jump a foot or so backward and bump into my bookshelf, knocking a novel off and sending it to the tan carpet. I recall the modern, stylized print of the writer's name, Anita Brookner, across the binding, but I don't recall which book it was.

That kick set me free of any proper behavior and so I cleared my throat and read the letter out loud in a dramatic voice, "I know this will be difficult for you, but I was quite unhappy for a long time." With the small blade in my right hand as I read, I cut gently, lovingly—even sensually—the first slice into my left forearm. I did it carefully at first, almost with civility, and it felt so sweet. Like an old friend, book, or movie, it seemed like absolutely the right thing to be doing midweek in Boston. It felt to me as simple and comforting as drinking a glass of milk with Oreo cookies. "Really," I said, my nose angled up considerably, "it's the perfect after-dinner exercise for a young man on the go."

Then I sliced quickly into my skin, repeating two or three cuts along the arm. I started to feel a rhythm, a nice pace as I watched the blood worm out of my wounds; I saw the liquid rushing up, filling out the cuts. I saw the white line of inner skin before the blood emerged. I started with the arms, but then moved to the shoulders, the chest, and then even the belly. None of it really hurt; I was too frozen, too zoned out for that. But after ten minutes of mutilation, I got cocky. I thought, *Nothing, nothing, nothing I do will ever touch me again!* I clenched my teeth and ripped into my skin, carving the word FUCK sideways along my belly button. I winced for a second and continued on.

Fascinated by the little gashes on my belly, chest, and shoulders, I danced a bit, spastically moving around to the music in circles. By then it was a new song—Fats Domino had been replaced by Nancy Sinatra. "These boots are made for walking . . ." she sang and I felt, if not sexually aroused, hypertitillated. I was suddenly wide awake. There was now a muted car ad on television; some satisfied African American Toyota customer was jumping as high as she could. I remember her heels seemed too high, too flashy to me. False.

The clean cuts looked beautiful and weird. Endorphins sped through me. I spun around, growing dizzy, frantic, and silly. I wasn't drunk, but I felt a nice stoned feeling, sans paranoia, and I thought, "I believe I've found my new pharmaceutical deep inside." I giggled fearlessly, manically at this and looked down at myself; hands, arms, chest, and belly covered in crimson. Superficial wounds, yes, but I didn't want to stop. They gave me a delicious rush, but I had to be cautious—I didn't want to stain the carpet and no way was I going to some fucking hospital.

I wiped my blood on the letter, watching it bead and drip over the painful phrases. "Love ya" and "I'm sorry" and "Take care of yourself."

"This one's for you, hon," I said, then put on a long-sleeved navy T-shirt. I rambled, "Me? Oh, God, things are really developing now, really gelling, thanks." I continued the conversation. "You know, Peaches," I said, "I feel quite sanguine this evening. It's a good era for the blood-smeared fucks of New England. We must rise up and let our stains be known."

I heard an odd sound in my voice. I didn't like it so I pushed the tears back. I wiped some blood on the wall, a diagonal, defiant streak across it, and walked into the bathroom. When I took the long-sleeved shirt off, I saw my reflection in the mirror. I stuck my tongue out at myself, at my trunk and upper body covered in little slashes. I threw the soaked T-shirt into the trash, and I started a bath and sat in the tub. I felt the warmth of the water sting me as it grew deeper over my shins, crotch, and belly. Then the water grew rosy, and I soaped the cuts, clenching my teeth as that mixture stung the wounds. Outside my door I heard someone whistling their way down to the laundry room and a neighbor shouting. My body ached as I lay back in the tub, though I did feel less tense. "I can do this," I whispered. "I can keep this secret to myself." That evening I dreamed of three dung snakes devouring my guts. I continued the mutilation for seven days after this, skipping the museum entirely and visiting bookstores and movie theaters during the day and then hurting myself at night. I repeated my new mantra as I sat in the tub after each performance: "No one has to know."

A WEEK LATER, I DROVE HOME TO GUILFORD FOR MY HIGH SCHOOL buddy Kevin's graduation party from UConn—he was a year behind us. This group was made up of the same guys from that magical summer on the Vineyard three years earlier. I was on 395, and I drove this little blue stick-shift Isuzu I-Mark, and no one was around me—no traffic, and it was blackness save for my headlights and some streetlights every couple hundred yards, and I was listening to James Taylor, the *Flag* album, and hollering, "Fuck!" off and on. I laughed scornfully at my hoarse pleas, at how no one heard them. Then this huge, obnoxious 18-wheeler with tricked-out yellow lights along the bottom of the rig rolled around a bend. "Fuckkkkkk you!" I screamed. I figured someone had to have heard me then, and I weaved away from the passing vehicle, compensating too much as the car veered into the breakdown lane. Glimpsing beer cans and lavender panties strewn along the edge of the highway, I straightened out the car and drove on. My arms stung as I turned the wheel.

I was frustrated by the stinging from the scabs. I didn't want to think about what I'd been doing to myself each evening, and I did everything possible *not* to think about my body. Just the other day I had played basketball with my freshman year roommate from Skidmore. He transferred after a semester to Boston University— said he couldn't bear to count the number of Beamers in the Saratoga parking lot. "Skidrow isn't a college," Danny had said to me then, "it's like a gilded resort for the crafty and semi-intelligent." He transferred to BU and left me, but we'd remained friends.

Anyway, Danny and I had gotten into a pickup game of hoops

with eight other guys, and they wanted to do shirts and skins. But I couldn't take off my shirt, no fucking way. Everyone would see the scars, and my world would become . . . complicated and fucked! I didn't want other people peering into my travesties. So I said I had to play on the shirts side, and some people complained, so I left and didn't return Danny's calls.

As I crossed into Connecticut, I screamed for a while and sang stupid verses of silly songs. "Pack up your troubles in your old kit bag and smile, smile, SMILE!" My conscience was busy trying to name the feeling, the thing that sat on the edge of my eyelids, the thing I couldn't see. It was a ghost that demanded to be recognized. Entropy, was that the word? The same one Dr. Shelly used when he first saw my mutilated hands: "shambles."

"Listen to me, son," he said with warmth, with practice. "You seem to be strained, and I don't want your life to fall into *shambles*."

"It's superficial stuff," I said, looking down at my sore fingers. "It's been such a relief to do it—it brings a kind of peace."

"You have to stop or I'll put you in the hospital," he said, leaning forward.

"I'm not going to a freaking hospital, this isn't out of control," I said. "I'm not in shambles. I'm coping."

"Listen to you, David," he said. "You're running razors through your skin, and it's 87 degrees, and you have on a long-sleeved turtleneck."

"So?"

"Are you cutting all over your body?" he asked.

"I'll stop," I said. "It just helps me loosen up—it takes the pressure off and aids me when your medicine does nothing."

"The meds take weeks sometimes," he said. "Things don't happen overnight."

"This did," I said. "One night after another of glorious feeling."

"Listen to yourself."

So I promised Dr. Shelly I'd stop, and I drove home and flew through Jewett City, Connecticut, going sixty-nine miles an hour in my Crest Lincoln Mercury-Isuzu product from 84 Whalley Avenue, which could be found in New Haven and sold by my father, who fed me and allowed me go to a beautiful college in Saratoga, where I met both sweet people and monsters and inhaled great books and bad drugs and graduated and soon found myself alone in Boston purchasing Bic razors for unsavory, fucked-up reasons. I rolled down the window on the vehicle—no automatic anything on the stripped car—and screamed, "Can I get some prayers for one lonely boy in Jewett City!"

WHEN I ARRIVED HOME IN GUILFORD, I REMEMBERED THAT MY parents and Julie and Dennis wouldn't be there until Sunday evening so I had the place to myself. I watched television and jerked off to odd, lurid images in my head. There were lactating, extended, engorged, and bloated sexual organs prancing behind my eyes. At one point I was floating in a pool on a velvet raft supported by breasts, hundreds of them with nipples intact, keeping me propped up and floating. No water, just drifting, wavy breasts. Later, I saw Emily smiling at me from a photo in my wallet. I thought, *Who are you bouncing on now, darling? Just who is the lucky man?*

THE NEXT AFTERNOON WAS KEVIN'S PARTY AND EVERYONE GAVE him gag presents—he had told us in high school that he set his masturbation record at age fourteen. Twelve times was the figure. So the seven of us gave him bottles of Johnson's baby powder. He had said at one point that he used the powder for the best grip. His parents did not understand why we gave their son twelve bottles of the stuff. He was very red-faced through the opening of gifts, and I grew more and more embarrassed for Kevin and angry at myself and the others as the day wore on.

I felt paranoid and nervous with the whole gathering, walking around wearing a long-sleeved shirt in 89-degree heat. I was convinced that my friends were going to make a crack about my attire. I went to the bathroom and sat down on the toilet even though I didn't have to go and peered out through the shades. It was a perfect early summer afternoon, the aboveground pool was open, and Kevin's little sister, Allison, was swimming, splashing everyone.

I watched my friends laughing, conversing, and hanging around that pool. A small breeze kicked through the trees out back, and Kevin's stereo played the Thompson Twins. People looked contented, and I wanted to take the picture, to capture it in my mind and save it. I felt suddenly that I needed thousands of snapshots in my head to combat the shambles I was becoming. I felt myself slipping as I looked into the medicine cabinet. I was overcome by the need to wound myself immediately, anywhere—could be my belly, my shoulder, my thigh. I searched for razors but couldn't find any, and then someone knocked on the door. I closed the medicine cabinet, splashed some water on my face, and returned to the party.

When I walked away from everyone a little later, say 3:00 p.m. or so, somebody yelled, "You belong in Manhattan, Fitz—leave the Irish and their suds in Beantown and come to New York with your friends."

I held up my hand and waved but kept on walking to my car. Then I was in it and I drove away and I was safe. *Jesus,* I thought, *I never want to head anywhere near New York City.* That was Emily's turf; somehow, in a city of 7.5 million, I was sure I'd run into her with her big happy beau by her side. There was too much shit, force, and talent in that city: the pace, the intricate sophistications. I always felt like I couldn't compete there. *No thanks,* I thought. *I'll lose that battle quickly.*

Kevin came over on Saturday night, and we went to the beach and listened to James Taylor. I think the album was *In the Pocket,* and I was in the passenger seat, and I felt myself . . . I want to get this right . . . *melting* into the vinyl of the seat. I felt like a Ken doll whose face was set on fire. Whose limbs were crumbling, whose heart was burnt beyond recognition. I sank down farther and farther until I was below the dashboard and Kevin said, "Are you okay there, David?"

I said, "I think I just need to lie down, feeling kind of broken and worn."

That night it took everything I had not to cut myself in the house—at one point I took a few unbroken disposable blades and held them in my hand reverently, even licked one with my tongue as if it were some aluminum clitoris. I went downstairs and watched *The World According to Garp* on VHS.

On Sunday I lay around most of the day and went for a run in the late afternoon—I saw a girl from high school bike past me, and she grinned and waved. It was Deborah Grath, and I stopped to say hello and then watched her shapely, pumping buttocks and calf muscles strain and push as she biked up a small incline. Just another girl I overlooked in high school, and suddenly she looked so alive, so sexual. Life, joy, energy, and sweat leapt from her tanned skin.

Then it was dark, and my parents and Dennis and Julie returned from their trip. I believe it was mid-June, and I was in the kitchen, and Julie, nine years old by now, pointed to my hands. They were covered in crisscrossed scars, messy, diagonal cuts. Red and brown and oozing some mixture of blood and puss. "What happened to you, Dave?" she asked.

"Oh," I said. "I cut them slicing a tomato—just a tomato."

My father was behind me and gently led me into the living room. I saw the reflection in the dining room mirror one second before I walked into the room. For that moment, the three of us were caught in the reflection. My father was in jeans and a dress shirt, a very fit fifty-two-year-old car dealer with tired eyes. His nose was broad and strong, and his silver hair was fading, disappearing. My mother was a crossing blur in back of him, going to open a kitchen cabinet. She was a fifty-one-year-old Congregational minister with short brown hair, a thin nose, and a red dress, both very comely, capable people. Out of the corner of my eye was a dark blue blurred image of myself. My father was bringing me into a formal place; we usually sat on those couches only when company came. "How are you doing in Boston?" my father asked, looking down at the floor. Our blue and white rug needed cleaning soon, and I was just about to mention it to my mother, but she continued to slam glasses in the kitchen and bang cabinet doors. *If you're going to bang them,* I thought, *why not destroy them? I mean, why not take a fucking axe to the cabinets?*

Suddenly, everything erupted inside of me, and I started screaming and hollering. Shrieking, I ran over to our cranberry couch by the window and stuck my face in some of the pillows, punching them wildly. I wanted to bite it, eat it. I thought, *Maybe if I swallow the whole fucking couch, it will stop my howling!* I cried, ripping at my hair. *I want all of it gone, every fucking strand. I am shit, I am a pig*, I thought. *Fucking pathetic scum-sucking shitfuckshitfuckfucking pig!*

"Okay, okay," my sister Julie whispered and touched my back. Dennis approached and did the same. I think those moments of touch saved me; Dennis's unusual timbre and Julie's tender voice eased me.

But soon Jules and Dennis were told to go upstairs. My face continued to be stuffed into the couch, and I was weeping, wailing. I thrust my face farther into the cushions, the fabric itchy on my cheeks, and I couldn't breathe very well but I kept pushing. My mouth was open, I was gnashing my teeth, and sounds, horrific, guttural wails, emerged from my belly, from what seemed like deep in my toes. This seemed to go on forever, the sound of my wailing, my mother repeating the phrase "JesusMaryJosephJesusMaryJoseph" in the background.

I saw swords taking off heads, chain saws slashing off limbs; I saw guns, cannons, M-80s in my mouth exploding my mind into minute pieces of grayish-black shit. And crimson everywhere, my bloody leftovers flying, splattering off walls, off ceilings, off the piano. I looked into some mirror, and I saw my body without anything—no head, hands, legs, or genitals, just a trunk rolling over the carpet, spewing, and somehow still screaming. I was still screaming through it all. My mother called my shrink in Boston and brought the phone to me. Dr. Shelly spoke in a low, calm voice. "I'm afraid they're out of beds at McLean right now, son," he said. "You'll have to go into New Haven. Easy, son, now breathe deeply."

My parents hustled me out to the car, and the crunch of the gravel sounded heinous, discordant beneath my sneakers. St. Raphael's Hospital was called and warned that we were on our way. My mother wrapped a blanket around me, kissing me. Then she ran inside and returned with my pillow from my bedroom. *"Oh, Mom,"* I wanted to say, *I'm so fucking sorry, sorry, sorry, sorry, sorry . . ."* My father guided me into the passenger seat, and I started whimpering. Then my father drove rapidly through Guilford, down Leete's Island Road, where I watched two teens running, ducking their heads away from our headlights.

We were suddenly on the highway, and Branford rushed past; East Haven looked so caustic and scary with its hungry neon advertisements off I-95. China Buffet, Friendly's, Big and Tall Men Store, Shell gasoline, and all that crap glowed like piles of radioactive waste. I looked away from the harsh, bright lights, closed my eyes tight, and when I opened them again, there was a triage nurse holding my elbow, and she said, "Okay, now what do we have on our hands here?"

Soon I was in an examination room with my father and the doctor, and he said for me to take off my shirt. I remember the silence, that long pause as they both checked out my body with the various wounds. Finally my father said, "Okay, okay now." The resident wrote down some notes, asked me to raise my arms and twisted his head. "Does that say 'Fuck' on your belly?"

"I'm not sure," I said.

"David," the young shrink said to me. "Did you cut your body below the waist at all?"

"Got my thighs a little."

"Anything else," he said, looking down at the floor (*Christ,* I thought, *why can't anyone look me in the eye tonight?*) "Did you cut your penis in any way?"

"I did not," I said

It was a frequent and popular question; perhaps the favorite that shrinks asked me as my self-injuring continued over the years. The frequency of the question made me think, *Am I weird for not cutting off my penis? Do the doctors expect someone with my profile to have sliced it off by now? I mean, would I be more normal if I cut off my penis?*

What the fuck am I talking about?

CELANTANO ONE WAS THE PSYCHIATRIC WING OF ST. RAPHAEL'S Hospital in a rundown section of New Haven. My father, a prominent businessman in the city, was on the board of the hospital. It's where I spent the next month and a half. At first I isolated myself in my private room on the unit, staring out beyond the curtain at the corner of Chapel Street and Sherman Avenue. I felt like the chief investigative reporter for some TV network as I studied drug dealers calling from a pay phone twenty yards away early in the morning. There were tricked-out cars and a gold Lexus with fat wheels. One day a Mercedes with mud flaps stopped, and this kid in baggy jeans got out of the car and started talking on the phone. He looked about thirteen years old, though he was probably seventeen or eighteen, and he seemed to be the one everyone looked to for answers.

I was on the second floor, about ten feet up, and the room was set back so I watched from a safe distance as crackheads reacted to the beeping orange "Don't Walk" figure on the traffic light. The process seemed easy—walk when the figure glowed white and don't when the figure was orange. Nobody listened, though; nobody paid attention. I watched the young man get back into the car, and the Mercedes sped away.

A tattered pair of sneakers had been tied together and thrown over a telephone wire that stretched across the street—I couldn't remember if that meant someone had been shot or if it meant this was a good place to purchase drugs. My father's dealership was only about half a mile away.

My first psychiatrist on the unit had a broad, large nose and bubbly lips and asked me repeatedly why I didn't tell anyone in my family that I was cutting. *Did I want to punish my family? Did I grow sexually excited by the mutilation? Did I taste the blood? Did I smear it? Why? Can I keep myself safe and stay visible on the unit? Did I wish to cut off my penis? What did I think the ultimate goal for the behavior was? Did I masturbate as I cut myself?* After ten minutes with Dr. Walls, I felt a lurching disappointment. I thought psychiatrists in a hospital would be like Judd Hirsch in *Ordinary People* or like Dr. Shelly. Present, loving, and intense—my favorite welcoming, wise, and benevolent anteater back in Boston. Not the case with Dr. Walls. I felt no bond for that physician; if anything, I felt revulsion.

I told him and my parents a secret that I had been ashamed of since sixth grade—the night a man stopped me on the street and kissed me and held me. The same night Julie was born. When I told Dr. Walls this, he replied, "Those things happen to many children." I loathed him when he said that. I wanted to kick him in the teeth, to slam my mother's pocketbook across his meaty, ugly face. To choke the bastard and spit on him. The only thing he wanted to do was put me on antidepressants, and so he did. Then he said, "David, do you wish to kill yourself, to die?"

Fuck you! I wanted to yell. *Fuck you!*

I didn't like him, and I talked with one of the nurses about this. Diane was cute and kind and reminded me of Molly. She told me in a few weeks we could go for a pass and get some exercise around the hospital. She showed me to a Plexiglas enclosure in the corner of the dayroom called the Bubble—it had an impressively secured television hanging from the wall, magazines, and some hand gel. She introduced me to a man with traumatic brain injury and abnormally puffy cheeks who sat in the Bubble discussing how a Connecticut Little League team was about to win the world title. He said to us, "I could hit the ball in my day, but these boys—Jesus, they got something special. They got true balls." Another lady, maybe eighty—Louise—had dementia and shouted out, usually during commercial breaks, for her deceased husband. "I'm not finished in the bathroom yet, Teddy," she said, staring through me. "You're always hustling me out of the damn ladies' room."

The hospital's colors on the unit were mauve and this light, anxiety blue with tomato-colored plastic furniture that was difficult to destroy. (Sometimes frustrated or bored patients would try to dig into it with pens or cut it with plastic silverware or just grasp it and try to tear it apart, but no. It was tough stuff.)

There were tastefully placed watercolor sunsets and different displays of homegrown art—decoupage, nontoxic finger paintings. Along the corridor were rough whitecapped oceans, pastel abstract chalk designs, even a few puppies, cats, and bunnies in burgundy and black. I recall one paper banner that stretched along the bottom of the nurse's station that read, "This Is How We Draw Hope," and "You Can Turn Your Life Around Starting Today!" There were also peace signs and thumbs-ups and smiling little children captured in crayons, stick figures with lemon dreadlocks.

I remember a young woman who dressed in violet beneath her gown with matching booties and finger gloves and didn't speak for most of her stay until the end, when she only repeated the word "Fuck" when they told her she was being transferred to another facility. She had been snipping and designing hundreds of snowflakes using a child's scissors with concentration, tenderness, and care. There were red, white, black, blue, and chartreuse flakes falling around that Plexiglas television bubble. Nothing to grab your attention on the unit during a summer's day but the multicolored storms in the cafeteria, near the women's bathroom, around the nurse's station, and directly over the unit's pet fish, Zeke. I thought the snowflakes were the most beautiful things on the unit, but another part of me thought they looked like pain in a box. *What was inside that girl?* I always wondered. *What was her secret that kept her so silent?* Part of it, I think, was natural empathy, but after a while I learned there's a cold type of curiosity that takes over. *Hmm,* I'd think, *here's someone new—I wonder what sent them into their tailspin?* (Later, that curiosity frightened me; as the experts pushed me to feel, it felt like I was perhaps losing my gift to engage. A sort of inverse reaction was going on inside my head and heart. As I tried to feel more, I ended up feeling less.)

I was twenty-three years old when I was first admitted. I weighed 175 pounds—I was svelte and in good shape. That changed rapidly with the psychotropic cocktails they gave me, which made me incredibly hungry and caused me to chow on everything—four helpings of cereal, of cookies, of snacks each day. Still, I felt I'd be out in a few weeks—just needed a little straightening, I thought. *A little fine tuning*—an expression everyone used.

On the second day on, a nurse gave me a plaid notebook and a pen along with some Raymond Carver poems and said, "This act is what helps save people." I recall writing something sarcastic that night as I watched *Thirtysomething* in the Bubble. I also spent my days pacing along the waxy linoleum hall that stretched fifty yards out from the nurses' station. It led to a porch overlooking some begonias and tulips and offered another view of Sherman Avenue—a street you didn't want to be looking at in the first place.

My father brought me a rubber basketball, squishy like, and I spun it on my finger as I walked. During the first days, I met two interesting women on the porch; they were harried and tragic, and they had short chopped hair. They were Sharon and Jamie, and they were both suicidal, with bandages around their wrists and forearms. One was a teacher's assistant and the other was a science-fiction writer and a potter; both were in their early thirties. We bullshitted and started tossing the Nerf ball around, back and forth, the three of us divided into a triangle of self-deprecating loons. I laughed and made jokes about how I wasted most of my time at Skidmore, and Jamie said, "I feel as if I've wasted my entire life." We bonded and joked about creepy therapists, about shock therapy, about my doctor and his nose and his funny lips. Sharon discussed her science-fiction novel about a planet where no one bleeds. She said it was impossible to draw blood in the world she was writing about.

Jamie laughed at this and said, "What the hell will you do with yourself on that planet?" Sharon didn't laugh back.

"You come across as pleasant in the beginning," she said, turning and giving the finger to Jamie as she walked away. "But you're a cold, mean bitch."

Jamie was silent for a moment and then looked at me: "I guess it's time for a PRN of Ativan."

"Sorry?" I said.

"Whenever she's feeling stressed, she gets anxiety medication," she said. "The phrase means *as needed*. You'll get them when you're overwhelmed—we all do. Ativan or Buspar or Xanax. They even give you Thorazine sometimes."

"Thanks for the heads-up," I said and then asked, "Is it true, though, what Sharon said—are you truly a cold, mean bitch?"

She grinned as she threw the ball back: "Absolutely."

MY FAMILY VISITED EVERY DAY DURING THE FIRST HOSPITALIZATION— very present and loving, always supportive and kind. I usually had a full room when it was visiting hours. They brought books, food, soda—letters from cousins. Mix tapes from high school buddies; I was too embarrassed to have Tim, Eric, Rich, or Kevin come.

My older sister, Laura, brought a family photo and some soda on the second day of my stay, and I put both carefully, lovingly, on my bureau. The photo showed all seven of us Fitzpatricks gathered around a big oval rock in our old front yard. It was taken in 1987, a year before I graduated from Skidmore. My parents are standing side by side, holding hands, while the children take smiling positions around the rock. Laura, the eldest with the stylish short hair of that era, has her hand on my shoulder; Andy has a new reddish-brown beard, and his face is tilted upward as if he's judging the photographer. Dennis has a mustache and a grin, and my little sister, Julie, is standing in front of all of us in a pink autumn jacket, beaming with her long black hair. She was ten at the time. I'm without a proper coat, just a flannel shirt and jeans, and I look a little dazed.

When everyone left that day, I was alone in my room, and I slammed the glass of the photo against my desk and took the broken pieces and quietly began cutting little slices into my hands and arm. Again, just like in Boston, the release was delicious and instant. It soothed like a balm, like some magical crimson concoction. I felt delight, a tiny, stoned pleasure at both the mini-endorphin rush and the fact of being sneaky. *How dare they think they can take away this new coping tool from me*? I smeared a small portion of the blood on the bedroom wall, a smiley-face character with a fat red nose. I sat on my bed and studied how the reflecting orange DON'T WALK danced along the trail of my blood on my wall. *It's beautiful,* I mused, and this caused me to quiver with fear and titillation. I tasted the blood some and thought, *How come no one ever told me about this?*

The cutting incident felt very much like a movie. And so I whispered out loud in my room at the hospital, to make it even more like an actual movie: "Hey, now, this is a bloody good movie." There was an ironic, wiseass laugh track built into my head from the beginning, or at least an appreciative audience always observing, always soaking it up. It felt like each slice was a religiously themed climactic scene from a melodramatic movie. I was a lapsed Catholic boy doing his thing, sacrificing himself on some crazy martyred altar of twisted and warped Old Testament catchphrases. At those moments, when I scraped myself in the beginning and then really mutilated as time went on, I felt myself losing balance very quickly. Tipping.

I usually had empathy for others when they'd hurt themselves, even if I didn't completely grasp it. But then when the case of "moi" entered the debate, the rotting soulless prick David Bruce Fitzpatrick, failure of all failures, the benevolence I felt for others went out the window. I thought, *Leave the brutality for me—I alone am worthy of raw hate and blood.* As I saw it, I had failed at college, at relationships, at writing, and at life. I firmly believed I was destined for bleeding and carving. I felt so hyped and manic because I'd finally discovered my major with the activity, and it was exciting and fresh.

I was able to clean up quickly that time by pressing a sock into the superficial scrapes on my hands and wrist so the blood wouldn't bead and drip onto the floor. I wiped the smiley face off the wall before anyone could see it. Then for a millisecond, I panicked that everyone would hate me, that this was a poor strategic move in the order of life on the unit. But most of me didn't give a fuck as I continued to rub small amounts of blood over my hands and arms. My God, I had found a good and powerful friend, and the release was raw, sensual. Then I grabbed the photo of my smiling family from the floor and laid it back on the bureau facing upward. That's when I heard the knock on my door for the fifteen-minute check, and the staff discovered my bloody hands and cleaned me up with soap, Bacitracin, and water. While this was going on, I had a final thought that proved prescient.

I must go deeper and harder.

HUMANS HAVE BEEN SACRIFICING, BEATING, SLICING, PULLING, picking, breaking, burning, and whipping themselves since the beginning. Free-flowing blood captivates folks, and it seizes their attention. It certainly grabbed me and seduced me. The Aztec people loved it; Catholics seemed to adore it as well. Self-flagellation at its extreme, bring on the masochism, the martyrs, bring on the sadism. Look at our history, save a piece of the beloved saint's arm and pray on it, remove his fingers and the golden ring and slap some formaldehyde on that sucker and keep it in a velvet case for eternity. There's a primal appeal of the body, of marking it up, decorating it, hurting it. "Wash yourself in the blood of Christ, come and drink his blood and eat his body and you will be saved." Check out the scene on any crucifix in town. Oh, the mortal wounds! The guilt, the crown of thorns, the suffering. And I know, of course, it's a stretch, but we're talking about illness of the mind here, a strained, ugly, and warped mind, so who doesn't get riled up watching the baptism scene in *The Godfather*? Yes, the chorus of angelic voices, the anointing oil and the blessings, the seraphim, but then the machine guns, the essential crimson of life! Oh, the violence and destruction!

I HAD FOUR TREATMENTS OF SHOCK THERAPY DURING THE STAY—IT didn't seem like a huge deal to me. It had worked well for my grandmother and my aunt—there was a kind of all-in-the-family thing going on, so I thought, *Sure, I'll try it*. And those initial treatments worked so well that they said no more were necessary. One thing I loathed about the treatments was the anesthesia. It felt as if my head would explode each time it was injected into my arm. I could feel the frozen fluid rushing up my arms into my shoulder and then into my skull and BOOM! I wanted to scream, to shriek at the stupid collection of doctors who administered the treatments in a quiet little room on the third floor of the hospital. But by then I was under.

Afterward, I felt a lack of short-term memory and an odd rubber taste in my mouth where they'd placed the mouth guard so I wouldn't bite my tongue in two. The treatments also gave me the worst body aches, nausea, and headaches of my life. I could barely move afterward when I returned to consciousness in the room with three other patients. I listened to the echo of patients' groans and doctor's voices. Phrases ricocheted around the room like "Help me—God help me," "Oh, Christ," and "How about that Michael Jordan?" and "Perhaps you need a Jag, Doctor."

Then, after I was discharged that summer, Dr. Shelly had a

session with me and my parents in Belmont. I would be turning twenty-three years old before long, and he felt I should return to Boston and enter a halfway house in Cambridge. He wanted me to build my own home there, my own milieu. He said it would give me structure, and he and I could work together three times a week. At the time, the meeting seemed insignificant but, looking back, it may have been huge.

At that point, I was already heavier and slowed down and, of course, didn't feel normal in any way. I wished to hibernate and remain with the people I loved. So instead of starting a new life away from my family and my hometown, I stuck with what I knew: the comfortable, the same old stuff, and it exploded in my face. When I ponder that moment today, I think maybe, just maybe, if I had worked and stuck it out with Dr. Shelly, that steady and talented doctor, perhaps he could've intercepted the freight train headed my way.

WHEN I LEFT THE INPATIENT PROGRAM LATE IN SUMMER, I LIVED with my parents and Julie in Guilford. I started going to a day hospital three times a week on Chapel Street in New Haven—usually a five-hour day with patients who were trying to get back into the world. Although the staff was patient and passionate, I wandered through the schedule like a zombie, feeling terribly anxious and unfocused. They had the same types of groups as the inpatient program—art, relaxation, and music therapy, plus family support groups once every two weeks.

"Keeping a fixed schedule is crucial," a therapist there explained. "It gives you the structure so you can build your life again, so you can reenter society."

I tried to listen to the advice and to be disciplined, but I felt only harried and so I began to injure myself again, this time in Guilford after the day hospital. I felt a real compulsion to cut; the sight of the blood eased me. I started to take apart Gillette disposable blades in the upstairs bathroom and mark myself up. Nothing too dramatic. Just cuts that I could clean up quickly. Truth was, though, I was leaving little droplets of blood on the floor in between the tiles. By this time, I had started individual therapy with, of all folks, Dr. Walls, at his office in New Haven. I had strong resentment toward him but warmed up to him as time went by. Plus, he had a measured certainty about him in his white doctor's coat, and his medication numbed me, and I simply didn't have the energy to see anyone else. I had wanted to return to Dr. Grinder, but he had gotten seriously ill.

When I couldn't stop the cutting, Dr. Walls and the staff at the day hospital decided halfway through September that I should be hospitalized again at St. Raphael's. I was only in for a short time, about three weeks or so, and was promptly given four more treatments of shock during that time. I obsessed about the anesthesia and how it was killing me— all I could think of was that fucking ice-cold death fluid rushing into my neck, strangling me. It gave me nightmares, and I made doctors promise they wouldn't do it to me again after the final treatment.

I'd go on passes from the hospital with my father to the Yale Golf Course and tried to concentrate on hitting the ball, stroking it with everything I had. But as I stood at the tees, anxiety devoured me and I only wanted to be finished and go to sleep or go eat ice cream by myself. I raged at myself: *David, enjoy this time with your father—it's golf. You used to love golf and you love your father. Pull your act together quickly or you'll be a worse failure, you fat freak!*

When I was discharged, I returned to the day hospital and was contacted by Curtis. He was heading to Barbados for eight days and wanted me to help him film the island and all its beauty. He told me as his cameraman, I wouldn't have to pay. "Wouldn't that be cool?" he asked. It's hard to believe, but I still hadn't fully grasped that the Four Pricks had been horrible and cruel to me. I hadn't shared those harsh stories with any of the psychiatrists I'd worked with—not in Boston, not in New Haven. I was numb and depressed and still thought of Curtis as the closest thing I had to a real-time friend. He was familiar and could still make me smile with his inside jokes.

Curtis even came to one of the Friends and Family Support Group sessions when I was an inpatient and spoke about his belief and respect for me. "I can only speak for myself," he said that night, as my parents, other patients, and social workers beamed with admiration. "I just want my friend to know I'm here for him at any time. I'd walk across hot coals for you, Fitz—I love you, man."

Now his invitation to Barbados set my head swirling, and I decided, with my parents' blessing and the day hospital's tacit approval—one staff member warned me, "There is no such thing as a geographical cure"—to go to Barbados. My parents looked with fondness at Curtis—"God, there's a young man who doesn't forget his friends when they're down. He truly comes through in the clutch, doesn't he?" they said.

BARBADOS WAS PAINFULLY BEAUTIFUL AND SERENE AND FILLED with Rastafarians and, of course, enough ganja to keep the reggae thumping, bumping deep into the next millennium. But

I was still depressed, emotionally stripped, bloated, about thirty pounds overweight, and I wanted to sleep all day at the luxurious tiny peach-colored hotel built into a mountain. Of course, I also wanted to eat. I was fat, and my only desires were to chow away, use the bathroom, and bleed. While there, I didn't allow myself to bleed because it was such a gauche thing to do on vacation. It was in bad taste.

Curtis tried—Jesus, you have to give him credit for that. He brought me down to the silver beach to do some filming and hired two beautiful surfer girls from the Outer Banks. We swung together in a hammock for the video camera and appeared mostly happy, but no one liked my smile. "Why can't you grin like normal, Fitz?" he said. "Come on, for Christ's sake, we're in Barbados. I'm not torturing you, am I? We were supposed to be working, right? All I need is that million-dollar smile that lit up many hearts in Saratoga!"

The girls were shapely, and so one girl's ass kept grinding into my crotch. But I was long gone and didn't feel shit anymore—the medication emasculated me; it might as well have cut the damn thing off because I was drained of all drive. To me, the girl's breasts were unimpressive even though they were technically beautiful. I saw two fleshy lumps—big deal. Nothing moved me. Curtis brought me down to a tennis court and filmed me hitting the ball with a brand-new racquet he purchased. I felt like the world had stopped to watch me and everything was disjointed, unconnected, and moving in slow-mo. People were staring at me through the fence—twisting their heads to the side. I could almost hear their whispers. "What's wrong with the chubby man, Daddy? Why is he moving so slowly?"

I tried to concentrate, but I couldn't even hit a tennis ball. I wanted to lie down on the court and sleep. Or maybe eat something. I went back to the hotel and napped, and later that evening, headed out into the island nightlife with Curtis. The flitting lights at the bars were invasive and ugly—they were pink, navy, orange, coral, cranberry, and yellow, and the drinks tasted like spoiled candy to me. Plus I couldn't drink much with the medications I was on. There were too many flowery shirts throughout the island; everything felt overdone, cooked. Barbados had steep mountain roads with craters for potholes—we learned it was an almost impossible island to drive around on. I never thought I'd get tired of hearing Bob Marley or Jimmy Buffett songs but . . . the music suddenly seemed horrific to my ears. The faces and colors flew by quickly like some roller coaster at a county fair and made me blink my eyes repeatedly. They were watering, and I felt self-conscious, so fat and so tired with my runny eyes.

At the bars, on the streets, the men looked like tanned extras from *Miami Vice* except they didn't wear blazers, and then the black faces looked huge and haunting. Their pupils were dilated and their voices didn't register completely with me. Were they too deep or too high? *Christ, someone please turn the fucking music down!* Too much blue, the aqua blues assaulted me. Blue, blue, blue. A pretty girl sauntered up to me and looked deeply into my eyes; MTV was on in the background at a bar on a pier; I saw someone, maybe the Beastie Boys, singing. The girl looked at me and said, "You better go sit down, man, you look so tired. Cheer up, okay; this is what everyone calls paradise. Have a happy Thanksgiving, friend." Then she reached up and touched my right cheek, just below the eye. I pulled away and she said, "It's okay—I won't hurt you."

Curtis got drunk and brought me back to the hotel and then headed out with some surfer girls to get stoned. I sat in the room and felt hungry and embarrassed. I wanted to bleed, or punch my head, but I was too tired. So tired. Then, just as I reached down to take off my sneakers; I realized a slight damp gauze, a thin layer of cloth, had lowered between me and the world. It dropped down—this veil—from the ceiling, but I put out my hand and I couldn't touch it. Yet it hung between me and absolutely everything, and nothing would touch me in quite the same way for the next seventeen years.

It settled onto me fully as I was changing channels with the remote and I thought, *I can feel myself drifting further and further away from everyone, everything.* I had distance, finally, and I could turn on the television and change to a porno station, but that stuff made me sick. A red-haired woman was fellating a dwarf before a comfy fireplace in some American suburb. It didn't titillate, it was absurd and awful and harmful. And yet I was jealous. *Why can't I do that? Why don't I have one of those?* Nothing turned me on, and so I shut it off and went to bed.

THREE WEEKS LATER, ABOUT MID-DECEMBER, CURTIS CALLED ME and invited me to a weekend with several of the roommates up in New York State. "It's not Saratoga, Fitz—we're not going there," he said. "It's a condo that a friend is letting us use. They all want to see you, to cheer you up." I didn't want to go, but my parents insisted; they thought, *God bless, maybe it'll help him to see his old friends.*

I slept the whole way in the car, and Curtis tried everything, even playing James Taylor CDs or Dire Straits to get me to wake up. "It'll be all right, Fitz—we'll have a blast—nothing too wild or anything."

When I saw them, it was shocking—they looked exactly the

same, but what they saw in me made them look down at their feet. Could it have been shame? No teasing whatsoever, not even a mention of old days; a year and a half had gone by since graduation. I hadn't heard from most of them since we grabbed our diplomas. The three of them looked absolutely stumped. They approached slowly, awkwardly, and punched my shoulder kiddingly. One asked me what I thought of the Giants' chances that year—did I think they were playoff material? Their eyes darted around. That night we went to a bar, and they crowded together near a jukebox, talking, whispering. I sat at an empty table sucking on peanut shells across the room. Maybe they said, "This stuff is serious—the guy looks whacked. Nuts. Crazy. Gonzofucking-toodaloo. What the hell do we do now? Are we responsible—did we have a hand in this somehow?"

That's when they must have started to fully grasp what had become of me. We left the bar and drove back to the condo, and I slept in a spare room in blackness. I saw the light from the den beneath the door. They were getting stoned. The odor turned my stomach, panicked my whole body. I heard them chatting, whispering. A part of me wanted to scream out, *How are you feeling now, scholars—how does this particular strain of guilt sit in your bellies? Feeling a tad empty, a little hollow perhaps in the diaphragm? You have actively participated in destroying a young life. You made me your gimp—deal with it. Suck it up, fuckheads!*

PERHAPS I AM EXAGGERATING, OVERSIMPLIFYING BECAUSE I'M A dramatic guy. Certainly, these upstanding college graduates were merely a pinprick in the gusher of my story. They didn't slash any veins, they didn't hand out the razors, and most certainly they didn't give me a family tree of mental instabilities. *Don't be ri-diculous, David. You took those college drugs with verve while you were fully cognizant of what you were doing. You coaxed those men toward the bong sometimes. People must stand on their own in the world, fella. Buck up, pal! When the going gets tough, you know? You gotta take, take, take, or the world will eat you alive. They'll suck you up like yesterday's placenta! You've made your own bed and now you've got to die or lie in it. But just keep the college grad-uates the fuck out of it! Those are good souls, I mean, Christ, aren't people supposed to have fun and act crazy in college? It's youthful play—boys tackle rough. You took the drugs, for Christ's sake. Stop playing the victim role—it's in such bad taste. Don't blame the boys for your mental insufficiencies. Let men live their lives. They are good people with good hearts and minds. Don't go depressing them with tales of your frailties!*

But instead of getting up and yelling, I rolled over and fell deeply into a sedated sleep.

The next morning everyone decided to pack it in and leave early. They walked up to me and embraced me and said, "You know, Fitz, we just want you to be okay, to be healthy and happy like you were at school." One of them teared up and said, "God, man, you're the most important person in the world to us—we'd never let anything bad happen to you, man. We love you, Fitzy. We'll call and write, okay. We'll visit—whatever happens, we are there with you for the duration. We are there."

I grimaced at them and felt that fabric, the damp veil, be-tween us. It pushed me, took me and placed me safely in the car. They waved as Curtis and I drove home silently.

◆

I NEVER STRUCK BACK AT THE PRICKS. NOT EVEN A PUNCH OR A raised voice. That passivity embarrasses me today; I can't figure how such an intake of drugs and a *Lord of the Flies* vibe came down on me without a scream or kick. *Come on, David,* I say to myself now, *what the fuck!* Maybe they were nothing more, nothing less than shitheads: very stuck and wasted postadolescents without standards, without any rules to follow. And maybe I just happened to be the perfect lightning rod for their anger, confusion, and sadism.

Every once in a while, I Google their names and see what they are up to. They're mostly successful—one is a bald banker in London. Another works with computer software in Seattle, and another works for a successful advertising firm in Austin, Texas. I'm sure some of them have children and are trying to raise them with good values and morals, teaching them to be kind and supportive of other people and to steer clear of humiliating others. Part of me thinks the Four Pricks will write at some point—or one of them will show up and smirk at me from a distance. I'm not a great fighter, never have been, except with my older brother.

I won't have to see these guys to know they are there. I will be able to sense their toxic black cloud, the noxiousness. I used to believe that those four guys didn't have any souls. What I'd really like to do is throw four quick punches and fracture each of their noses and shatter the damn things. Just a lightning-quick jab, and I could watch blood spurt out of their faces. The contact of my fist on their skin would feel great because it would be a punch of such force, such hate . . . I don't know. I imagine walking quickly through Grand Central and seeing Curtis or Jasper hustling along with a guitar or attaché case about to slip right past—I'd take a deep, delicious breath and put all my weight into it, and crush the fuck out of their noses.

I TRIED TO GO FOR FREQUENT WALKS WITH MY FAMILY IN GUIL-ford, though it was growing harder to get out of bed and drive to the day hospital and get through my whole schedule. I walked past Shell Beach in Guilford with my parents one December day and felt agitated, on edge, as if the shock had pepped me up inside, in my veins, but the outside—my body—felt in slow motion. Autumn and then winter had rolled in so quickly and blew right over me. Before I knew it, I'd somehow become a recidivist mental patient who always felt like hell. No one was certain about my future—I even started saving up pills like anti-depressants, Tylenol, Dexatrim, anything I could find. I was pas sively suicidal; If I had to do anything, I'd go with cutting and bleeding, but my family made me promise there'd be no more of that. And so I saved up the pills just in case— I was like a child playing house, flirting with suicide, fantasizing about it.

I walked along the beach with my family on the weekends, and I saw the water was frozen and chunks of ice were stuck against one another like pileups on the highway. I tried to have a good attitude; I wanted to stress the positive with everyone, hoping that somehow that would bring me back to some kind of health. A smoothness. Although this interior, false peppiness wasn't the most convincing feeling in the world. It felt pretty hor-rible. "I must try and *celebrate* life now," I said, almost crying, as my mother and father watched me closely. "I'm going to try and be *appreciative* for each second that ticks by."

At the day hospital in New Haven, the social worker, Teddy, a frightfully pale man with a slight belly, spoke about my ongoing situation. How I wasn't improving, still feeling suicidal, looking like I hadn't slept in years, though I slept all the time. "Long-term places are a possibility; they're always available in your situation, David," he said. "The Institute of Living in Hartford is very well-respected."

"I don't know," I said. "I don't want to be sent away like that."

"It's something to ponder, something to think about and discuss with your folks," he said. "We can't have patients at this understaffed day facility actively cutting or seeking death."

Seeking death. I had heard of suicidal ideation, self-destruction, self-evisceration, and mutilation, but "seeking death." That was a new one. It sounded so . . . serious.

I WAS DISCHARGED FROM THE DAY HOSPITAL JUST BEFORE CHRIST-mas. The staff clearly thought they had helped me as much as they could and, unbelievably, desperately, I had employment lined up right away. After the New Year, I started to work as an editorial assistant at *Better Health* magazine, which was run out of St. Raphael's. My father had pushed and helped me get the position and my duties were basic: answer phones, do a little editing, and help with stuffing envelopes. It was a last chance, a test, of sorts, though I felt as if the whole thing were a farce. As if everyone could see I was a mental patient with a warped head and a damaged soul. I tried hard to be responsible and not think about injuring, but I felt out of control, partially manic and itching to bleed.

I started taking baths at home early in the morning and cutting myself with razors, little slices. Just like before. Sometimes

I did it when the house was empty, and other times when my family was downstairs in the kitchen. I would, ridiculously, "hide" the razors in the bathroom closet beneath towels. I felt so hungry for the behavior. I tried to scrub the tub when I was finished, to make sure the blood was gone. Oddly, I felt like I was contributing to the house, cleaning up after myself. The act centered me, though I later realized I was terrifying my family, especially Julie. In a perhaps unconscious way, I was taunting my parents, challenging them to kick me out. See who would blink first.

For "work" I dressed in long-sleeved T-shirts, usually black to absorb any unsightly bloodstains, and then put on a white dress shirt and a tie and cleaned the tub and drove into New Haven. I started going into the bathroom at the magazine and taking long breaks and removing my shirts and cutting myself ever so slightly in there as well. This happened about five times over the month I worked at the magazine. I had to move fast, but I'd do little marks with the thin disposable blades, scrapes against my chest and shoulders and then wash them and pat them dry with paper towels. No gaping wounds or anything, not too much blood, just small things. One time I even emptied the trash from the bathroom so they wouldn't get suspicious about the reddish paper towels. I know at a later time I wanted to really destroy myself and wound deeply and hard, but for that January, I was eased with the minor bits of cutting. Then I'd dress quickly and go to lunch with one or two other workers.

I'd walk along Chapel Street and then over to Howe to a new place called Hot Peas 'n Butter, and the frigid January air would soothe me. I felt partially eased by the course of events. We'd walk by the day hospital and see several patients and staff smoking cigarettes outside the building, and I'd say hello and nod in a psychologically stable manner.

"Looking good in that tie, sir," a staff member called to me as we passed. "Just take it one day at a time."

"You said it, man." I smiled and kept walking. We'd get to the restaurant and talk about politics and laugh a little and I'd be asked about college, about my experience working at a small newspaper. My future plans, my writing dreams. And I pretended—that's entirely what I did—I pretended my life was going along perfectly swell. I continued to mislead, confuse, and scare everyone.

When I wasn't hurting myself at work, or answering the rare phone call, I drew faces on construction paper at the desk in the back corner. Haunted-looking ghouls with huge eyes and crooked and scraggly teeth, or a mouth with lips partially sewn together. *If this is what work consists of in the real world, well, it's doable*, I thought. I'd just be a closet cutter, a razor blade junkie with steady pay.

I was in a state of shambles, rapidly losing my mind. After seeing that the cutting continued unabated—I had little slices and sores all over my hands—Dr. Walls and my parents decided to admit me to the Institute of Living in Hartford. I called the people at the magazine and told them I'd no longer be working there, and my father and I drove up I-91 to the hospital on a cold morning.

7

"Club Med for the Brain"

O N February 7, 1990, I stood in the young-adult Brace- land II unit at the Institute of Living, talking with Jeffrey, a staff member with a blond mullet and a thin mustache. It was my first day there, and he was asking me to step out of my clothes.

"It's like a Club Med for the brain, guy," he said. "That's really the healthiest way to look at it—that's how you gotta go into it, you know?"

We were in a single bedroom, and he checked my pants and shirt pockets for sharps. The room had the utilitarian hospital

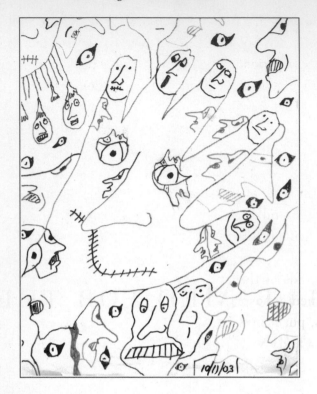

look down well—a desk, a bathroom, a cheap wooden bureau. He grabbed the barn coat I was wearing, turned it upside down, and two thin razors fell out. He looked at me and shook his head. "Level with me now, man—you don't have razors *elsewhere,* do you?"

"You mean like in my anus?" I said.

"Well, yes, like in your anus," he said.

"No," I said. "That really isn't my genre . . . I just like to bleed, to cut, to watch it spill—"

Jeffrey held up his hand. "Great start," he said, "you 'like to bleed.' Easy, man—let's go meet your doctor and talk to the nurses. You can tell them all about the wish."

"No. You don't understand," I said, trying to sound calm. "It's not . . . a wish. It's a *need*. I need to slice myself up." The sound of my voice was breaking. "Please, will you let me do a little?"

"I'm sorry, friend," he said, shaking his head. "Come on now, get your pants on and let's get you out to the dayroom."

The Braceland unit held twenty-five young adults between the ages of eighteen and thirty. Some people called it Graceland, and every day I'd hear someone humming or whistling that Paul Simon tune ("I'm going to Graceland, Graceland . . ."). It was one of the more populated buildings on the grounds of the Institute of Living in Hartford, the third oldest mental hospital in the country. I think my little brother, Dennis, put it best when he visited me there one Christmas morning and said, "This place looks haunted, David."

The building on the outside was two stories of clunky, fading gray bricks; while the interior had been hip in the early eighties, it was deteriorating by now. Behind the bolted doors and the alarms was a faded blue-gray carpet with two main hallways leading to the bedrooms. The cameras in each hallway made those with paranoia problems even more whacked out, and the big expansive windows gave us a view of the grounds that had been softened and sculpted by the same architect who designed Central Park. Olmstead, I believe. Or at least that's what it said in the brochure they gave my father when I was admitted. The walls were faded mauve, and the prints were all Monet, Manet, and Cassatt (never van Gogh—too emotionally weighty). In front of the building were little statues of two children—one was a boy sitting on a stoop with a terrier in his arms and the other was a girl who was petting a chipmunk held in her tiny arms. I loved little statues like that and had stopped for a moment to look at them as I was walking over with Jeffrey and my father, who were chatting about health, keeping a positive attitude, and going into "this experience with an aim for a redeemed life."

The unit's epicenter was the nurses' station that everyone called the Hub. It had once been made of glass but a psychotically brave or stupid few had thrown chairs and banged their heads and broken their hands trying to get to an unwavering doctor or a recalcitrant nurse, and the whole thing was redone with Plexiglas. The Hub was where we received samples from an unceasing supply of pastel medications—the choices weren't as plentiful as they are today but still, there was more than enough for the willing and the unwilling: Thorazine, Stelazine, Haldol, Tegretol, Depakote, and amitriptyline. All of these colorful antipsychotics, sedatives, and antidepressants really packed a punch.

The facility was built in 1822 and first named the Hartford Retreat for the Insane. It aided those suffering from tuberculosis, but by the twentieth century had morphed into a psychiatric hospital. In 1930, the hospital began to market itself directly as a refuge for the wealthy, though it continued to have some state-paid clients. Very rich patients actually built small cottages on the grounds and lived there. Several of those buildings remain today. One senior staff person told me about the heyday when all the sparkling, snazzy black limousines lined up on Sundays, and drivers took their clients for a ride through West Hartford, the hills of Connecticut, and even into Manhattan. Hospital aides worked with them in their own cottages, and meals were served on china and fancy silverware—a little different from the plastic forks and spoons (no knives!) we used. Back in the 1950s, my grandfather worked the night shift at the Institute after he spent the day toiling for the IRS. I couldn't help but wonder if this bit of moonlighting had cast a pall on my destiny.

When I arrived at age twenty-four, long-term hospitalization was being phased out as a treatment option, and by my last visit, people were staying only one to two months, if that. By the early eighties, the state hospitals were mostly empty. This caused the insurance companies to nod their heads spastically, happy as clams that they wouldn't have to ante up for long stays. But for those with money or with dinosaur insurance policies like mine, it wasn't unusual to stay ten months to two years, and a handful of patients decided to stay their whole lives.

JEFFREY LED ME OUT TO THE HUB, WHERE I MET DR. COLLANDER, who was my psychologist. I liked him immediately; he was about six feet, 170 pounds, with a bushy beard and mustache, soft shoulders, and blondish hair with some balding spots on top. He had a gentle, calm voice that was as reassuring as a Hyundai or American Express commercial today. He was easy and real, a Jeff Bridges type. He said we would meet three times a week on the unit, and that he'd come to visit me for the time being. "All you have to do is stay here and meet people, stay calm as possible, don't give yourself a hard time," he said. Then he pointed to my hands, which were freshly cut up with diagonal cuts and slashes—I had marked them up just before I left Guilford to drive with my dad.

"Obviously, you have to leave those cuts alone—and we'll work on that together."

He smiled then, and I watched him stroll away down the hall

to the exit, loping casually in his new Docksiders. I thought they looked, perhaps, too new. Squeaky clean, malleable maybe. My head whirled with images of shoes, razors, suicide, and fratricide.

Next came Dr. Presley, the chief psychiatrist, who seemed to exude sparks as he strutted toward me in a brilliant silver suit, peach tie, and cheap-looking shoes. He looked peppy, animated, as scary and confident as a smooth pit bull, a real charmer. His silver hair was shiny and matched his beautiful suit, and I later learned he perfected that tan several times a year in Palm Springs. His style of relating scared me because it was very touchy, kind of in-your-face with a benign vibe. He strode up to me, gripped my wrists, inspected my scarred arms and said, "Easy now, easy. We're here to help you. No reason to hate David anymore." Then he patted my upper arms and said, "Good skin, good skin." Then he released me, pulled back, and said, "We can't have you leaving those little harmful vaginas all over your body now, can we?"

I retracted violently from him as his arms reached toward me. "Huh?" I said.

"Easy, David, easy, friend," he said. "Just trying to get you thinking about what's behind the behaviors. One doesn't just injure oneself repeatedly for no reason at all. You know that, right?"

"I don't know," I said.

He grinned and patted my cheeks warmly, held my right arm, then patted the left shoulder. "No need to destroy and hate, no need to destroy and hate. Repeat that whenever possible, okay? Don't be afraid to stroke those lovely arms . . . we've got to relearn how to stroke ourselves. We got to turn you around."

Later, as the smokers lined up for courtyard break, I walked over to the wall and hit my head against it to keep from crying.

Dr. Presley whispered as he approached, "Okay, okay, we're going to give you a little sedative. You can just sit down on one of those chairs and relax. It's a lot, David, I understand. God, it's a lot to take in so quickly isn't it?"

I bent over again, stifling the tears, allowing just a slight cough or gasp to escape my mouth. A nurse handed me a capful of Thorazine mixed with apple juice. Dr. Presley said, "You are going to be okay. Nod with me now. You are going to be okay. Say it."

"I am going to be okay," I said.

LATER THAT DAY I MET LINK, WHO TOLD ME HE'D BEEN WORKING at the hospital for thirty-three years. He was an older, chubby man who wore tortoiseshell glasses. He was just an everyday Joe with snazzy glasses that didn't seem to fit. He gripped my hand firmly and nodded toward a row of maroon and navy itchy-looking seats.

"I usually work the night shift, David," he said. "But when the possibility of overtime comes, I gotta jump on it."

I wobbled over to the chair and plumped down into it, feel-ing as if I'd broken through and was falling further. Link sat to the right of me. Phillip, a large patient with a grizzly brown beard, floated by, pointing to my hands and arms. "I see you enjoy mucking yourself up," he said. "It's a terrible, terrible habit to grow accustomed to."

"All right, Phillip," Link said. "Move it along, move it along."

I sat there for three hours, not stirring as the drug settled into me. It was my first day, and I felt as if I'd already tumbled into a groove, an awful sad space, a faraway place. Nothing could touch me. I couldn't touch me. My father had left to drive home, and he couldn't touch me. *I am an untouchable,* I told myself.

I looked over at Phillip across the room. Most everyone was watching television, staring out the window, sleeping, mumbling. Phillip stared back at me.

"Jerry Garcia," I uttered out loud.

Link nodded his head and said, "Good call there—and that's what he wishes you to believe. Just don't say anything cruel about the Dead."

"Thanks, Link," I said. My voice sounded *dead.* "You weren't involved in any way with *The Mod Squad,* were you?"

"I never saw the show," he grinned. "Not a big television fan. But I know the actor was a skinny black cop with a big afro." He ran his hand over his smooth head. "I could never pull that off."

"You're definitely one Caucasian gentleman," I said, and he smiled.

"Pretty much, huh?" he said. "Humor is bubbling to the surface now." He laughed. "That's a positive thing."

I was silent for a few seconds, and my eyes filled. He tilted his head toward me. "You there, guy?" he said. "Hey, David, everything okay?"

"The smoker's chuckle reminded me of my maternal grandfather," I said.

"No harm in that, son," he said. "Let it out. That's why you're here."

I laughed a slight hiccup. "That's why I'm here," I echoed. "Great album."

Link looked away, and I began to hum the tune. James Taylor, title track. Released 1985. Multiplatinum, I believe. It brought back fond memories of summers. Huck, chubby blueberries and cream, Wiffle ball, a particularly shapely ass of a neighborhood girl on Bay View beach. Emily, naked in a hot tub in Saratoga, eyes closed.

I looked around the unit and saw patient bedrooms along two separate hallways, plus those leering, rotating cameras. It struck me in an excruciatingly beautiful way that there was an undeniably lecherous amount to study and examine, soak up and poke at in a mental institution. There were events and thoughts to decipher and scribble down. The staff took notes on each of us, but it was impossible to get everything.

I took a deep breath and my thoughts raced. *Those cameras have a stressful, difficult job and I'm sorry for them; I really am. They can't pick up everything and they are probably installed on the majestic thirty-five-acre grounds outside as well. But hey, you know what, guys and gals of Greater Hartford? That's A-okay. I can jump, duck, and roll. I can twist, whistle, and play hide-and-seek in the rutted-out trees. Oh, Lordy-loo, alleluia, praise the blessed and swift razor! I'll discover a way to vivisection myself and paint the hospital with my juicy, tangy crimson. Why? said the young boy. Why would you do something so negative, bastardized, and unseemly? Why are you so fucking angry?*

Don't ask why, you silly piece of uselessness! Ask why not!

I SPENT MY FIRST SESSION WITH DR. COLLANDER DISCUSSING MY psych history, and during our second session I told him that my maternal grandfather threw feral cats off abandoned buildings in North Cambridge during the Depression. I described how nine-year-old Guppy and his mates grabbed as many strays as they could in Boston alleys, stuffed them into burlap bags, climbed up to the roofs, and gave them a hurl. "Even while trapped, the cats found a way to extend themselves and break their fall," Guppy told me once, almost scientifically.

"Yeah?" I said, and he patted my shoulder and then crossed his heart.

"That's gospel, David," Guppy told me. "The cats descended like broken umbrellas and wouldn't always die when they'd land." He shrugged. "It's a terrible truth of mine—but that's the way truth works," he said. "It nips you in the behind."

I first heard about the tossed cats during a surprise trip to Disney World when I was in third grade; Guppy took me there after I'd been suffering intense headaches. I told Dr. Collander that I shared that story not for shock value but to suggest that institutions, just like people, can be ugly and gifted, crass and decent, terribly flawed and once in a while, they can be blessed with grace. I told him my grandfather, whose name came out of my sister's mouth as "Guppy," grew up to be a man of deep faith, an Irish immigrant with sharp wit and a gift for storytelling. He eventually worked as an undercover investigator for the Internal Revenue Service, but on his way up, he moonlighted at the Institute of Living, where he cared for semi-obliterated folks like me. He raised three children, had eight grandchildren, and was married for fifty-one years.

While attending my great-aunt's wake with Guppy a week before his fatal heart attack in my senior year of college, I overheard him chatting with some female octogenarians. "You know, I'm basically against the idea of aging . . . ," he began.

He was a very charming, religious, loving, and successful man.

And, he once threw cats off rooftops as a child.

◆

"That's lively and odd," Dr. Collander said with a slight smile. "It makes for a great icebreaker at a party, but that's not what I'm looking for. How about specifics, about why you're sitting here on this cold day in February in a psych hospital?"

I yawned nervously. "I'm not entirely sure."

"What do you want to do?" he said.

"Could we watch *Ordinary People*?" I said. "I loved that one. Or is that the most pathetic request you've heard?"

"No, no, that's good," he said. "I've never seen it, and I heard it shows a great therapist-patient give-and-take. Loads of guilt in the Timothy Hutton character, right?"

"How about *Angel Heart* or *Running on Empty*?" I said.

"Enough," he said. "Why didn't you ever tell your doctors about the roommates?"

"I don't know," I said. "They weren't there to defend themselves, I guess."

"What could they say that would justify cruelty?" he said.

"See," I said, shifting in my seat, "that's my problem—my experience with therapy is that it's forever about socking it to the other guys, pinning the donkeys with blame. I was complicit—I didn't fight back."

"Yet you made a point of telling me about it on the first day," he said, carefully folding the cuffs of his blue oxford. "You told me it was hellish. So what changed in your mind from those times with your doctors? How did it go from being a fuzzy, uncomfortable one to horrific?"

"I just began . . . realizing, obsessing about similarities with other heinous parts of my life," I said, leaning forward to tie my shoe.

"Right," he said. "Some in your life were harsh, cruel, and swarmed over you—true?"

"Yeah," I said, "but they were just immature and stoned."

"That's their alibi?" Dr. Collander said. "David, let's be clear—there's no excuse, your roommates were dicks."

"The Four Pricks of the Apocalypse, actually," I said. "It came to me recently."

"That's a good one," he said. "They treated you like an animal, didn't they?"

I nodded.

"Okay," he said, holding his index finger up. "Just simplify with me. Would you say it's unfair that you've become sick?"

"I deserve it."

He looked at me for a few seconds. "Why do you deserve to mutilate yourself and be clinically depressed?"

"I've failed," I said, rubbing my palms along my thighs, "in every aspect of life. I've disappointed greatly."

He hesitated. "You're twenty-four—aren't you being too harsh?"

"Just honest," I said. "You asked, right?"

"Okay," he said. "More specifically then, what have you failed at?"

"I've failed with writing, relationships, definitely living, even dying," I said.

He closed his eyes. "So who did you disappoint by coming here?" he said.

"My family, Emily, Molly, buddies from high school," I said, looking out the window. "Maybe God as well."

"Catholic guilt makes an appearance," he said, smiling. "Didn't you graduate from a well-respected college less than two years ago with an English degree?" he said. "Isn't that an achievement?"

"No," I said quickly. "Anyone can do that—I barely slid through with a 2.45 GPA. Just read great books during the day and inhaled powder and smoke all night."

"So you've disappointed yourself by being sick?" he said. "By being human and needing assistance?"

"Shape my crumbling in a hundred different ways, but it's still failure," I said.

He grimaced. "Now you sound like a drill sergeant from hell."

"I just want to carve myself, okay, Doctor?" I said, clenching my teeth. I fingered my dry lips. "Just give me a razor, a stage, and a few lights. I could do a performance-art thing."

"I get the picture," he said.

"No," I said. "I don't think you do." I sat there quietly, gripping and releasing the plastic sides of the chair. "Serve wine and fresh popcorn—add a cellist. Charge twenty bucks a head—proceeds would benefit the Red Cross. A charity event—attract the right crowd, you know, offer pints of my red blood to the blue bloods."

Dr Collander exhaled, waving his hand at the comment as if it were a pesky fly. "Okay, easy," he said. "What we've established is that there's lots of crap inside."

"No," I said, picking at my scars. "There's a coating of blackness that lives."

He leaned toward me and took my hands off my arms gently. "So you feel there's literally black liquid inside of you?" he said.

"Yes," I sighed. "That's what I've been saying—it needs to be lanced."

"Okay," he said, nodding. "We need to bring that out, examine it. First, though, I've got to say I'm a dad, David," he said, "and I want to voice the obvious. What's evil about you?" he said. "Never a felon, never a speeding ticket, nicest smile and friendliest in high school. Parents said you were a blessed and happy boy. Mom used the word 'beloved.' Pleasing others, watching out for retarded brother—"

"Dennis is developmentally disabled," I said. "They want you to say 'disabled' now."

"See," he said. "You're looking out for him. And I like you already. I don't always like my patients."

"Which ones truly nauseate you on Graceland?" I said.

He smiled and fingered his mustache. "Sorry, I can't tell you that," he said. "But you, David, seem funny, kind, are handsome, and probably a pretty good writer."

"Weren't you listening to anything I said?"

"I respect everything you said about others," Dr. Collander said, "but I don't listen much to what you say about yourself. You appear to loathe yourself with a raving intensity." He took a breath and said, "Tell me about your parents."

"They're married, in their fifties," I said. "Dad's a car dealer in New Haven; mother a minister in the Congregational Church—she jumped ship."

"Former Catholic?" he said.

"Yeah." I said. "She desired a slice of the pie—went to Yale Div and Hartford Seminary and wanted to marry people and bury them as well. I think she's brave and great. Same goes for my dad."

"Are they off limits, though?" he asked, leaning forward. "It seems the way you answered that was to keep the topic off of them."

"I love them," I said.

"Can you be angry at them when you love them?" Dr. Collander said.

"No," I said. "I can't."

"I get pissed at my wife, and I love her more than anyone on the planet," Collander said, fingering his wedding band. "Why aren't you allowed the same normal emotion?"

"Anger eviscerates and mutilates," I said, palms sweaty.

"You mean rage. Rage does those things sometimes?" Dr. Collander said.

"Dr. C," I said, annoyed. "I don't allow myself the privilege of anger."

"What?" he said.

"It ruins people," I said.

He looked at me and took off his glasses. "What do you do when you get angry?"

"I don't," I said. "Any form of anger leads to entropy."

He paused and pointed to my arms. "What do you think the wounds on your body are?"

"Punishment for failure to produce a good life," I said, picking at my scabs again.

"Jesus," he said. "Please leave your scabs alone, okay?"

"Why? I mean, Christ, let me do it, would you?" I said, blushing. "What's the point of fighting the momentum I've got here?"

"David," he said softly, "you're quite ill and you deserve better, okay? We've got serious therapy to do, plus I'd get in a heap of trouble if I let you bleed freely in my office," he said. "You get that, right?"

"Yeah." I smiled, looking up at him. "I get that."

He looked at his watch. "You have a biochemical storm in your head, mixed with the effects of drugs from school, mixed with your family's manic-depressive history."

"Did you pull my file?"

"No." He grinned. "You don't have a file, remember? You've never been here before." He held his hands above him and moved them down toward the ground, motioning ease, calm. "We're using some of what other therapists said. But we're going with honesty now—what you can share. Life doesn't have to be horrific, okay?"

"Okay . . . but can you truly assist me?" I said, suddenly subdued.

"Yeah, we can work together and do it," he said. "You'll learn to give yourself a break, to not loathe yourself so viciously. You're not a lost head case—you don't need bloody extravaganzas on stage, right?" He took a moment to place his palms on his knees. "Save the gory parts for your short stories."

"Okay," I said, trying to smile.

"Let your little sister, Julie, handle drama," he said. "She's the actress, right?"

"Yes," I said. "She's amazing."

He nodded and said, "Write for me as many pages as you need to about your first memory of your mother."

"My mother," I said. "More blame?"

"No blame," Dr. Collander said. "Just talking between two people who are getting to know one another."

"Promise?" I asked.

"You bet," he said. "Along with something about your dog that got killed when you were a boy—Josh?"

"Jiggs," I said. "All right, then, my mother and Jiggs. I'll do it."

THAT EVENING I SAT DOWN TO WRITE THE ASSIGNMENT, AND somehow I began discussing my first memory with my roommate, Jacob. It seemed like a safe thing to do. "Practice reaching out to that fellow," Dr. Collander had told me. "Make a connection—rehearse by telling him about your life."

Jacob was a slight fifty-two-year-old with grayish-red hair and a stubby nose. He was also quite frank—too frank, it seemed to me. "I want to have intense sexual relations with my mother, David," he said to me as soon as I entered our room on my first day, even before we shook hands. After then grasping my fingers extremely hard, he continued: "Her name is Janice and I don't see much of anything wrong with it, you know?" He smiled, pointing two fingers up. "I've been here two months, and I feel it's my sworn duty to commit the act. I love her passionately, completely. I truly need to."

"Huh," I said carefully. "That sounds like it must be . . . confusing for you."

"Oh, yeah," he said quietly. "Just a bit—plus they're discharging me in a few days. So I worry about her and me under the same roof."

I learned from Jacob how the general order of things proceeded at hospitals. Simple conversations got flipped and turned on their heads. You heard of the excruciating, sick, or terrible almost immediately—heinous abuse or tales of blood, guts, and psychic terror in one form or another. And then later, when you're sucking down pizza at the cafeteria with someone who seems bent on self-immolation, eating glass, or screwing their mother, you learn what kind of television shows they like or what their last name is.

Backward, different, odd, twisted.

All of the above, I guess.

After hearing Jacob go on about his maternal pining, I felt more comfortable with my own misfortunes and lay down on my mattress in the darkness. I figured Jacob's thoughts were more out there, so I felt comfortable telling him my first memory: This was the one about my mother wiping my ass in the bathroom in Missouri when I was three and a half years old. I found myself fighting a few tears then as I watched the streetlights and their shadows dance across the walls of our bedroom. *Pull yourself together, David.*

I told him I'd had a pretty decent childhood, even with Andy breathing down my neck. I described how in sync I was with my mother as a kid—that we just . . . understood each other. I remember having a sip of her drink once at a cocktail party at our house in New Jersey. Mostly Ford Motor Company men and their wives. The Carpenters and maybe Jim Croce were playing in the background.

I was a tiny boy, and these large, wise adults were laughing, smoking, their suit coats bright, and the different father's colognes clashed and banged against one another. Ice clinking in a glass. Her drink tasted bitter to me, awful. I knew she'd send me to bed, but I wanted to hear her say it. When I made a silly face, the adults laughed, the women had their legs folded just so, and my mother kissed my head and sent me up the stairs to bed.

"Time for bed, baby," she said. "Sleep tight."

The minute I stopped talking, Jacob jumped in and pined on again for his own mother. He said something like "They tell me there are tangible limits to passionate, filial love—but what's wrong with it and why? I believe that's what my heart calls me to do with my mom . . ."

I tuned him out at that point and eventually fell into a solid, heavy slumber. I dreamt of a massive figure, some type of Bigfoot, chasing me around our cramped, mildewed basement in Guilford. His razor-sharp fingers, each digit covered in prickly, coarse black hair, gripped me by the neck and hung on tight. Then he took out a dull butter knife from behind his ear and sawed into me, cutting off my legs right at the knees. Next thing I know, I'm in a wheelchair at St. Patrick's Cathedral, placed on an altar, bleeding from my uneven stumps. Around the church, painted faces are clapping, singing with a collection of multiethnic priests, ministers, monks, rabbis, and nuns blessing me, waving their hands around my wheelchair like banshees.

The conflicting smells of ginger, incense, cinnamon, and Coppertone suntan lotion settle into me, ease me somehow like a combination sedative and hallucinogen. The scent of the coconut oil reminds me of the delightful summers of my youth, and when I raise my head, I see the source of the odor—each of my summer girlfriends is lined up in their bright pink and pineapple sundresses in the balcony. They're tanned, gorgeous, and giggling, blowing kisses and fanning their young children with church bulletins. There's Emily, of course. She looks riveting, and then I see Barbara Milligan, the first girl I ever French-kissed, when I was ten. I see Molly up there, closing her eyes, swaying and getting into the music. I want to stop and tell everyone about the smooches with these girls, their smiles, their bellies.

Then I want to shout out to the congregation about how the neighborhood kids were always playing Wiffle ball, touch football, Relievo, or tag. I want to tell people about the smell of the summer rain, the burning sand on the beach, the tender pine needles on the path in the woods that stretched on for several miles behind our cottage.

And my family—God bless every fucking one of them! We'd be at one another's throats as we approached the Cape. The stench of sour bodies and urine wafting in the air, spilling out of the Folgers coffee can we boys used when we lost patience with the crowded rest stops. There was Mom, Laura, Andy, Dennis, Julie, and me and somehow, each time, every goddamned time, we started singing this song about Cape Cod. Whether we were driving from Missouri, New Jersey, or Connecticut, whether we hated one another's guts for the dirty looks and farting in the back of the station wagon, whether we couldn't bear to look at one another for another second, we raised our voices, looked off that bridge toward the bay and sang our Irish hearts out to the tune of "It's a Long Way to Tipperary."

"It's a long way to go to Cape Cod, it's a long, long way to go to see the ocean. It's a long way to go to Dennis, Cape Cod, to the sweetest land I know, God bless her . . ."

Suddenly I'm no longer shouting, and the scents and memories fade into the background. I'm back on that altar, the organ music just a quiet hum in the rafters. The crowd settles down, takes their seats, though my girls in the balcony are still waving at me. They seem to be saying good-bye, wishing me luck, and I want to point out to them that this isn't a time for good-byes, and then the ministers, rabbis, and nuns pull back from me, making a path for the pope. He comes loping forward to splash holy water on my leg. *Is it a miracle type of thing going on? Will he bless me or redeem me, or perhaps bring back my legs? Please, God—won't you heal me?*

The substantial pope is swathed in lush royal and purple fabrics, and they drape over him. His crown is bejeweled with pearls, diamonds, emeralds, and black opals. But when he reaches out to touch me, I see his hairy, gnarled fingers, and I know it's really Bigfoot. He mock-blesses me with a sly grin and then reaches up to slash my neck, to destroy me—and then I can hear Jacob calling my name, and I'm awake.

"Just a nightmare, man," he said, rubbing my shoulder. "Everything's okay here. You're in the hospital, remember?"

"Okay, okay," I said, exhausted and confused. I sat up in bed, catching my breath, situating myself. My thoughts raced: *Has the world eaten me alive? How else do I explain the hospital and scabs? What's wrong with you, David, why can't you get out of this hole? What's gone so fucking haywire in that head of yours?*

DR. COLLANDER ALSO ASKED ME TO WRITE IN MY JOURNAL ABOUT the death of my dog, a chocolate cockapoo spliced in two by an Amtrak train when I was twelve years old. I was frightened and shocked, but also partially fascinated, with the train's precision that day.

One of the sixth-grade girls and I had been looking for a place to make out, and wandered down near the tracks after middle school on a warm autumn afternoon. Then suddenly, we heard the roaring, screaming metal and saw Jiggs try to outrun it. The girl screeched and cried and rushed up the hill toward home when she saw the remains. It was a horrible scene, a terrible mess, but weirdly intriguing to me. Jiggs's upper and lower halves lay forty feet apart, and I saw his open mouth and petite tongue still hanging out, eyes shut serenely. I also saw the inner workings of my pooch, the clean lines of the cut. Then I turned my head and watched the caboose disappear, the hammering sound fade quickly.

I was in shock but I didn't sprint home. I knelt down beside him, observing. I studied the stark white bone, the intestines, and a little redness around his skin and matted fur. It looked like two large sides of roast beef perfectly divided. I wanted to mend

Jiggs, of course. I mean, sadness was definitely present. I wished to ease him, stroke his fur, to help him return to life. *Could I glue him somehow?*

That clean slice became lodged inside me forever. Only five seconds later, I watched as the blood furiously spilled out of his muscles and stained the gray-black stones beneath. This image festered and danced around in my unconscious for years. Is this too easy an explanation for my fascination with blood? Too much connecting the dots? Perhaps, but the image hovered and appeared to wait for me.

I eventually ran back through the woods to find my mother and sister, but I ducked behind a woodpile when I felt tears coming on. For a minute or two, I listened to the gnawing, buzzing roar of a neighbor's chain saw, cars horns sounding in the distance. I studied my leather Puma sneakers as they became partially covered by swarming black carpenter ants. I thought they would devour me, destroy me quickly if I didn't tell my family, if I didn't take action.

I inhaled several breaths, my nostrils filling with the sometimes-comforting and seasonal scent of burning wood and decay. But at that moment everything was rotten, putrid. I heard our phone ringing in the kitchen. I brushed off the ants and ran toward the house and told my mother and sister what had happened. I wept there with both of them. Later, they buried Jiggs down at the tracks. But twelve years later, with my world fragmenting in Boston, with me whipping out my disposable Bic and slicing through parts of my body, I still saw my old pooch's same fresh inner skin revealed. Before the blood arrived.

Old Jiggs then became a very conscious joke, thanks to me and my high school buddies. I signed his name on birthday cards, and friends barked whenever we drove over railroad crossings.

Years later I gave my parents a silver plate as an anniversary gift. It was inscribed with swirls and intricate carving from the five children. The engraving near the base read, "Much love, from each of us and Jiggs."

I got a B+ senior year on my final computer science project: a reenactment of his death. The program showed a little black dog barking on screen. Behind him was a tangerine sun, a chugging silver locomotive with AMTRAK written on the side. This was followed by a single yelp and the crimson curtain that descended over the whole monitor. People watched this with peculiar grins and tilted heads. They didn't know whether to laugh or not, whether it was mean or ironic or kind of a fucked thing to do. I wasn't so sure myself. Truth is, my best friend, Tony, had created the computer project for me a few nights before when I couldn't come up with any ideas. It seemed clever to me back then—make fun of what is vulnerable in myself and I'd be stronger and wittier, and then no one would ever be able to hurt me. To touch me.

I'd be safe.

IN THE NEXT WEEKS, DR. COLLANDER INSTRUCTED ME TO SOCIALize more on the unit. He said to mix it up. "It's the same story as outside the brick walls," he said. "It's best if we mingle every now and again to keep the interpersonal juices flowing."

"I'm not exactly in the best mood, you know," I told him. "Can't do the cocktail groove so well."

"You have to stay social or you'll slink away," he said. "Less isolation, watch TV. No scribbling in your journals for hours on end. Write sometimes, but now it's partly about engaging others and being part of a community . . . like going to the groups, feeling that people respond to you and like you."

"Okay," I said. "I'll give it a shot."

Early on in my stay at Graceland, the only true excitement was when we heard that a Kennedy cousin had been admitted in the next ward, and the *National Enquirer* had hired a rented black van with tinted windows to take photos of him around the grounds. The next issue was filled with photos of him walking around the hospital, with other patients' faces blacked out.

Then there was Phillip, the burly, bearded Grateful Dead fan Link had told me about. He approached me and explained how he had become associated with the hospital ten months earlier.

"What's up, Phillip?" I said, and he chuckled and stroked his thick beard.

"For one, I'm still up," he said, shrugging. "I've been up forever, it seems." He spoke quietly and offered me some M&M's out of a clear plastic container. "I attempted to overdose on thirty-six tabs of acid in a canoe on a silvery-blue pond in New Hampshire," he said. "It caused tremendous havoc in my limbic system." He sighed and popped more candy into his mouth. "I took eleven U-turns and haven't seen home since," he said. "I can't find it anywhere, man, understand?"

"That's horrendous," I said, and he chuckled again.

"Horrendous is normal, David," he said. "You'll see that before long."

I saw proof the next morning when I met the most devastated and melancholy girl in the world, bar none. Even while I was stuck in my own mire, Holly made me look like a chirpy, benign talk-show host in comparison. Her isolation was like nothing I'd ever seen. A few seventeen-year-olds on the unit whispered to one another that she was in fact Death. I don't know if she ever heard them say that, the little shits! It's just not okay to say that to a person—I don't care how many times you were molested by a sadistic uncle.

You do not refer to people as Death on a unit.

Holly didn't speak for the first three months I was there. Nurses had her corralled in with the eating disorders, but I think that was just to help her develop some form of identity. She was a very pale, emaciated twenty-nine-year-old, and her brown, spindly hair crept halfway down her back. Sometimes, when I couldn't sleep at 2:00 a.m., I'd find her at the window at the end of the hallway, looking out into the blackness. Perhaps she was staring at her reflection or maybe she had her eyes closed for a moment. Who knows? Perhaps she slept standing up.

Holly walked away from other patients. She actually rolled away because she often had a bag of chocolate Ensure running into her nose from an IV pole. She kept her right hand over her eyes whenever someone came within four feet of her, as if the glare from their gaze would decimate her. Even then, I knew Holly's isolation was the saddest thing I'd ever witnessed. More immediate than the stories I saw on television of starving children in Africa or drugged boy soldiers killing neighbors with Uzis in Sierra Leone. Holly's struggle was asphyxiating.

Janet was another silent girl on the unit—rumor was she had strangled a bunch of cats in her neighborhood in Pennsylvania. I heard it was nine, which is a considerable number of cadavers, when you think about it. She was heavyset with thin, stringy black hair falling around her freckled face. Nineteen years of age and always rubbing her palms together vigorously. There was an older, harsh schizophrenic woman from San Antonio named Meaghan. She would stroll past Janet and meow.

"Would you care for more pussy, Janet?" the woman would whisper.

Janet's face flushed, and she stared at the worn carpet until the staff led Meaghan to the quiet room for a half hour. Each day, as I waited in the medication line behind Janet, I studied her small, pink fingers and her thin, gentle-looking wrists. Her nails were bitten down to the very edges. *Where does the rage reside?* I wondered. *How do you kill a cat? Could I ever kill one like Janet or Guppy? Was my grandfather telling tales, just spinning yarns to a little boy back then? Why would he tell me that story? How do people do horrible things at one point and change to live a completely moral life down the road? Are they guided toward that by a force, by God? And then why don't others complete that change? Why do they get trapped in the behavior like it was an unbreakable cast? How does that occur? Is it happening to me now? Can I even stop it?*

I wanted to tell Janet about Jiggs. I found myself making guilt-riddled connections with what she did and the fascination I felt with my dog. Maybe I had killed Jiggs, just in a more nuanced way. (If the young girl and I hadn't walked down to the tracks, he wouldn't have followed me—that type of thing.) I thought I could help her, or at least I could feel her anguish, maybe suck most of the guilt out of her. That's who I was. I could take the pain, take everybody's despair, and store it inside me. I figured I was nothing but a useless vessel at that point, and maybe that's how I could save the people on the unit. (This was just before I felt I was the Messiah.)

I used Holly and Janet as a measuring stick in my own therapy as a way of buoying myself. Sometimes Dr. Presley stopped me on the unit and stood close to me and asked me how sessions were going with my psychologist. "You have to understand," I said looking down at him. "I know things are appearing a little bleak for me, but look at Holly, look at Janet. Those poor girls are really hurting."

"You ever notice you look everywhere but at yourself?" he said to me one afternoon. "Why do you think you do that?"

This was after I'd been at the hospital for several months—he initially treated me somewhat cautiously but became more and more confrontational. I don't mean to suggest he didn't care for me. He was an extremely warm fellow, always impeccably draped in sparkling suits, peach or purple ties, and cheap, disappointing shoes. I never understood that—great suits like a Freudian gangster, but the damn shoes were tainted, run-of-the-mill. I wanted to scream at him sometimes, "Come on, you bastard. Splurge and get an attractive pair of kicks!"

He was a very physical, touch-based type who loved to keep patients off balance. He invaded everyone's personal space, and sometimes he'd pick up my hands, my scarred arms, pat them and say, "It's okay, son. It's really great to see you with Dr. Collander. You're growing closer, sharing yourself. Making advances. But if you ever just wish to vent, feel free. I'm always here." Then he winked. "You are not bad at all. You're filled with goodness, that's it. Love David with everything you've got. Take it easy on him, okay?"

Other times, he'd hold me tight in a bear hug, which completely threw me off.

We had a unit meeting once every week. Twenty-five depressives, anorexics, and some schizophrenics, from eighteen to thirty years of age, would sit in a circle with the nurses and the doctors, and Dr. Presley would say odd things. "Is everyone clear what our bodies are made of?" he said once. "Does anyone know, for instance, what the clitoris consists of?"

"Aluminum" is what I was dying to say. But I didn't. I couldn't—I wasn't capable of it at the time.

Dr. Presley walked bunched up on his toes, leaning forward, and ready to spring into therapeutic action at a moment's notice. Maybe that's why I was so cognizant of his disappointing footwear—because of that posture, that stance. Pushing off the carpet with those fit, strong toes, casing each inch of the therapeutic milieu.

He had his nose everywhere. Granted, he was the unit chief, but still, his awareness of everything happening on the ward was impressive. He strolled down the hall, offering affirmations and recriminations to half a dozen patients as he consulted with the cute student nurses giggling beside him. "Would it kill you to say hello to me?" he teased one patient or, "Glad to hear you're out of the quiet room, Milton." He was pure energy, just naturally, perfectly manic.

Oh yeah, and he was Freudian to the bone. Cigars were absolutely never just cigars.

HOLLY NEVER SEEMED TO SLEEP. I DON'T THINK I EVER CAUGHT her zonked out on a couch like the others. She just walked—except it wasn't really a walk. She drifted and slouched and pulled herself around the unit, staring out at the world. The unit had two long hallways with those twelve-foot Plexiglas windows in the center, and there were some meeting rooms right near the cafeteria. Holly would stare out the windows into the beautiful collection of trees, the huge maples, elms, oaks, an ash, a ginkgo, and the pines out back.

In the winter, you could see through the bare trees into the surrounding neighborhoods of Hartford. Perhaps Holly was looking for movement there, signs of life beyond the hospital, over the eight-foot brick wall. Sometimes I joined her. I would sit near where she stood and just write in my journal about the breasts of old girlfriends, and the frivolous days before the storm rushed in.

My family visited frequently at first, and then their pace leveled off as my drama became routine for them, for me, and for everyone who knew me. Life rolled on. Plus the drive was ninety minutes from Guilford, and I was there for just under 940 days—an eternity. Everyone was exhausted, raw, on edge, and then the feelings grew rigid, stale, numb, and ugly inside and out. The whole thing still hurt me and everyone in my family just as intensely, but after a while my therapy's progress seemed slogged in super slow-mo. This was true of both my individual work and the intermittent family sessions. My sickness and the fact of my sickness were like a game of hot potato in my family. If we concentrated too much on the collective anguish, it would overwhelm us and leave us more wounded than we already were.

Other family members suffered silently and were overshadowed by my illness. They struggled with depression themselves, felt abandoned while the attention was showered on me for years. Dennis lost forty-five pounds out of sheer panic when he went away to live at the Riverview School in Cape Cod, an academy for developmentally disabled adults. Julie started therapy, and

Laura did as well. Even my parents sought counseling to keep things afloat. So when visits happened, we spoke of topics that were quick and bouncy, like maybe the accomplishments and the accoutrements of the place—*Aren't the grounds lovely? Was James Taylor ever here, David? How are things on the unit? How is therapy going, by the way?* I felt awful causing such misery over and over. It felt like a long-drawn-out advertisement for my frailties, and that shamed me.

When I told Dr. Collander this in one family session he said, "Oh, come on, David, that's bull. You got sick—some of your uncles and aunts struggled terribly. Manic depression slashed a wide swath through both sides of your family. Mental illness constricted and took a life—that's a truism. It's not just you alone with the illness out of the blue."

DENNIS CAME TO THE FAMILY SESSIONS ONCE EVERY TWO OR three months, but he was very wary of coming to see me at other times. "How come you haven't been by to see me for a couple months, Den?" I asked him on the phone once.

He was quiet at first and thought it through. "I feel uncomfortable at that place," he said, "the people look sick, weird, and crazy, and I know you're not like that. It just looks very spooky, and I want you to get out of there as soon as you can."

"I'm working on it, buddy," I said.

"Good," he said. "Work harder so we can go to the movies or shopping or anything, really. Just get the heck out of that place and we'll go have fun."

"I'd like that," I said

Dennis still competes in the softball throw and standing long jump every year at the Special Olympics; after the competitions he wears the gold and silver medals around town. The medals shimmer, jingle, and bounce around his neck as he walks, though actually it's more of a strut.

He attended that school in Sandwich but then returned to New Haven and started working at my father's car dealership in Woodbridge. He's been there ever since, distributing the mail and picking up trash and listening to the mechanics in the shop curse their wives and girlfriends. Dennis shares an apartment with a handicapped fellow in New Haven, and they have supervision during the evenings, someone who comes in to cook meals. Other than that, he's unusually independent and proud. He also has a capacity for joy that is astounding.

Dennis has always rocked his body. Just a steady, forward-moving rhythm. My earliest memory was of this tiny, cross-eyed boy with huge Buddy Holly–type glasses (black rimmed with thick corrective lenses), sitting splay-legged in a crib, moving throughout the night. We'd say good night to each other with Dennis on the other side of the room; when I woke up in the morning, he'd be smiling at me two feet away, still rocking. Today he does it slightly—a small, leaning-forward type of thing.

I brought a photo of my little brother as a four-year-old boy with me to the hospital: his legs are splayed out backward, and he's sharing his chocolate pudding with Jiggs. It was taken when we lived in Baldwin, Missouri. He has on those black-rimmed glasses, and he's tiny. In the photo, his lips are smothered in chocolate, and he's smiling. A black, curly lock of his hair dangles in front of one of his eyes. At that age, he became obsessed with fire trucks and ambulances. Sometimes the local firehouse took him for rides. He was just a diminutive boy with a hole in his heart bopping down the avenue, pulling on the horn of a fire truck. It was loud, discordant, irritating—but he loved it. The horn, the lights, the colors. The whole deal.

GRACELAND CONSTANTLY SEEMED TO HAVE THAT GOD-AWFUL smell of urine floating and mixing with an institutional, lemony Pine-Sol. Sometimes, when I closed my eyes, I could imagine I was back at the Cape with my brothers. Of course, at other times, I felt myself sinking further and further into the seats in the dayroom, just like that initial night with Link and the Thorazine.

I regularly told my family, "I feel like I can't feel." It was a popular saying on the unit. Young souls without any affect lurking and shuffling around under the lights. I sat around, grew fatter and added a beard and eventually became morbidly obese as the days wore on. There were moments my family and I did break through and hold each other—that felt crucial, so important. And there were lots of tears but never from me. My mother brought me books, and my father came with magazines and diet root beer. And that veil of gauzy fabric that had first appeared in Barbados hovered in front of me constantly.

I felt far from others at times, unable to connect with many save Dr. Collander. When I left his office or conference room, and my feet returned to Graceland, I grew numb. Back to the safety and horror of the perpetual gauze.

After half a year, Andy came to one of the family sessions. He was home on vacation after getting his degree in international relations from Tufts University, and he spent most of his life from that point outside the country, working for World Vision, a type of Peace Corps organization.

He was peculiar in the way he mentioned coming home, never saying Connecticut or Guilford when he spoke about returning. Home was always referred to as "America"—pronounced in the same way Dolph Lundgren said it as the Russian boxer in *Rocky IV.*

"Andy," Dr. Collander said to him as we sat in the conference room on the unit, "do you have any things you wish to talk about with David?"

Andy shifted his body for a moment, cleared his throat, and said, "Well, Doctor, to be honest, I worry that David will go out and commit one of those mass shootings on a playground at an elementary school, and I'll hear about it on CNN somewhere."

"And what causes you to think that?" Dr. Collander said.

"The way he threatened me on the phone not so long ago," he said, pointing at me. "It was scary, I tell you. I'm not sure he should be discharged for many moons."

I watched my brother look down at the floor. I could understand how he felt after receiving that phone message from me. He was broad shouldered and handsome with a red beard and some crow's-feet. A slight receding hairline. Everyone else in the room, my sisters and little brother Dennis, glared at him for the last comment. *What happened to us?* I wanted to sing out, to scream. *Do we have anything left to say? Not once were you loving and supportive—why is that, do you think? What did I do that made you so furious to begin with?*

Dr. Collander exhaled and said, "Do you wish to say anything to your brother about your early years?"

"I would love to," Andy said. "But I don't remember any of it. I just don't recall being harsh or mean to David. He always had a really good sense of humor, I remember that. But I don't remember specific tensions, and I can definitely say sorry if you'd like me to, if that would help, but I have no memory of it."

When I look back at that meeting and that discussion, I laugh at the crapshoot that is DNA: I'm plagued with a memory that cannot forget a scent or sight or sound, and my childhood bully is blessed with no memory at all.

8

FIRST SIGHT AND
HOLLY'S EMERGENCE

AFTER SEVERAL MONTHS OF RESTRICTIONS ON THE GRACE-land Unit, I started going out with patients and staff for strolls around the grounds. I found it spare and frosty in the winter when the wide lawns had substantial snow cover. Just like the brochures they handed out to my father when I first arrived. Huge, creaking trees waited for spring. Beside the fields was a gymnasium that had a bowling alley the color of pea soup in the basement. There was a chapel that I never visited and a small, dusty library—*Catcher in the Rye* was perpetually out on loan. Fountains and a few statues accented the grounds. Most patients

I saw from other units had the familiar MPP—mental patient posture—the fatigued, bloated way about them that I saw in the mirror every day. Some patients became circuit riders traveling from one top-tier hospital to another: McLean near Boston, Sheppard Pratt in Baltimore, the Menninger Clinic in Kansas (now relocated to Houston), and the Austen Riggs Center in the Berkshires.

The volleyball games in the gym were slow in the winter and spring, though there was usually a handful of manic young men or women to offset the depressives and the one or two catatonics on the ward. On one of the walks, I spotted a statue of a boy, oxidized green, picking a thorn from his foot. He was about three feet high, very thin. Meek. It was off in a corner of the grounds, right near a paved walkway that we passed each day, and it was surrounded by a bush that I think was a huckleberry that would bloom lushly in the summer. I had seen examples of the statue in photos and outside a neighbor's swimming pool in my childhood. *Could that have been the second grade in Missouri, maybe?* The green boy struck me immediately, caught my attention, and I couldn't stop obsessing over it. *He looks like a true friend, a confidant maybe*, I told myself. I held that knowledge tight to me, a locked secret. A simple, mostly harmless and unknown connection that he and I shared for a while

MY SESSIONS WITH DR. COLLANDER COVERED A LOT OF TOPICS, but one that came up frequently was the Skidmore Pricks and why I allowed them to behave as they did. I was constantly pestering Collander to explain my complicity and why I never stuck up for myself. That seemed to haunt me—where were my balls during that whole time? Dr. Collander said the haze of drugs made everything unreal for me and that I had subjugated myself to these stronger, malevolent personalities as a way of avoiding conflict and surviving. He believed that both Andy and the roommates made me feel that my very life was threatened.

"You felt cornered by these . . . predators and didn't know what to do," he said.

"'Predators' seems a little strong," I said.

"Why don't you give yourself a goddamned break?" he said with a befuddled smile. "Stop worrying about their feelings, how it might affect them. Maybe the only way you could push through, could live, was to accept their treatment? Don't you see that possibility?"

I wasn't sure. This seemed very vague to me, and I was greatly disappointed by that fogginess. The drugs back then only made it foggier. I wanted easy answers, not the grayish in-betweens. No answer in therapy was ever razor clear, razor sharp. Nothing except the razors themselves.

I remember receiving a call from Curtis in the spring. He said something like "So, how much do you weigh now, Fitz? Getting up there, right, with all those drugs? You must be a balloon by now. Just kidding, buddy—you know I'm just kidding."

I got a final letter from him in the summer of 1990. The letter said a bunch of the Pricks were together for a weekend and that they were all very upset. I remember that Curtis drew an arrow to the stains on the yellow legal pad and said something like, "These are my very real tears spilling."

When I showed the letter to Dr. Collander, he got furious. I'd never seen him so angry. "Those animals talk about you like you're an ex-lover," he said. " They treat you like someone they still long for—it's so bizarre and fucked up what they did to you."

A FEW MONTHS LATER, I HAD PSYCH TESTING IN A ROOM OVERLOOK-ing the grounds. It was summertime in 1990, and I had a small carton of low-fat milk in my hand. I studied the different ink blots, part of the Rorschach test, and noticed one that looked to me like a grotesque butterfly serving hors d'oeuvres to Jesus and some corpses. As the twenty-seven-year-old psychiatric resident wrote down my observations, I took the carton and poured the milk over my head. It splashed down my face, and I licked some of it. The resident looked panicked. "Why did you do that to yourself?"

"It's a college thing," I said. "A sign of love and respect for my friends there."

He handed me a paper towel and scratched his cheek. "That's interesting sarcasm, David," he said. "Why are you serving hors d'oeuvres to Jesus—why is he there with the corpses? Are these your roommates you're serving food to?"

"I don't know," I said, wiping my face with a towel. "I feel God has not been very present for me—how's that?"

"You're jumping around—but you don't have to explain any of this to me if you don't want to," he said.

"What's your concept of God, Doctor—do you serve him or her hors d'oeuvres with corpses?" I asked.

"Why don't we stop for now," he said. "You're floating away from things."

"Yes," I said. "That seems accurate."

◆

One Tuesday afternoon, after five months of my sitting near Holly at the end of the hall, she cleared her throat and took her hand away from her eyes. She looked down at me, pushed the tube away from her nose, and managed a "Hi . . . hi, David."

"Holly . . . hi, hello," I said, watching a smile grow on her face. "Wow . . . you're back here. Welcome, welcome back. I'm so glad you're here with me."

"Yes," she said. "Me, too." She laughed self-consciously and wiped her lips, rubbed her eyes, and looked down at the floor. Then she wiped her nose on her shirt, looking at the tube in her hand. Her eyes were wet. It was like watching a fawn's struggle to stand or, perhaps, watching a flower burst open in accelerated time. It was a bright flash in a black and ugly swamp of time, and it led to the two of us becoming buddies. She opened up more and more each day. She was still silent at times with others on the unit, but she talked with me, and she even giggled. I dragged an extra chair down to the hallway's far window one time, and she sat beside me. After a week or two of constant and increasing conversation, she said, "You've gotten me in a lot of trouble."

"How's that?"

"Nurses and doctors don't miss a thing," she smiled. "They see me talking—smiling even. They want to know what you told me to get me to speak."

"What did you say?"

"I said you sang the Canadian national anthem," she said.

"You're screwing with them," I said, looking over at her. "Well, good for you."

She patted my hand. "Thanks."

"Oh, don't mention it," I said, shrugging. "Those of us on this unit must look out for one another."

"Is that a rule?"

"Yes, as a matter of fact, it is," I said. "It's a new rule, just recently enacted." I looked at her face, which had some color, and said, "You don't use the feeding tube anymore—that's fantastic."

"Yep," she said, blushing. "Nurses want me to start sharing in groups, expecting so much from me now."

"Yeah," I said. "Someone expecting things. That's one of the dangers of being among the living."

She cleared her throat and said, "Are you, uh, you think you'll get out anytime soon?"

"I don't know, Holly," I said. "I'm afraid of my mind—even of stupid commercials on TV."

"Really?" she said. "Like what—is it, like, cereal, like Tony the Tiger or something?"

I smiled for a second. "No, it's actually the razor commercials," I said. "Like 'Gillette, the Best a Man Can Get!'—that stuff screws me over. The close-ups, the gigantic blades gnawing, the hungry teeth flashing across the screen."

"Huh," she said. "I didn't know that could be scary to anyone." She tapped my arm and pointed to her chest. "If I'm learning to chew food and swallow and not freak out with the socializing, then I know how you can stop your bloody thoughts."

"You sound sure of this," I said, and she reached out her hand again and patted my wrist.

"Certainly," she said. "Just take a few sips of this chocolate Ensure each morning, and you'll think of me."

"That's all it takes?" I said.

"Swallow a whole carton or two down," she said. "Just chug it, think of me and you'll feel safe, secure—ready to, uh, conquer worlds. That's my guarantee."

"You should do a commercial," I said.

She stood and walked to the window and turned around

quickly, holding an Ensure can. Outside it was a July evening and some lush leaves were moving slowly in the trees. It was maybe 72 degrees out there. I recall her grinning widely as I watched her skin stretch taut around her skull. "Hello, I'm a recovering anorexic with a whole bathtub of issues," she said, "but after choking on chocolate Ensure, I'm like some Wonder Woman . . . with a little gas."

I smiled, touched. "How about a jingle to go along with it?"

"Come on," she said. "I can only tax my brain so much."

I NEVER GRASPED WHO GOD WAS WHEN I WAS GROWING UP—AND I'm still fairly confused about it. As a child I imagined he was a seventy-five-foot blondish-bearded giant with thick sandals and a tambourine, draped in white linen sheets, dispensing lightning and snow days like Zeus. Part Charlton Heston, part Sonny Bono. I'm not sure why he had the tambourine, maybe it was that 1970s variety show influence. (To this day, when I see Cher in a movie or an infomercial, I feel a certain odd peace. A tiny part of my mind still thinks, "That's one of God's women.") As I went through my teen years and into college, God's presence in my life shrank drastically. So much so that, at one point, I told peers his wisdom could be scrunched up and fitted inside a miniature bong and smoked away forever. This was a pretentious, obnoxious quip I saved up for late-night ramblings.

At different points in my life, I was halfway sure Catholics had the answer, followed very briefly by the Jews. From there I appreciated the Congregationalists and then while I was hospitalized repeatedly, I imagined it was the Buddhists. Or at least I liked the idea of a heavyset holy man, someone with a substantial belly. It made me feel less . . . monstrous. I was enraged at God for a long time—felt he'd utterly let me down by being a fraud and a bitter, angry force that picked on the helpless for no reason.

God's gender also morphed for me over the years, switching from male to female in my mind. The more I saw my mother in reverent garb in her minister positions at Yale, with a colorful stole draped over her shoulders, I found my mind changing, accepting. Each time this happened, it seemed like a natural shift, a resolution of a long-festering question. She was healer, consoler, kinder, all encompassing. Perhaps God was a woman.

WHILE HOLLY WAS GROWING HEALTHIER AND BRIGHTER, I BECAME friendly with another anorexic girl from Boston. She was a beautiful, emaciated artist named Shine. I believe her real name was Prudence, but even the nurses used the name Shine. Plus, I liked the sound of it. Classy, cool, and maybe I figured she had reasons for the nickname. Her own private stuff.

I was moved by how clearly you could see her skull through her pale skin in the morning light. Shine had almost translucent bones. When I'd see her over by the expansive window in the dayroom, I was reminded of something I used to do as a kid— holding a flashlight up to my hand in the dark and admiring the orangey glow that went into my palm. With Shine's hollows and gaps on her face and her all-skeletal look, I swore I could see the sunlight pass right through her. It's a telling memory because, despite her sickness, she was luminous to me.

We became fast friends, two self-mutilators who went about their business in totally different ways. She preferred to manipulate and starve her body, and I just liked to mark mine up and watch it bleed. All she wore was a huge black T-shirt and a thin gray-and-blue-checked nightgown, but she made it look artsy and cool, and I found myself not so much wanting her, but just wanting to lie down on one of the shiny mattresses in the quiet room and hold her for a while. The boatloads of medication I was taking gave me the sexual drive of a cadaver, so I was confused by this desire.

"Maybe you've finally met someone who's in worse shape," Dr. Collander suggested. "Maybe you just want some fucking human contact."

Early on, before they started feeding her through her nose for refusing to eat, we went on two off-the-grounds passes together. I had been behaving well for a long time—no cutting for four months—so we were awarded a three-hour trip with my high school friend, Tony, as the driver. He took us for beer and pizza on Franklin Avenue, the Italian section of Hartford, and I remember studying Shine as she carefully ate minuscule bites of a white clam pie at the restaurant. When she got up and slid her way to the bathroom, I wondered if she'd vomited up the pizza. But an hour later, back on the grounds of the hospital, we kissed, and I tasted her tongue and decided, "No, I guess the pizza stayed down—her breath seems fresh."

Back at the hospital we lay on the thick grass beside a large fountain and barked at the neighborhood kids as they cut through the grounds on their way home from school. We tried to sound as crazy as possible for them. I remember touching Shine's breasts and being stunned by her projecting rib cage, the sound of her breathing, and her tiny nipple underneath my index finger. When I had her climb on me, she felt light and still, an ultra-mini waif. We were interrupted just before things got too heated by the horn of a passing security jeep. I was enraged and jumped up screaming at them, but Shine just said, "No, no it's okay. We'll do it again. We have all the time in the world."

"No, we don't," I said. "They never let you touch anyone on these units."

"We'll figure something out. We'll get thrown out and get an apartment."

"Shine—"

"Don't worry, it'll work out," she said.

But of course, it didn't and we didn't.

We did go out on one more pass, to a café in West Hartford after watching David Lynch's *Wild at Heart* together and obsessing over the best scenes. Both of us were infatuated with the somber, the melancholic, the darkness waiting around the bend of any moment, waiting to be plucked from inside us. Later, on the unit, Shine wrote tragic notes to me and drew peculiar sketches of trees with funny faces, heads dangling off the branches: "People fruit," she told me.

I knew nothing about eating disorders when I was admitted. I had heard passing references to Karen Carpenter's death, and there were some girls at Skidmore who handed out leaflets on emotional eating, but other than that, what I witnessed was a new and bizarre world of suffering.

Shine once said, "Dr. Shimley tells me everything is out of control in my life and that's why I do this shit." As she talked, she repeatedly picked the skin of her tiny tricep and then released it. Pick, release, frown. Pick, release, scowl.

"Yeah, but why do you think you do this?" I asked.

"Who knows," she said with a smirk. "I have no idea."

"Come on," I coaxed.

"It's what I'm great at," she said carefully, cautiously. "See that histrionic troop of seven that sit with me? I'm the leader, I set the tone. No one will be thinner than me—I refuse to allow it."

"What about Holly?" I said, and she smiled.

"Holly's got a crush on David," she sang in a whisper. "Listen, she's a troubled girl, but rumor has it you've given her new life. She'll be leaving soon, and you're getting quite the reputation, young fellow."

"She's my friend."

"Yes," Shine said. "That's a good thing—we must remember any time someone leaves, it's a time to rejoice."

The eating disorder "troop" she spoke of consisted of seven girls—a few were strictly anorexic and a few were strictly bulimic, but most were a morphing of the two. (Later, two young men from California would show up, but it was only women at this point.) At meals they pushed around their vegetables and made liquid out of their mashed potatoes. Some ate too much, others refused to eat. The stubborn patients weren't allowed to leave the cafeteria until something was eaten. They had to suck down those Ensures no matter what. When one refused all day, she would get fed by a tube through her nose. (That was always a startling sight. The patient had to lie back on a couch for an hour while they ran the tubes into her. If the patient cooperated with the treatment, she was eventually allowed to walk around with an IV on a pole, like Holly did for a while. It was harder for me to look at someone supine with a feeding tube than with someone walking and being, at the very least, active.)

One time a girl named Eugenia, a bulimic from Seattle, snuck down to the end of the hall and killed a ficus plant by repeatedly vomiting into it. Eugenia's father was big with a pharmaceutical company near Puget Sound, and she was always defending her dad against the PETA supporters on the unit—a vocal bunch. They'd scream at her, "Your father is a murderer!" and she'd defiantly defend him.

Each of us was funny like that—once in a while you'd see sparks of life from the young faces, but rarely did they get passionate about taking on their own overwhelming pain. It was just too fucking much, you know? Who would understand about beginning something like that? Where precisely would you start? Sure, we had experts prompting us each day, but it felt mostly futile, and so most of us obsessed about pharmaceutical companies ruling the world or George H. W. Bush or the texture of the toilet paper.

And we swore off thinking about depression, delusions, and an abusive uncle or, like Shine, dealing with a sexually abusive father. I was there on her twenty-first birthday, about a month after our pass. She opened a present that came in the mail from him—a red lace teddy with a note that read: "Sweet Dreams, Baby—Love, Daddy."

"That's fucked up," she said. "We may be freaks, but what the hell is he?"

I didn't have an answer.

Shine was my lifeline for a long time back then, my friend, and I recall her high-pitched, generous laughter; her adoration of her brother and grandmother; and even one time that involved a lot of dental floss.

While I was in session, she snuck into my room and wrapped dental floss from the doorknob to the bathroom and to my clothes in the closet. She used two packages of the floss, which turned into something like one hundred feet of the stuff tangled. The aides spent an hour untangling it and were not happy with her. But I thought it was a spectacular, touching thing. I later returned the favor by short-sheeting her bed.

This was stupid, of course, but it was fun. I was sick and lonely, and this emaciated girl entered my life and started cheering me up—it was a hell of a deal. We were inseparable on that unit. Shine used to bark sometimes when we were talking, mimicking another patient from Saudi Arabia named Loo, who wandered the thirty-five-acre facility intensely sucking on cigars and Diet 7UP and barking in the early mornings. Sometimes at breakfast with the windows open in the summer, we could hear him doing his howling dog routine—I believe that fellow ended up staying on the grounds forever.

AFTER ABOUT EIGHT MONTHS, I STARTED TO BELIEVE THE STATUE on grounds—the green boy—was my soul mate. The thought attached itself to my head like an ingrown hair might—just a throbbing dot that grew a few inches in from my brow. It felt vaguely frightening, and I decided not to share this detail with Dr. Collander, Holly, or Shine—I figured they'd be scared, and Collander wouldn't let me go out to the grounds. Eventually, the thought expanded and infected me, radiating waves of flamboyance, of delusions that fluttered, soared, and cooed. At times, the boy became a fallen angel—a diminutive, sentient being who aided patients. His arms were smooth and hairless—something I envied. I loved to run my hands over his head and his shoulders when I strolled through the grounds with the other patients and staff. I remember cursing myself for being so disgustingly hirsute. My arms, my chest—Jesus, even my back! I found myself furious with my body and self—every damn inch of it.

I bided my time for months until finally I got a pass that allowed me to walk the grounds alone. Then, a week and a half after my twenty-fifth birthday, I simply walked out the back gates and into Hartford. I had it in my head that I had to look like that angel, and so I went in search of a barbershop. I found one in Hartford and told the barber a story about it being my buddy's wedding and that I'd promised that if he ever got married, I would shave my head. Then I added that I didn't really want to exist, that I wanted to return to the womb and start again. He finished my head and was silent. Then I asked him if he'd shave my arms and chest with his clippers. "I want everything as smooth and clean as my skull," I said.

"I can't help you there, friend," he said, grimacing as he pocketed my money. It was a crappy neighborhood—street gangs were being arrested there on *Eyewitness News* several times a month. But I was cocky, giggling to myself as I waited on the corner for a cab to whisk me away to a multiplex cinema in East Hartford. *What the fuck can be done to me?* I thought. *Do they want to cut me? I'll slice deeper. Do they want to fuck me? I'll fuck myself deeper. Do they want to kill me?*

I'm already dead.

I FELT THE GREEN BOY'S PLIGHT AS I PREPARED FOR THE EVENING. I thought of him, suffering back on the grounds, stuck on his cold ass for perpetuity. I wanted to weep with him, imagining a life of no escape. My thoughts raced. *That poor thing is surrounded by the same damn plants, bugs, and trees every year.* His inner blight had to be lanced. And, I, in turn, needed release as well.

I took the cab to East Hartford and watched two mediocre movies with serious portent in the title: *Desperate Hours* and *Postcards from the Edge.* Afterward, I walked next door to the

Stop & Shop and bought some straight-edge razors, gingersnaps, and a quart of skim milk. The store was closing, so I sat on a bench outside watching two patrol cars parked side by side in the rear parking lot of the movie theater, the officers chatting during a break. *You could nip this thing in the bud, David,* I thought. *Go over and confess all your sins.*

Soon, though, I was making inane conversation with a taxi driver about the World Series as he flew down I-84 East toward Hartford Hospital, which was next door to the Institute. I told him I was visiting an "unusually subdued buddy" there. I remember that the driver told me he was from Kingstown, Jamaica. I got out at the hospital and walked into the ER and told a security officer, a woman, that I was a visitor and had to use the bathroom. I was wearing a baseball cap my father had given me—I think it read "Lincoln." The bill was angled downward and was blue with white mesh in front. I went inside to take a crap and while I was there, I took out a fresh razor and made my first slash of the night—a diagonal carving into my left calf.

On my way out, I strolled past two more cops and said, "Evening, Officers," and headed over toward the Institute. I found a little nook of pear trees that sat across from the Institute—the city was planting trees to improve the area's appearance. I squatted beneath one that was freshly planted and ogled the darkened Institute grounds like a sadistic lover preparing to ravish.

Then I did my thing—psychotic would be an accurate description. I made several small gashes in my scalp and arms, legs, forehead, and shoulders. I said hello to two passing teens and they kind of looked at me, raised their hands in a half wave and kept on strolling past. Then I dashed across the traffic-less street to the Retreat Avenue sidewalk, just twenty feet away from the Institute of Living president's beautiful white-stucco building.

There was nothing there but a four-foot brick wall and a row of bushes; I leapt into them and rolled onto the property. There were cameras in the back of the hospital, and I dodged their scopes in the darkness.

The only security was some dogs and a couple of Jeep Cherokees marked "Institute of Living Security." The officers were stationed at the front gate on Washington Street, leaving me free to roam in the back property. It was just me against the whitish-peach of the buildings, the turned-off fountains, and my green boy. My self-hate had been stewing for half a year of inpatient life, and I pined to damage. I hustled through the darkness to the little statue and found myself growing viciously upset at the green boy, enraged. My earlier affection for him disappeared completely. "Oh, you're such a fucking little useless piece of crap," I whispered, wrapping my arms around him, trying to rip him out of the ground. I smeared blood all over his naïve face, legs, and arms. *You let me down, you son of a bitch, you fucking pussy!* I thought as I looked down at the smooth boy. Then I seethed, *Who are you to be calling anyone names, David, you useless fat fuck?*

I unloaded on myself, mutilating my body for an hour and a half, slashing and filleting until blood spouted in arcs from my scalp, forearms, and shoulders. It was enormously invigorating, thrilling. I felt gruesome, animalistic. My blood was thick and sticky, and I played with it, loving it. I scrubbed myself with it, I sucked my arm, I giggled, did free impressions for the night sky. Dennis Hopper in *Blue Velvet,* chanting, "Mommy, Mommy," as I sucked on crimson limbs. Wiping my blood with a fiendish glee, I was Charles Manson, I was Travis Bickle; I twirled my hands around my bare skull, and suddenly I was Kurtz in *Apocalypse Now.* Nightmares, video images, novels, and movies swirled, mixing inside my brain. I was a wounded, charismatic, and newly self-christened pope of Greater Hartford, baptizing the well-respected insurance men and women of the world. Extending my arms, making the sign of the cross, I sang, "Everybody now, shall we gather at the river . . ."

Suddenly, I heard a door slam at the darkened main building and watched a shadowy figure hurry through the fallen autumn leaves, shoes making a swish-swish-swish sound toward the gravel parking lot fifty feet from where I was. I stopped singing and fell backward against the chain-link fence of the tennis courts and held my breath. I could tell it was a woman by her walk and the cut of her medium-length overcoat. *She must have heard me bang against the fence, it's over, it's over,* I thought. I pulled my knees up against my body. I looked down at my arms, felt my head smooth and wet, shiny against a far-away streetlight. I rubbed my arms, feeling the bloody moisture and thought, *It's over, when she gets to the car, she'll turn on the headlights and I'll be caught. Maybe this night is history.* My body shook and I thought, *Perhaps it's a sign, it's a fucking sign. If she sees me, God wants me to stop, if not, if by some miracle she doesn't spot me, well, then, I'm going off. I'm painting this fucking town!*

Her heels on the gravel parking lot ground were as loud as a fresh bowl of Cap'n Crunch. She got into her car and the headlights flicked on, catching me directly. Straight on. I held my breath and kept my head down, watching the light illumine the wet crimson of my left arm. I held my breath and felt a mad type of horror as I heard the car backing up, wheezing like an old Peugeot. The headlights quickly moved off me. Then I heard it shift from reverse into first gear and drive away from me and shift to second and then drive around the perimeter of the hospital and then out of sight, toward the entrance around the main buildings. *I can't believe she didn't see me,* I thought, terror rushing through a part of me.

Then I rose to my feet, pushing off from the fence, and waved good-bye to the blind doctor in the car. I stumbled up fifty feet beyond the tennis courts and came to a huge white fountain of cherubs and porcelain torches reaching up into the sky. The same one Shine and I had lounged around a month earlier. I started cutting again, smearing, picking up steam, my head feeling dizzy. Before long, I was panting and embracing the porcelain babies, hugging, yelling. Hanging off the top of the fountain. Splash, smear, laugh, giggle. I decorated everything that night— suddenly, I was an *artiste* who worked exclusively in plasma. It was hellish, but it also gave me a phenomenal rush, like a swirling, twisted dream. Mutilating and dreaming like that were the most illicit feelings I'd ever had, and it was what I was shooting for each time I hurt myself. *Carry me back to the fluidity of that forbidden dream,* I mused. *Get me back there!*

Then I fell, stumbling and splashing in the fountain, making that brackish water grow rosy. I felt light-headed, and for a moment I lay back and let myself drift. I took off my shirt, threw it on top of the cherubs. As I watched it slip and splash down beside me, I thought I might die, that I would die. I decided there were worse things. I took a breath and closed my eyes, dipping my smooth skull under the water.

Then I surfaced and threw up some ingested blood, heaving and coughing. I shivered, splashed, and started looking at my arms, my chest, my torn-up jeans. I was soaking and covered in wounds and gashes. I left the fountain and then, with an aching dizziness in my head and the blood pouring from me, I lay back on the dewy grass and saw a shooting star with a fiery orange tail.

Surrounding it were hundreds of white dots. The rushing star was magnificent, ferocious.

"Why doesn't anyone like me?" I screamed. I rose and wandered up a way and smeared some of the administration building walls with "FUCK, FUCK!" and "HELP, HELP!" Convinced that my left arm was made of rare fudge, I bit down and tasted something edible, sticky and thick. I tried to tear wounds open with my teeth—but they wouldn't rip. The dance of laughter and shrieks became desperate, and I looked up for God, for anyone. I started howling, crying. I sobbed. I felt my way along a wall and then a sidewalk led me to an empty administration building, where I banged on the window. When no one answered, I stumbled on until I found an empty security Jeep at the gym and tried to blow the horn. But even when I slammed my fist against that thing, it wouldn't sound!

"Luck of the fucking Irish," I whispered and slashed myself again with a downward cut through my chest and left wrist. Blood spouted, and I hummed the theme from *The Beverly Hillbillies*: "And up through the ground came a bumbling crude / Oil that is . . . Texas tea." I felt dizzy, nauseous. I heard voices shouting, and I turned a corner near the chapel and suddenly, came into brilliant electric light. That's when I saw my parents and my friend Tony. After I'd been missing for hours, the Institute called them to come and help search for me throughout Hartford. Now I saw them step out of a gray Isuzu Trooper in the front parking lot. They rushed over. I crumpled to the ground and started cursing and pounding my fist on the gravel. *Oh, fuck, fuck, fuck, fuck!* I was yelling, weeping, my mother reached me first and whispered, "JesusMaryJoseph, oh Jesus, baby!" Soon my father had blood on his shirt as he wiped the cuts on my head. Sirens erupted. He cursed at the swarming nurses as they ran from nearby units to assist.

"Eight months! He's been here eight fucking months and this is what we get?" he asked in a voice that was pained and hoarse.

Then I crumbled and collapsed like an infant, and a responsible paramedic inserted a needle into my groin.

I was rushed to a trauma room at Hartford Hospital. I lay there naked save for a washcloth covering my genitals, as they stapled, sutured, and glued me back together. For forty-five minutes it was silent save for the sounds of snipping, cleaning, and breathing. A new nurse entered the room eventually and said, "Did this guy cut his thing off?"

The washcloth was removed and she said, "Oh, man—thank God!"

Then, for each person who entered the room, they asked if my penis was severed and then removed the washcloth. Eventually an older-sounding doctor said, "Can we have some dignity for the patient, please? The genitals were left alone—let's leave it at that."

Then everyone was silent, and I felt stitches being tied, staples inserted. Before long, they placed me in a wheelchair, and my parents rushed in and kissed me, their shirts stained with my dried blood. Next Tony came in and said, "I'm just glad you're not dead."

Twenty minutes later, I was returned to the Institute of Living from which I had disappeared the day before. The grounds were dark and looked caustic to me then. (I heard later that the hospital grounds were off limits that morning while workers cleaned up the blood. I felt a deep surge of wickedness that *I had showed them who's boss*.) Nurses led me to a single room where I would be kept on suicide watch for six months. My mother looked stunned, in shock, back at the room, and she wept quietly before she left. "You don't deserve this, baby."

My father hugged me.

"Hey, watch out, you'll get blood on me," I whispered, and his eyes filled. Tony gripped my hand and then they walked down the hallway. "I'm so sorry," I said.

"It's okay now, baby," my mother said over her shoulder. I followed them out to the dayroom, and I watched them step through the bolted exit and turn left toward the elevator. And just like that they were gone.

Link sat in my room through the first night. I was quiet,

stunned, and I rested my head against the thin pillow. A street-light threw some moving skinny shadows across my bed and I wondered what would happen if I sprinted toward the window and jumped with all my weight. *Would it shatter? Jesus, give it a fucking rest, David!* I thought and closed my eyes. But I couldn't rest, couldn't fall into slumber. A nurse came in and gave me a strong cocktail and then I faded away as Link talked on and on about the finer points of his Chevy Duster. He knew my dad sold cars and so he rattled on about the business and his faithful vehicle.

I might have complained about the incessant gabbing, but that evening, I was scared, fucked, lonely, drugged. I had scared the crap out of myself and my family. Everyone, really. I wished myself dead, and so I listened to a man discuss the itty-bitty details about his Chevy until I fell asleep. In the morning, I heard him say to Louis, the next staff sitter, "My heart breaks for this guy. Nothing holding that soul together except nylon stitch and antipsychotics."

I wasn't allowed to leave the room for the first ten days—I felt shock, anxiety, and a throbbing, lingering blood lust. Just a raw need to get the juices flowing again.

"What on earth is there left for you to do with a razor on your skin?" Dr. Collander asked when I confessed this.

"I want to finish up the bastard," I said.

"You mean finish up you?" he said. "The young man, David, is still the bastard in your scenario?"

"Apparently," I said.

"We can't keep you in here forever," Dr. Collander said, annoyed. "We'll eventually get you out into the community room. You'll remain out there with staff right beside you." The aides tiptoed around me, nurses were constantly applying Bacitracin on my wounds. "Gotta keep the infections at bay," they said. A few younger nurses said they feared being left alone with me. "Let's keep your hands on the desktop, okay? No picking of the stitches," they said when I sat at my desk and tried to read magazines. Dr. Collander didn't let me write in my journal for four months:

"Any journaling now would just turn macabre and masturbatory," he said. "It would be too bloody."

I felt so studied, trapped, vacant, and scared. I wanted to climb up on the bureau and throw myself off it at the bedposts, smacking against anything, sharp or dull. I wanted to eat myself, the nurses and doctors. Anything raw—Jesus Christ, I felt so ragged, trapped, and horrible. At one point I was in four-point restraints for a night and felt like a dog. I was tied up, chatting with the technician or nurse, and the next moment I wanted to bite my fingers, eat my feet. Paul Simon's *Rhythm of the Saints* album came out around that time and it eased me, settled me down considerably. I couldn't stop listening to "The Obvious Child": ". . . how strange that some rooms are like cages . . ."

Holly was probably the first person to see me other than staff and my parents. She was due to be discharged soon, and a week after the incident she asked the doctors if she could come in to see me. She walked over to me at my desk, smiled, and slowly, awkwardly embraced me before stepping back. "I'm heading out into the world," she said.

"Congratulations, Holly," I said. "You're going to do great, I'm sure."

"Don't think you can't do the exact same thing," she said to me. "Don't give up, okay?"

"I'll remember," I said, smiling slightly.

We exchanged numbers, but I never saw her again. We had

done our time together, touching on things somber, intense, and unique. Perhaps everything after that would be awkward and disappointing. That said, whenever I see a chocolate Ensure spot on television today, now mass-marketed for every soul on earth, I can't help but grin and think, "Holly's commercial was better."

During this time, Shine wrote me notes each day that kept me buoyed. They cheered me on and said things like "These are harrowing times, my dear, but you'll make it. It is carved in marble somewhere in Rome that you must get out of the hospital so that we can continue to analyze *Twin Peaks*. No more blood, okay? And next time get a real haircut, not a shaved head. It scares me some. You look a little too much like a full-blooded, nutso mental patient and I know, of course, that you're so much more. Love, Shine."

THERE WAS A WONDERFUL NURSE NAMED PHYLLIS WHO SAT WITH me most weeknights during this time. She was graying and in her early fifties and brought me *Entertainment Weekly* magazines and challah bread from her home. We talked about most anything and I felt . . . safer when she was around. I told her about a dream I had as a kid, where I stood in a school cafeteria and floated up and bumped my head on the bulky ceiling lights. I didn't have wings, and it wasn't a Superman kind of flying, I just lost gravity around me.

It took place in the eating halls, usually old gymnasiums, places with high ceilings and rooms packed with circular tables and loud, hungry kids digging into lunchboxes. The classmates never batted an eye when I drifted around; they carried on conversations with me as I floated ten, fifteen feet above their miniature heads. I couldn't control it. I pretended it wasn't happening; that I was just different, a little off that day, and people never said anything. They refused to mention it, and so I was confused and wondered, *Is this real? Am I really drifting around through my life? Or is it all in my head?*

"You believe in visions, then?" Phyllis asked me when I finished, turning the pages of her magazine.

"I want to say no," I said. "But there was a huge guy bleeding in a dream of mine some years back, killing himself, yelling—a real nut."

"And you think that's why you did this stuff to yourself?" she said.

"Subconscious self-fulfilling prophecy, maybe?" I said. "Is that pushing it?"

"That's probably too simplistic, too easy, David," she said, placing her magazine on her lap. "You know you could've asked for help—could've picked up the phone and called and stopped the whole show before it got out of hand."

"I know," I said. "I feel terrible about that."

"Do you feel bad for yourself, though?" she said. "You've got to see that you hurt family and friends but mostly you. Your body, your mind—you've dug a substantial hole for David at this hospital."

"You think so?" I said.

"I know so," she said. "The administration now thinks of you as a liability risk. They won't let you out of anyone's sight for months."

I nodded and said, "I can't wait to go to the bathroom alone."

"But do you grasp that you built this prison for yourself?" she said.

"Yeah," I said. "I guess."

"I think you need to. It's important," Phyllis said. "So you don't repeat the mistake, so you don't build any more walls around you or dig any more graves."

I EVENTUALLY STARTED MY OWN COUNTDOWN CALENDAR TO WHAT I dubbed "Free Urination and Defecation Day." Most of the staff didn't budge an inch with rules. Three feet away—always. No time alone. Sleeping, eating, in the bathroom, showering, walking, sitting, writing, talking, etc. November, December, January, February: someone was always watching me. Eventually, after four and a half months of my showing the staff that I could be trusted, a couple of male technicians gave me five minutes alone in the shower to masturbate.

"Every guy needs relief from the stressors of the world," they said. "You can't tell the female staff about this, but go ahead, imagine Demi Moore's waiting in there and knock it out of the park. Shower the people, man."

That ounce of freedom, the kindness and humor, the chance for quick release, wasn't the most pleasurable experience, but my God, how I looked forward to those three hundred seconds! For the Super Bowl that year, a tall Greek aide, Milo, let me watch it on his then–techno marvel, a mini-TV. I was touched and grew quite close to him and another guy on staff named Eddie, who handled my long-term status with care and respect.

At moments when everyone else was asleep, and I had insomnia, we'd go into the cafeteria, and Eddie and I would load up on snacks. It was simple kindness, and it made me feel special and cared for. Eddie and Milo kept me alive and kicking just as much as Dr. Collander did. They treated me like a friend, a school buddy, and that made a true difference. The aides complained about their frustrations and failed romances and nudged me in their own way, toward improvement, toward thinking outside the walls. It made me feel part of something bigger than my own skull. They spoke of the world, the women, the heartaches, the joys—and their involvement in it bolstered me.

I trained myself to stop caring about the other staff observing while visitors hung around, although my parents found them especially irritating. "What the hell is the guy going to do with me sitting here?" my father said, flushed.

"We're doing this for his safety," they would reply.

When I rejoined the community, it felt sweet to be surrounded by the others, to have peers, though I was still followed closely. At the time, a very wealthy patient had come in from Maryland. Grant carried a folder around with him that contained clippings from a Baltimore newspaper about his dad's company, which had been purchased some months earlier for $675 million. Grant loved Bob Marley, surfing, dirt bikes, and avocado sandwiches. He was sweet and kind to me at a time when I desperately needed it. He made me delicious treats and later shared with me the collection of pornography he kept in his room.

He was a patient of Dr. Presley's and remained totally dedicated to the man. I felt partially envious—not that my own therapist wasn't kind and helpful, but the interactions with the main shrink were the ones that stuck in my head, that made the biggest impressions. I felt a weird combination of tension, loathing, and admiration for him.

Once, around this time, Dr. Presley sauntered over to me and said he wanted to discuss the sexual dreams I'd been having. I leered at him through the haze of numbness, medication, and depression, and thought, *Just try and fix me, you son of a bitch.*

He sat me down in a conference room on the unit and said he'd been reading some of the notes Dr. Collander had written about my dreams.

"You dreamt of flying breasts, soaring vaginas, and large penises drifting through the sky, is this true?" he said, shuffling some papers.

"I guess—last week," I mumbled, blushing, and he grinned.

"David, who would you rather be masturbated by, your therapist or your father?" he said.

I looked at him, stuttering, "What?"

"Come on, answer," he said, his brow furrowed. "Would you rather have your father jerk you off or Dr. Collander?"

"I don't know," I said, seriously pondering the query.

"Nothing seems to move you, son," he said, placing his palms out so I could see them. "I go away for a month, try to have a goddamned vacation, and you nearly crucify yourself with razors on the grounds of my hospital. When I return, you stay silent as ever. I see you moping around here day after day. So I want to wake you up, okay?"

"I'm trying," I said.

"Oh, bullshit!" he said, his face flushed. "Now, tell me. If you were in a room with your father and both of you were naked and erect . . ."

"What is this, Dr. Presley?" I said.

"You got me so far, just listen," he said. "Imagine you both have hard-ons, and you're standing side by side in a room. Then, let's say the velvet curtain opens, and your naked mother enters the room. Would you rather have her stare at your erection or your father's?"

"You're very bizarre," I said, looking toward the door.

"Oh, I'm bizarre?" he said and came around the table to place his palms on my arms, my hands. His large, tanned face was close to mine. "Why do you do this stuff to yourself—why do you think you bleed? Why do you wipe your blood all over my hospital?"

"I'm trying to figure that out," I said.

"Bullshit!" he said, "You treat this place like a fancy hotel—if you're not careful, you'll be one of the professional goats that are screwed up for the rest of their lives. So tell me, the truth now, did you ever fantasize about fucking your old therapist in the ass?"

"Huh?"

"For fun—would you do it just for fun if you could?" he said, and I started crying, overwhelmed. It was quiet for a few seconds before he exhaled and moved toward me. "Those are little vaginas on your skin that you slice," he said quietly. "The only thing you're doing is having your mother menstruate on your body. Did you know the significance of that? The fantasy, the meaning behind it?"

When I looked up at him, I said, "You're basically a bully."

"All right," he said, gently patting my arm. He smiled warmly then, as if we had just discussed major league baseball for a few minutes. "We'll end now, we're through."

"What . . . was that?" I said. "Do you do this to each of your patients?"

"I think you needed this, son," he said gently, grabbing his suit coat and putting it on. "You needed to be brought out of your perpetual state of blah, of nothingness."

"But do you do that to each of your patients?" I said. "Do you assault them—even the girls?"

"No, of course not," he said, smiling slightly. "And I didn't assault you. As I explained, you need to be awakened from your deep freeze. My words were meant to shock—did they do that?"

"Yes," I said. "I guess so."

"Yeah, I guess so, too," he said and patted my back. "We're done."

"Okay," I said.

Then, just as he opened the door and was about to let me out into the unit, he closed the door. "I just don't want you to turn this into a career, David," he said, his red face gazing up at me. "I've seen it too many times. Young promising minds and bodies overwhelmed with sickness. As they try to heal and reenter society, the anxiety they feel looking forward is much greater than the anxiety waiting in the past. And so they stay sick. They mingle in hell and remain with the sickly forever. 'Professional mental patients' is what I call them." He patted my shoulder and then my cheek. "You've read Dante?" he asked.

"Most of it," I said, blushing.

"Don't dawdle in the shit pits for the rest of your life," he said. "Know what I mean?" He winked and said, "Forget about blood, leave the blood in the dreams. That wacky shit belongs inside you. You need it to live. Do it for me, my friend, okay?"

"Okay," I said and went back out onto the unit.

It's odd. Many have commented about how cruel and bizarre those questions were and how I should have reported him or complained. But it was such a terribly disturbed time for me; I had little faith in myself, and I believed I had no righteous ground to stand on. Plus, I usually liked the guy a lot. So I returned to the dayroom and watched VH1 with the others. The videos kept me company.

◆

Just as Presley said, I was becoming like many young men and women who go from a first visit at a mental hospital and then to the fifth and then the tenth and then are suddenly transformed into chronics. That was a significant lesson I learned quickly—it's excruciatingly hard *not* to return to a psychiatric ward. Once you've been broken to a certain point—attempting suicide or cutting or having a breakdown or psychosis, you will probably be admitted again. It's a horrible fact, really, but it's truth.

A person is pushed to what he thinks is the edge (of his life, of his sanity, or of what he imagined the limits of sanity would be) and it seems a signal goes up inside the brain. A last-minute red flag: warning, warning, and all that. Beyond the flag is light-years beyond zany. It is sheer terror, an area where, if you push through the muck, if you take that chance and examine and remove and pick apart and shine a light on it, you might never get back to a clean room with three meals a day and a television in a bubble at a hospital. And so, perhaps you concede in minute ways—I'm not saying it's a game, but you don't push quite as hard because you're terrified of what lies beyond the flag. And you don't go to the terror area, you don't access that fear. People stay away from terror. You make a deal with your psyche and don't venture there by giving up slightly. You say, "I can live with a smaller world: a day hospital with medication, or coming back into inpatient treatment four times a year."

Professional mental patients don't become that way because it's fun or easy or because they're lazy. It's sheer terror that keeps them from pushing on; a life of muted, sedated, depressed psychic pain is a safer choice than exploding through and maybe never coming back

I didn't meet many folks who broke that cycle—who are admitted once and do not fall into recidivism. I was slowly turning into a noted and pathetic leader of this bloated, lonely constituency, a professional mental patient, an entitled careerist in the hospitals of the country.

AFTER THE NIGHT OF SLICING, I BELIEVED THAT I POSSESSED HOLY gifts and could lend a hand to lost souls through my blood's magical powers. The Christ complex will forever be popular on psych units around the globe, but when I fell under that spell in 1990–91, there were probably four or five of us on that ward who believed they were the Chosen One. God delusions zipped around the unit like a flu bug.

It may have been common, but I truly felt that, way down deep, below my soul, where things were essential, I was the substantial, secret and *true* David Christ and could do amazing acts. I believed vigorously that my touch, my blood, could make sick folks feel dynamite and reborn. I felt I could fly if only the staff had some faith and would allow me to leap off the stone roof. The only thing I needed to do was more smearing—that was the key. If the staff and Dr. Collander would just let me go out into the world again and baptize the hurting souls in my new favorite color (it was cobalt blue, but it changed to crimson overnight), then miracles would take place. I kept this between me and Dr. Collander—I certainly didn't want to step on the toes of any other messiah on the unit. But I believed, I *knew* what I had inside. "Let me touch these people, and they'll leave the hospital transformed," I told Collander. "I'm certain the more blood I lose, the more gifts the world receives."

"Oh, David," he said. "Just hang on, pal. We'll get you through this."

Those were times of great confusion and fantastical thinking. Truly.

There was a gentle Presbyterian chaplain by the name of Harry who visited the patients once a week or so. He was in his late sixties and had a handlebar white-gray mustache and was a great conversationalist. But his presence and his white collar freaked me out at times. I could not *not* think about smearing my blood onto his seersucker suit when he visited on Wednesday mornings. I didn't want to hurt him, but I did want to insult his God for taking me down so completely, for destroying me.

I went from feeling like the worldwide ambassador of miracles, David Christ, to feeling horrific and pissed off at the old God, the Charlton Heston one. For *crucifying* me, for reducing me from a college grad to a sometimes mumbling and obese heifer in such a short time. Consequently, I couldn't speak with Harry for long periods. I shared brief, English-major like comments with him about, say, Kate Chopin or Hemingway, but then the rage steamed through me and I knew I had to rest. One second I'd be discussing my fury with the first President Bush or the theme of nothingness in *The Sun Also Rises*, and then the next I wanted to baptize the visiting chaplain.

Yet, talking with Harry was one of the highlights of my time there. He was utterly patient and kind, a true gentleman. And in the end, when I think of people who represented God well in this world, I think of him and my mother.

GOD TAKES EVERYTHING IN—THAT WAS THE BIG LESSON I RECALL from my childhood catechism classes. He is more omniscient and powerful than Santa Claus and the Easter Bunny combined.

Growing up I did my best and whispered my proper Catholic prayers nightly to a wilted-looking, expired Jesus on a cross and blessed my family from top to bottom, including my nemesis Andy. I didn't want to make any mistakes, and I kept everybody covered, even Jiggs. I knew God kept score. Plus, I had a strong sense that the crucifix in our kitchen had some type of minicam installed and was soaking up the filth that lay inside me.

I saw God in Jan, a friend who left her convent in Michigan and befriended my family. She's my de facto godmother and has known me since I was four years old. We used to play basketball together—she had a great jump shot. She called me once at the Institute and reminded me how she used to bring old sneakers by our house when I was a young boy. I'd take them into the musty basement while she was upstairs having tea with my mother. I spent the hour ripping and stabbing holes in them with baby scissors; then I showed Jan the tattered remains, dangling from my proud fingers like freshly caught mackerel. "Well done, David," she said. "Next time, I'll bring you more pure, untainted souls."

I didn't get the humor—I was a kid at the time, but I appreciated that I pleased her.

FOR A CONSIDERABLE AMOUNT OF TIME I WAS AFRAID OF THE SKY and didn't go out for months. I was terrified of it. I had developed agoraphobia after the trauma in October. I was certain that an omniscient, punishing force (Charlton Heston's or my brother's?) would grab me or that the sky itself would suck me up like a divine vacuum cleaner. I even refused to venture into the small grass courtyard where the smokers gathered, which was surrounded by ten-foot-high concrete walls outside of Graceland. I literally couldn't move when someone suggested we go outdoors. Once I even fell to the ground when faced with the task. Nature and other world forces were furious with me and would stop at nothing to destroy me.

My doctors differed on how to deal with this development. In one corner was Dr. Collander, my patient and loving therapist, who tried to get me to step out onto the grass one foot farther each day. Dr. Presley took the more aggressive and feisty route.

"Just walk out onto the goddamned grass!" he pleaded. "That's the only way you're going to beat this stuff."

Looking back, I have a lot less patience with my old, shattered self. To people who suffer from the panic and fear, "just step up and beat it" doesn't help solve the underlying mess of feelings. But, in my simplistic hindsight, my crucial quest to recover my wasted youth, "Just do it!" doesn't sound half bad to me.

In the end, I finally went for a walk with Dr. Collander and didn't stop. The progress, though, felt like a crawl—it was that tentative. I just kept on going to the grass initially, then to the big oak out front a week later, and finally to the brick wall surrounding the hospital a few days after that. And I walked farther the next day. No collapsing in tremors or anything—just a slow, cautious, itsy-bitsy crawl. That's how I learned to start living in the world.

THE HOSPITAL TOOK ME OFF CONSTANT SUPERVISION JUST AS SHINE was being discharged. She remained frighteningly thin, but she told me she was ready to give the real world another shot. Shine moved to an apartment close by and attended a day hospital on the grounds, and we promised to keep in touch. We talked on the phone frequently, and Shine sent me more notes, silly, dark, and quirky things. The day she left, she gave me her Andy Warhol poster of Marilyn Monroe.

"I'll always be around, my friend," she said.

I EVENTUALLY ASKED DR. COLLANDER TO LIMIT MY MOTHER'S visits to once every two weeks. I was feeling miserable and had grown uncomfortable and jumpy around her. My brain felt warped, hollow, as if there were a huge crater in my belly. One evening I felt that an open lesion had formed as I struggled to find slumber. Anything soaring by in the air around it—sarcasm, support, derision, love, therapeutic language, *CBS Evening News with Dan Rather*—hit me with a salty force and stung.

At first I had struggled with feelings of wanting to nap beside my mother in her bed—the sweetest, kindest woman on the earth. To be embraced by the one who birthed and suckled me. Perhaps even prayed over me—what could be more right?

"They aren't evil or bad feelings, David," Dr. Collander said. "You're simply wrestling with very basic, primal urges. It will pass as we discuss and repair them."

This led to me wanting to make love with my mother, to have her as my girlfriend—kind of a kill-two-birds-with-one-stone type of thing. "It would be so fun and safe," I said to Collander. "No pressure in performing Herculean sexual moves or anything. Just showing true physical and spiritual adoration for the one I adore." When I was first hospitalized and my roommate Jacob talked about yearning for his mother, I thought, "Jesus—that's pretty sick." But when it was me with similar issues a year later, I gave myself a pass. I wanted to buy her shiny new shoes, a pretty dress.

Then the feelings became filled with rage, out of control one day, and I wanted to rape my mother with a small, silver crucifix and stab my father on his bald spot with the sharpened end of that cross. To eat his purple, jellied brains for dinner, maybe cook them up in a skillet beside one of my severed fingers. The urges sprang on me in a flurry one visit, and I was startled and shocked, and I asked my parents to exit quickly. It was insane—they were the most important people in my life! I didn't want to hurt them—how could I think of murdering them and setting their bodies aflame, floating them off together into Long Island Sound? I was flooded with images of an overloaded funeral pyre teetering along the ocean. UFO? SOS? *No, it's just David's parents on a late-night cruise into oblivion!*

I felt shamed and physically ill, furious with myself, but the pictures oozed into my skull nevertheless. Made themselves known like slow-moving lava. It scared off my eyelids, and I couldn't *not* look. *What is happening to me?* I panicked. To rid myself of the thoughts, I punched my head.

It didn't help.

My friend Tony visited me on weekends, and I asked him to sneak in some red lipstick—Shine and I had watched David Lynch's *Wild at Heart* together, and it had stirred me up and given me ideas. "The only reason I'm giving you this, David, is I know it can't be used as a weapon," Tony said and rolled his eyes as he dropped it into my T-shirt pocket.

The next morning, after my roommate had showered and left the bathroom, I went in and quickly stripped down. I looked at my disappointing body in the mirror, so hairy and obese, and grew enraged. *What happened to you, my boy?* I thought. Then, just like that brief scene from the movie, I took out the maroon lipstick and covered my face entirely. Just drew over my forehead, cheeks, chin, and neck. Then I improvised, growing manic and senseless and drew a huge X across my body—I felt out of control but juiced and so alive. I imagined the liquid spilling over me as I drew, coloring my ears, some of my buttocks. I slashed and drew quickly, circling my nipples, cognizant all the while that the staff would be in to check on me in about thirty minutes for a status report.

Soon I was using the lipstick like slices, crisscrossing my thighs, my belly, drawing a circle around my penis. Coloring the head of it intently. Spelling out an upside-down "ASSHOLE" below my chest. "You are simply vile scum," I said, looking at my body. I started leaping like I did as a kid, something that used to comfort me when I grew nervous. I would go up to our family room and jump up and repeatedly touch the top of the sliding glass door frame, seeing myself as Doctor J, Julius Erving, star hoops player for the Philadelphia 76ers.

I started the same thing then in the bathroom, acting out jump shots and reaching above the door and touching the top of the frame with my fingers, leaving smudges. Over and over. Soon I was perspiring and my body reeked of fear, along with the waxy, herbal whiff of the lipstick. I bounced up and down repeatedly, sticking my tongue out at myself as I had when I mutilated for the first time back in Boston. My calves burned and my heart raced, panicked. There was Johnson's Baby Powder next to the sink, and I took it and poured that on me as well. I grew sweaty and frightened, and the powder got into my mouth, and I jumped up a few more times and then coughed. I even danced a little, spastic and wild, as I had with my friends on Martha's Vineyard. Back then, I was bubbling with life, fun, and joy; a sane, silly innocence that felt easy, natural. My buddies and I were mostly happy—I was a buoyant and hope-filled young man. Four years later, most of them had fallen away from me, and I was a panting, motherfucking freak!

I finally stopped and sat on the toilet, trying to catch my breath. The little drops of red sweat were pouring down my body. The powder on my face and the lipstick made me look like Shakespeare's Falstaff. I closed my eyes and tried to breathe slower.

"You going to start that shower, David?" a staff member called in from my room after a few minutes. I nearly fell off the toilet.

"Just hopping in now," I said, somewhat pleased with the pun. "Just hopping right this second—had to powder my nose first."

"Well, hustle up," he said. "The day gets under way soon."

I took a hot shower and removed any traces of lipstick. I cleaned up the powder around my feet in the bathroom the best I could. Fifteen minutes later, I returned to the relatively normal unit. Later, when I confessed this to Dr. Collander, he said my mind was rattled, shaken up, and I was reenacting some childhood fantasy, some dance from the mind of a three- or four-year-old.

"But the lipstick?" I said.

"You're exploring your sexual identity, the psychic bounds of your gender," he said. "That mind of yours is strained, confused, and all over the place. Plus, you saw the scene in a movie, and those shots make huge impressions on you."

"Yeah," I said.

"You have so much of Hollywood and pop culture entrenched in you," he said. "It's very much part of your essence—cinema, music videos, literature, commercials, television, billboards—those things imprint themselves." He stopped and came over to me and patted my shoulder. "It's going to be okay, my friend, but

you can't do this crap anymore with the lipstick," he said. "That only adds confusion and misery."

"No argument there," I said.

I WAS FRANTIC, WITHOUT ANY BASELINE. I SEIZED EACH SOUND BITE of life's minutiae: slick crime shows, patient chitchat, meteorologists' forecasts, and casual banter on Channel 3 *Eyewitness News.* Everything had free rein—bloodbaths, cannibalism, a jingle from a shampoo commercial, patricide, Swiss Miss hot cocoa, dress-shop mannequins, a nor'easter, scenes from *Casablanca* mixed with *The Exorcist,* plus the Bible and Freud's basic tenets.

I felt stilted around my parents then, afraid that they could read my sinful thoughts and would disown me. And yet, after it occurred multiple times, it seemed not so terrible, not so awful. The feelings, images of killing and raping, of devouring, lasted for a few months off and on, cropping up whenever we discussed my older brother's treatment of me in the early years. Especially how my parents hardly ever intervened to stop Andy from being so cruel. Dr. Collander suggested I should be angry at my folks for abandoning me in a house with a tyrant, but I couldn't seem to do that. I couldn't get in touch with rage—it usually came out against me.

I told Collander that Andy did things behind everyone's back—it was only when the rage got the best of him that he hurt me in front of my family. He was savvy, a smart kid. And so I took the anger I felt at my situation, the rage I couldn't express at anyone, and turned it on me. Just little insults, spitting into the mirror in the mornings, "shadow cutting"—pretending I had a razor and that I was bleeding to death as I fell into sleep in my bed at night. Years later, when I asked my current therapist about those fantasies, he gave me his thoughts.

"Your mind was pushed to its extremes," he said. "Those images probably reconstituted now and then throughout the arc of your illness. You had a horrid case of manic depression, where dream space felt and became reality. You had a constant freak show going on in your mind, filled with the possibility of being everything, anything all at once."

"Why?" I said.

"No one knows for certain," he said. "Pressure, myths, psychosis, despair, an overly taxed mind, a family tree dotted with illness. It was like, if you couldn't screw your mother in reality, you became a twisted version of one with the lipstick, powder, and dancing in the bathroom. You were like a method actor who couldn't escape the role of psychotic patient. Boundaries vanished—they didn't exist. You were a woman, a crazy man, the freaking pope—you were even Christ himself for a while."

He told me that for a considerable amount of time, I didn't have a true self. "You were a wisp of thrown-together personalities," he said. "Your brother mocked it out of you, the roommates did the same, even the drugs. Your illness aggravated it, stirred up the soup. Dr. Collander was right on target, I think."

"How's that?" I said.

"Listen," he said. "You had a type of submerged personality, where the essence of who David was grew lost among the malevolent folks around you. Your goal was to survive, to avoid conflict that you felt might threaten your life. And so you acquiesced or, more pointedly, you didn't feel you had a choice. It was submit to their ways or die."

"I morphed into everything at once," I said, "mother, father, seducer, monster, creator, and destroyer?"

"Partially," he said. "You were a very ill, confused, and lost young man, taking on brutal internal warfare. You possessed a very naïve understanding of developmental issues. Really, a childlike one. You gave up early on a sense of self-assertion—it was blown back inside because of the creeps in your life. Your mind survived the best way it could, the only way."

AFTER TWO MONTHS OF INTENSE SESSIONS WITH DR. COLLANDER, I grew more comfortable with having my folks around again. It was like I partially grew up or used up some of my messy, ugly thoughts in that department. Mostly I just missed them a lot. I had to become comfortable knowing that my head could go dancing in many directions if I allowed it, if I embraced it blindly. That doesn't mean my brain stopped fluttering, but I started to grasp the nuances and extent of my disease. I tried to keep things simple, settled, and if the thoughts went off, they went off. I realized I had an imagination and a mind that, when hooked up with my flair for the dramatic, could go bananas. Ballistic, colorful, bloody scenes constantly played in my mind's eye, and Collander assured me that was okay. But I also didn't have to act out any of them. *Chill, David, chill.*

"You don't think Stephen King would be locked up if he hadn't found a way to channel his thoughts into writing books?" Dr. Collander said. "You don't have to act on them."

I felt at that point like I was building up washed-out roads that had been destroyed in a freak storm, a bad night in my skull. Nothing was lasting, nothing that would damage me or my family for a long period of time. At least, that's what I told myself.

9

The Life of Maddy and Continued Submersion

I MET THE MAJESTIC MADDY SHEEHAN ON THE UNIT A FEW months after I'd been taken off constant supervision. She could have stepped out of an Irish Spring commercial: a fair-skinned redhead with multitudinous freckles, brown-specked hazel eyes, and full breasts. God, what a brilliant girl! As we shook hands, she told me she was home-schooled, felt a strong desire to avoid most men, and sometimes put out cigarettes on her thighs. Then she told me she had herpes. "Not the harmless kind," she added with a smile.

That was her style, always flirting by saying seemingly shameful things. She'd pick a phrase and shock you with it like a high school sophomore. It was mostly fucking annoying, but it was a turn-on, too.

"I'm sorry about the sores on your privates," I said, looking at her, "but it's a pleasure to meet you."

She studied my face for a moment, forgave me, smiled, and said, "Small opaque dildos are my only close friends."

And just like that, I was sold on Maddy. I don't remember her diagnosis, exactly, although I'm sure it fell under the banner of bipolar disorder. But I do know she wouldn't discuss her family except to say, "Oh, who grasps exactly what happens to filial units in the magical land of West Egg."

The Great Gatsby was her thing. She insisted she was related to Jay Gatsby. "I am from the bloodline of that great man," she told me.

She worshipped that fucking book and never hesitated to talk about its characters or F. Scott Fitzgerald. She insisted she was baptized, christened, and deflowered in that fictional town across from Manhattan.

Maddy and I began a series of provocative, humorous, erotic conversations, and the closest we could get to sex was a seven-and-a-half-second blow job that was interrupted by a passing psychiatric nurse with good peripheral vision. I was so delighted to have had some contact and so thrilled that my apparatus still worked properly, that I didn't mind the lecture that followed. We were in the quiet room, and the nurse's voice echoed as I zipped up. "Safety," she said. "Safety needs to be practiced in every area of our lives, both in here and outside in the world." She nodded at me and said, "That includes condoms, David," and led us out into the main hallway.

A week later, we sat at the end of the hall, and Maddy said, "Okay, mister, ask anything sexual and I'll offer you the unvarnished truth."

"Describe your ideal man."

"Six feet, 165 pounds," she said. "He wouldn't have to have a big one, but it's got to be pretty thick. Good staying power, muscular. Plus great ankles."

"Really?" I said. "Why the ankles?"

"They're my soft spot," she said. "I can tell so much from a man's ankle."

I shook my head and said, "Any other kinks I should know about?"

"I like pearl necklaces," she whispered as another patient walked by.

"I thought girls dreaded those," I said.

She grabbed my arm and said, "Maybe they do, but I don't." Then she smiled and said, "Now I've got some for you."

"Shoot."

"Well," she said, "I know you're a breast man."

I nodded.

"My next query isn't sexual—do you still wish to play?" she said. When I smiled, she said, "I want to know why you hurt yourself. Why do you take it out on your body?"

I hesitated for a few moments, frowning. "I think cutters feel emotionally dead to the world, so they want to see the blood, the source of life," I said.

"Come on," she said, nudging me. "Be straight with me."

"Perhaps . . . they or I . . . have trauma in our past or can't cope with anger and so we wound," I continued in a monotone. "Emotional pain is the common thread. But each of our nightmares are specific, each psyche a mishmash of slights, memories, horrors. When you put our styles together, our list is lengthy—some cut, burn, break fingers or bones, poison themselves, punch themselves, hit themselves with hammers, pick at their skin, or pull out their hair." I exhaled and said, "We offer a wide variety of choices in our membership plan."

Maddy was staring at the ground when I finished. After a few moments she took my hand. "What about you, though?" she said. "Come on, give it a shot."

"It's difficult," I said, squirming a little.

"Try," she said. "It'll be good practice and I don't bite—as you've learned."

I smiled slightly and said, "The only thing I know is I really like doing it. I simply like to carve myself and bleed."

She touched a scar on my hand and said, "Is it painful?"

"No," I said, my voice shaking. "It psyches me up, makes me feel alive—so it doesn't hurt much."

"Okay," she said. "Does it arouse you—do you get an erection when you cut?"

"Now you sound like a shrink," I said. "It doesn't work like that for me, though the thick, sticky richness of it feels sensual, silky. But no hard-ons."

"So your whole body goes numb?"

"Most of the body feels numb, except my belly," I said. "The belly rarely lies to me about what I'm feeling."

"That's a quote to save," she said. "Maybe for your stories or something." She looked down the hall and said, "Do you see images when you cut?"

"I don't hallucinate," I said. "Just colorful, racing scenes that repeat so frequently in my head that it's like Showcase Cinemas."

"Yeah?"

"Oh, definitely," I said. "The wounds, the idea of turning my arms into ribbons of flesh—the whole deal. Like fluttering flash cards of gruesomeness. It feels impossible to escape now, even if I wanted to."

"How's that?" she said.

"Maddy," I said, "I don't think I can ever walk away from it—I love it too much."

She looked at me and seemed to ponder that statement for a few seconds. "You will," she said.

"Don't you have scars you could talk about?" I said, and she shrugged.

"I like scars I can see," she said and then quickly added, "It's easier for me that way."

"Huh?" I said.

"I don't mean I'm glad you suffered," she said. "But when we were first introduced, I . . . noticed the marks and thought, 'Okay, he seems to have seen it.'"

"What do you think I've seen?" I said, a little accusingly.

"Maybe you've seen the bottom," she said. "And now, perhaps, there's only one direction to go."

"Yeah," I said. "Maybe."

"What *did* you see?" she said. "I mean, what do you see when you're there?"

I hesitated. "Not sure exactly," I said. "I feel myself banging into it every once in a while. Like when I'm writing or dreaming about going for a run, it's waiting for me there—the raging force. But I never corner it."

"Do you think you will?" she asked.

"I don't know," I said. "It's like I'm about to name it when it transforms into an engorged wild rat with wings mocking me."

"Ka-boom," she said, slapping her thigh. "I think you just named it."

"I want to strangle it, you know," I said, my jaw tight. "Throw it on the ground and stomp the fucking thing until it's crushed!"

"That's good," she said, squeezing my hand. "Only keep that image outside of you—not in. Keep it out, okay? Have you told Dr. Collander about the engorged wild rat with wings?"

"In a way," I said. "But I'm afraid of talking about it too much."

She smiled and said, "I think Collander would love to hear more about it."

I looked at her and said, "You're basically a very sweet person. Did you know that?"

"Are you saying you want to be my friend?" Maddy said suddenly, her face flushed. "I don't have many friends, and I think we make quite the pair of nuts."

"Because I hurt myself, and you like scars?" I said.

"No, you idiot," she laughed, wiping her wet eyes. She kissed my cheek and said, "Because I can't wait to see you defeat this son of a bitch. The shadowy gunk, or whatever it is. And then we'll have fun."

I felt safer, freer with Maddy, more willing to say anything. I think a part of me believed if I revealed my truest thoughts with Dr. Collander, he'd steal the sickness from me, and I'd have to return to the world unprotected. Granted, I was very ill and never consciously had that actual thought, but looking back, it pops up. Yes, I was very open with my doctors, but with other patients it was so much easier to share tales of woe and hardship. They respected and admired my illness from a distance. The way a fellow carpenter might admire the work of another. "Hey, I like your aptitude there," they might say. "You've done quite a job."

But with Collander, I just wasn't sure where we were headed, what the goal was. Or maybe, more specifically, a part of me was *exactly* sure and the idea of moving toward health scared the crap out of me. I wasn't ready to be solved. A part of me, a tiny, nasty cryptic part, wanted to cut myself forever. The act felt mesmerizing and it gave me a stoned feeling. Wiping the blood was amazing, thrilling. It brought me a type of respect—it was a feeling I later shared with a few others, other self-injurers, at other hospitals. Even with the eating disorders or those who've had large amounts of shock, the most gruesome story or the saddest or the most heart-wrenching tale brought a bizarre sense of achievement. It was a status thing, ten times better than any Izod or grunge flannel on the unit. Part of me wanted to scream at Dr. Collander or Dr. Presley or anyone who challenged me with healing: "I finally have something that is mine—so back the fuck off!"

Maddy and I sat quietly for a minute while a new adolescent patient was brought into the unit with her suitcases and stuffed animal. I watched the girl and her parents slowly move down the corridor toward the Hub. "You never talk about you, Sheehan," I said. "You get me blabbering but you don't expand on Maddy."

"I'm a bore," she said. "Who wants to hear molestation or rape day in and day out? People grow bored if you run on too much, no matter how horrible and fascinating you might be."

"That's your excuse for not dealing?" I said. "It's flimsy, my lady."

"People much prefer fiction, David," she said. "Elaborate and perfect stories to disappear into—that's why Fitzgerald's world centers me so much, sweeps me away into a prolonged fantasy.

Gatsby and his buddies aid me, save me, with the romance and melancholy."

"Can you introduce me more formally to everyone—can I meet Gatsby?"

"Of course," she said. "You've got to heal first and then there'll be Tom and Daisy and crew."

"They're still around, Maddy?" I said, watching her face closely.

"Oh," she said, grinning and patting my hand. "They're around, buddy. You just have to know where to find them."

"At the Plaza?" I said.

"Silly man," she laughed. "You have to visit me in West Egg, Old Sport, and I'll show you the works, the whole smorgasbord—we'll have a hell of a time."

Maddy and I arrogantly assumed in the rush of our youth that this mental illness thing would be fleeting, a temporary setback in our still-promising lives. Sure, we'd fuck around with the sickness for a while, but then we'd dust ourselves off and just walk away when we'd had enough. It would be a piece of cake to re-enter society. The psychiatric interns and doctors get revved up and passionate when you're the newest case on the block, but it changes after a while. Suddenly you're not quite as young, and you find the word "chronic" on your résumé after six months or more, and the mental health world starts to forget you. You disappear from the ranks of the fresh and new, the ones people cry over, and you grow confused.

It's an odd, queasy feeling to be stuck in mental health limbo like that—you feel afraid of life, afraid of death, and afraid you'll be forgotten. Plus you've got a debilitating illness that's fucking with your head daily. So who's on your side? Whom do you trust? Who's giving you the real message, the healthy one? But then, you don't completely *want* the healthy one, do you? And you don't want to be *too* fucked up, either. It was enough to make a fellow like me want to take a bunch of meds and go to sleep forever. Passive suicidal ideation, I think they call it.

MADDY LOATHED DR. PRESLEY WITH A PASSION, CALLING HIM "chauvinistic," "misogynistic," "uppity," and a "Napoleonic Mighty Mouse with power." She said his style of therapy was fading into the woodwork. "Old-school Freudians are as lame as bell-bottoms nowadays," she said in the middle of one of his famous unit meetings. She made the excruciating monotony, silliness, insanity, and intensely controlled environment bearable.

During one of our community meetings, Dr. Presley and some other doctors discussed the recent influx of adolescents. They had recently begun allowing them on the unit, and it caused a great deal of havoc at first. Just that past week, a group of fourteen-year-olds had passed out little pieces of glass they'd gotten from an older patient and used them to scrape and cut themselves. Suddenly, cutting was the rage. "How do you feel about the kids following in your footsteps, David?" Dr. Presley said in the meeting.

Maddy snorted. "I think it's highly inappropriate to blame David for an epidemic problem that happens worldwide," she said.

"I'm not blaming," Dr. Presley said. "I'm merely asking David's opinion."

I looked at him, coughed, and said, "I feel horrible about it, of course . . . it's an awful thing and I hope they give it up right now. It doesn't solve, it only destroys you little by little."

At that time, a lanky green- and blue-haired Hispanic fifteen-year-old from Honolulu nicknamed Mojo was on the unit. He dressed in silk shirts unbuttoned to his chest and white alligator shoes. Dr. Presley asked him what he thought, and he popped up on his feet and yelled, "David, David, will be dead, dead, dead, if he doesn't get it out of his head, head, head!"

"Okay, take it easy, Mojo," Dr. Presley said.

Then the boy rushed over in front of me and started crying. "If you don't stop, you're going to end up slicing off your bloody legs and terrible arms and you'll be so freaking wasted! Please stop, okay? Will you stop?" Then he fell onto his knees before me. "I don't want you to be buried, to be smushed in dirt forever. Do you want that, do you want that, huh?" he shouted. His eyes were red and his thin lips looked chapped, strained, as if the words had burst forth after much restraint.

I was stunned and embarrassed, but managed a response. "No, of course not, Mojo," I said, and a technician came and took him to get some medication.

"I think your little meeting got way out of hand," Maddy said. "Mr. George Orwell would have a ball watching you."

"Don't be so disrespectful," a nurse hissed, sitting next to her, which caused Maddy to snort again. (She was a great snorter— she did it with just the right air of disdain.)

Dr. Presley ended the group then. "We are each affected by everyone around us, Maddy," he said. "There are connections, mentors, and bad examples throughout the world, throughout this unit. And there are very intense community meetings. David needs to know how his behavior affects others. He needs to smell the roses more often, to stop and appreciate people who care for him, who give a damn." He nodded at me and then looked around the room with a smile and said, "Why don't you folks have a pizza party tonight on me?"

◆

SOON AFTER THE MEETING, MADDY'S INSURANCE MONEY RAN OUT. She ended up being on the unit with me for only four months. From there she took a drawing course at Wesleyan and wrote me vague, loopy, but entertaining letters. Then she returned to "West Egg" and tried to reconcile with an old therapist. She wrote and told me she had a constant crush on him because "he possesses the sexiest ankles I've ever been around in my life. Equal to only your chubby ones, my lovely!"

When I was out of the Institute, she set up a date for us to meet at a café in New Haven, and for no reason except that I felt petrified, rotten, and unworthy of her, I called and canceled. I believed then that I'd only disappoint her, that I couldn't be strong enough for a relationship. I felt lonely and didn't want her to see any goodness in me. I didn't get it, wouldn't accept her need—or mine. *No one should want to be with me,* I told myself. *It's wrong and unhealthy for everyone involved.* The two of us wrote after that, but it became less frequent over time.

MY FATHER TOLD ME ONE DAY THAT HE ADMIRED DR. PRESLEY'S unorthodox style. "He's got the aggressiveness to shake up your passivity," he said.

"Dad," I said, rolling my eyes.

"It's the only way you're going to shock yourself out of the track you're on," he said. "Dr. Collander is too gentle for the changes you need. You need a doctor who'll get in your face. One who'll be a pain in your ass until you can make changes."

I was upset at him outwardly for saying that, but Presley did

rattle my cage. I'd had the same thoughts myself a few times. I
noticed, grudgingly, that my dad had a frustrating way of being
on the right side of things. What if Presley had worked on me
instead of Collander? Would his wild Freudian style have got me
healing quicker? Was that why I was so afraid of him—would I
have resisted healing even more with Presley as my own therapist?

There was an unconscious part of me that didn't want to get
better, and I wondered if that made me embrace my relationship with Dr. Collander even more. Could Presley have broken
through my walls, saved me decades of hell—straightened me out
quicker? An impossible question, I know, but it clanged around.

Father-and-son stuff is always complex, but for me it felt
multiplied a thousand times over back then. My dad was the
face of success-health-work-reality-male-responsibility, and that
scared me terribly. I also felt so proud of him, loved him dearly,
and studied him closely when he came to visit during the week
with the *Times* or *Newsweek* in one hand, his dress shoes clack-
clacking on the floor outside of the main entrance. He usually
had a Diet Coke in his other hand and he'd bend over and kiss
the top of my head.

My father always looked so handsome, so spiffy, and he
treated everyone with respect and dignity. I used to get mad
at him for that—I thought the friendliness was a façade, just
a cover for a slick salesman's pitch. I later learned that was just
him. I felt far from my father during some visits, so lost, angry,
and without hope, and then the next moment, I'd be hugging
him as he stood to drive home. I wouldn't want him to leave. I
knew I'd given him a permanent hole in his heart from the night
of cutting, from my sickness.

I'd see him coming back down the hallway a few days later

and try to sit up straighter. *I definitely need to get better,* I told myself. The more Dr. Collander and I chatted about moving on, moving home, the more I realized that I wanted my dad and mom to be pleased with me again. I didn't want to commit suicide like my father's baby sister did years ago. I didn't want to be another loss in the mental health column of my family tree's scorecard. No, that wasn't the plan—I was going home, and I'd make my father and mother proud, even if it destroyed a part of me.

DR. COLLANDER AND I DECIDED TO WATCH *ORDINARY PEOPLE* TO-gether in his office on the grounds. We had been discussing it right from the beginning, and so we got a VCR and watched it through two sessions. When it was over, we gave it a good review, thought Timothy Hutton and Judd Hirsch gave excellent performances. What I remember most distinctly were the shots of the bare park bench, blowing autumn leaves, a military statue in a park, a nice house in suburbia. Then the vertical scars on Timothy Hutton's wrists, the overwrought, blanched-out look on his face, and Bucky, his dead brother's name. Then finally, his mother driving away in a cab, and then the father and son embracing in the wintry backyard at the end as Pachelbel's Canon in D played.

ON SEPTEMBER 29, 1992, I WALKED OFF GRACELAND UNIT FOR good. It had been nearly thirty-one months. First, I stayed at the group home on the grounds for a month and a half, and it seemed like I was on the verge of tentative wellness. And for a while I think I was.

Eventually, I moved home with my folks and my twelve-year-old sister, Julie. I drove up to see Dr. Collander four times a week at the hospital, worked out daily, and started a liquid diet. A bright spot was a telephone call I received from the novelist Wally Lamb, a Connecticut native. Months earlier, I had sent him a long letter saying that I adored his book *She's Come Undone* and that I wanted to hold a dinner party and invite his protagonist, Dolores Price, to attend. Joining her at the table would be guests like Holden Caulfield, Franny Glass, Edna Pontellier, Jake Barnes, Rabbit Angstrom—each of my favorite fictional souls. Wally looked me up in the phone book and called to say hello. Then he sent me a card that read, "David, thanks again for your letter—it meant a lot to me to receive it. Hope to meet you in person someday. In the meantime, you might consider doing some serious writing yourself. There's talent and humor and decency in what you wrote—best, Wally."

The book he sent me was inscribed: "For David, in celebration of all we learn from pain and heartfelt thanks for your terrific letter." I wrote a few sentences in my journal after I spoke with him: "Writing, should I take it up again? For some reason it's hard for me to do both the journal and the stories. Maybe if they could somehow be one in the same? If I could mix them together, a collage of sorts, maybe that would work."

Wally's letter started a long pen-pal relationship that has lasted twenty years.

WHEN I RECENTLY ASKED JULIE WHAT I WAS LIKE BACK THEN, SHE said: "Fat/beard/cut marks/eyes glazed/arms bulging with scars/occasional moments of lucidity/moments of devilish glee/mute/darkness."

"Was it that awful, Julie?" I asked.

"It was horrendous," she said. "I didn't want to come back home from school each day, David. I'm sorry, but I thought I'd find you dead in the bathroom. Every day, every night—for a very long time."

I know today that I tainted my sister's life terribly, but back then I was buried too deeply inside myself and torn up about my whole sticky, selfish sickness and the wounds it left on everyone. I told myself that I could never cut myself again in the house or around them. That was the extent of my guarantees on bleeding.

I lost 110 pounds on the diet in eleven months. I also dug through my things at home and found the story I had written on the Vineyard about the fat man from the A&P who falls from the sky and kills himself with shards of glass. It was freaky to hold it in my hands. *How did this all begin—why has it happened?*

Whatever it was, the dream and my reality, I could not stop my lust for cutting, and it roared on inside of me. I tried to battle the urges by doodling and writing nonsensical rants about somber topics in my journals. Death, gore, whatever I could think of. During the winter, I asked my father if I could paint the cellar for him, and, desperate for me to do anything remotely positive, he agreed. For the next month and a half, I spent most of my time in the basement, painting gigantic black question marks, broad red brushstrokes, creepy rust-colored faces, and figures with multiple heads, wiry teeth. It was peculiar, a very bizarre thing. I started gluing morbid poems, photographs, and posters to the walls.

There were three mustard-yellow elementary school desks down in my dungeon, and I placed them in a precise row. I pretended I was teaching a class of mutant mutilators, and we were going to form a groundbreaking trio called the American Blades, kind of an Ice Capades but with blood. We'd travel around the

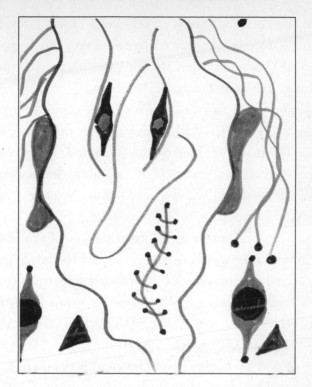

world, skating and spewing crimson for money, bringing dark cheer to men and women who hungered for a taste of the crazed.

Around that time, I became obsessed with the Clint Eastwood movie *In the Line of Fire* and its presidential assassin, Mitch Leary, played by actor John Malkovich. I went to see the movie nine times and even brought a tape recorder into the theater to capture Malkovich's rage-filled voice. (One clip I recall is of him seething, "The president is coming home in a fucking box!")

After one horribly guilt-ridden session with Collander during which I feigned fatigue and left early, I headed into downtown Hartford and reserved a room at a swanky hotel near Bushnell Park. It was on the ninth floor and had a calming view of the late summer dusk and the miniature folks thriving and screwing each other in their insurance-heavy world below. I felt giddy, thrilled. I was ready to unload again on myself—very much manic and dangerous. The buildup and planning for this cutting spree kept me focused like some deranged Zen monk.

I bought three packages of Treet razors and a large plastic drop cloth to cover the bathroom plus two medium-size paintbrushes. I listened to Malkovich's recorded, angry voice and spent hours there cutting my body up, taking breaks every now and then to watch MTV and to eat a ham and cheese sandwich and drink a glass of skim milk.

I used the brushes to paint broad strokes of crimson across the bathroom mirror, where I also created haunting, cavemanlike faces and question marks. There were finger-painting swirls of blood, smeared curses, and messages to no one in particular. A phrase I recall smudging: "I BLEED THEREFORE I AM." And "THIS THING CUTS LIKE A KNIFE!"

At half past midnight, I panicked and phoned Dr. Collander at his home. I told him where I was.

"Jesus," he said. "The Lincoln? Are you bleeding badly?"

"Yeah . . . in the chest, but these cuts aren't as bad as the last time on the fountain."

"Just walk out of the lobby and find your way until you're outside the Hartford Civic Center. I'll call an ambulance and send them there," he said. "Goddammit, you've got to stop this behavior, David, or you'll die. You're out of control!"

I left a note on the television for the chambermaids, *"Don't worry, I'm basically okay, and I really do apologize for this mess. I'm sorry for scaring you."* I think I left a ten-dollar tip.

◆

I COULDN'T STOP SHOOTING FOR THE INTENSITY, THE STONED fugue that rushed through me so quasi-transcendently during the Boston incident and the Big Slice of October 1990. Each time ended with me in an ambulance speeding to the ER, but I knew I didn't fully, completely *want* to die. I simply wanted to punish myself . . . for failing, for losing my way, for disappointing family, God, and world—for not having a clearer path in my head. I was never able to pull the trigger and had never slashed an artery anywhere on my body. I always wanted to destroy David, but not kill him. I felt great twisted shame about that—that I didn't have the balls to kill myself, to get me out of the way and make room for a new boy who smiled more.

MY MIND BECAME FOCUSED ON THE CAPE, THAT GORGEOUS, IN-nocent hook of land, as I was being processed from Hartford Hospital to the Institute that evening. The ambulance took me to a new building, Holland One, a more modern space across from Graceland. As I was being questioned and interviewed by nurses and a doctor at the Institute, my frazzled skull kept having a crystal-clear picture of a ten-year-old David at the Cape.

I was in the backseat of our car alone. I think it was a taupe Lincoln Town Car and my parents were chatting up in front, with my dad at the wheel and my mother laughing beautifully and stress-free in the passenger seat. We were headed to see cousins on the other side of Route 28 in Hyannis, and we passed a restaurant and hotel that was a Georgian colonial. Big, wide columns out front. Traffic was stopped for a few minutes, so I looked to my left and saw people gathering around a woman's body right on the restaurant's front steps. They had valet parking—I remember the glowing sky-blue and maroon sign from the road. A crowd was around her, men kneeling, maybe giving mouth to mouth, and all I could see were her two feet, white dress shoes, and her long, muscular calves sticking out. Her legs draped there in the hot summer evening, unmoving.

My parents looked over and discussed the scene, saying things like "I hope she's going to make it." Eventually the light changed, and an ambulance rushed into the parking lot as we drove away. A simple memory, but I obsessed about that lady throughout the evening. Nothing was as clear as the two legs on the steps. My head raced, *Would she live? Had she been happy on that day? Was she single? Would she die alone, a virgin, or had she recently emerged from a bitter divorce? Would people miss her that much? Would enough folks come to her funeral so she wouldn't be embarrassed or laughed at? Who will pray for her?*

Two hours later, I drove home with my parents, and this time, Laura, Andy, and Dennis were in the car. They had been with the cousins for the day. Andy was flicking his finger against my ear; Dennis was singing in the back while Laura was laughing with my mom and dad. We passed the restaurant, and everything was cleared away: the mess, the crowd, the ambulance. Right then I wanted to tell my family something about how important they were to me, how much I loved them, and how afraid I was that they, too, would die at any moment, any fucking second. I wanted to scream a little, scream at each of them. My parents, Laura, Dennis, and even freaking Andy, who by that time had stopped harassing me and was just staring out the window.

"Don't you feel it?" I wanted to holler. *"Aren't we fucking lucky to be alive, to be awake here at this moment in time? Aren't we?"*

It wasn't unusual for me to be struck with moods like that, moods that were so visceral I wanted to reach out and stop everything—

just cease life for a few seconds and get my filial unit to recognize our luck and happenstance. That our simple existence, our faulty, smelly, dysfunctional, ugly, selfish, and happy lives could quickly get horrible. Without warning—trees could fall on us, lightning could smack us, earthquakes, cancer, twisters, heart attacks. It's like I knew or sensed what was going to happen to me; like I had some deeper gut intelligence of what was coming way down the road for me. We must be thankful and we must not think we've got life figured out. I know that sounds a little much; a little too pious for a ten-year-old, but I think it was a taste, just a faint nuanced tap of God's presence. Of a tiny soul pushing through my skin, making itself known. Of realizing that God keeps the show rolling even when no one's looking, even when you're picking your nose or wetting your bed and playing Little League shortstop for the Guilford Pirates. God isn't always just the punisher, the observer with a camera sewn into Jesus' crucifix at our home, but she's a calming, comforting, steadying force. She's sweet and singular and she was there beside me on that evening.

THE FIRST TIME I MET A GROUP OF PEOPLE WHO BATTERED THEM-selves like I did was at Christmas 1993, at a clinic in Chicago. Chart Hospital was the name. At the time, it was the country's only program designed for self-mutilators. It was called Self Abuse Finally Ends (SAFE). I flew there with my father when I was drowning in drama and the doctors of Connecticut had had their fill of me. I was the token male in the cutting group that was made up of emotionally bruised, frantic women. They were mostly gorgeous and damaged, and they were quite lost, so I felt right at home.

The program was run by a charismatic counselor who was a former self-injurer herself, and a hip and pretty psychiatrist. Their intensity of message inspired me during the month I was there and I felt ready to take on the world. I didn't have to be silent with my anguish; I could articulate, draw, journal, cry, and scream it out without going back to the crutch of self-injury. I left the hospital thinking, *I'm done with cutting forever, there is nothing standing in my way. I'm a likable person without the blood— there's more to me than depression or razors. I can live full-on now—I'm still young!* It's what I told my father on the plane when I flew home with him. I was ready to turn everything around.

I faltered when I returned to Guilford, though. I kept working out and was seeing Dr. Collander, and our progress felt so slow and too gradual, like I was stuck in molasses. I couldn't get much traction, and I constantly felt the cutting magnet pulling me backward, sucking me in. A few weeks after I returned from Chicago, a friend of Maddy's called and told me that Maddy's car had crashed and she was dead. I believe it was late winter, and there was no snow in New York State at the time.

"Police are calling it a suspicious death because she apparently peeled off the road and hit a tree," the girl said. There was no funeral, no memorial service, no planted tree on a beach, no engraved stone somewhere. No "Amazing Grace."

That's how Maddy exited my life.

The news blindsided me. The girlfriend had only said, "She used to talk about you a lot and felt very close to you." Dealing with this by hurting myself felt easier and more familiar than working through the mourning and guilt. I already knew the standard lines a professional would use with me: "Exercise, write it out in your journal, share it with your doctor, don't swallow it. Don't give in." And I did do some of those things, but I was also seized by the compulsion to hurt. It was overpowering, seductive. I told myself, *They don't understand how badly I want to cut off my fingers. Only I grasp the truth. Maddy would grasp it but she's gone now, she gave up because I let her down. A friend was looking for help, for a connection with me, and I turned my back and now she's dead.*

I found myself soon slipping deeper into thoughts of severing digits. I'd lost my way again so rapidly. One morning I purchased a paper slicer at an office supply store; the damn thing cost me seventy dollars. I was prepared to slice off the first four fingers of my left hand. I knew it was time for the fingers to be dismissed. People had to make sacrifices, I felt, and I was due for one big sacrifice. I felt the fingers needed to go. I told Dr. Collander, and he hospitalized me for the weekend at the Institute and took away the paper slicer. Most of the positive energy I had taken in at Chart Hospital had vanished.

When I got out of the hospital, I wanted only to *not* be me. I drove down to Stony Creek, a small, beautiful harbor in Branford, four miles from my folks' house. I went there at night, parked my car by the water, and then walked up the streets to a railroad trestle. I felt myself planning future cutting, obsessing about it. This eased my anxiety and kept me focused.

Do your goddamned hands tonight, David! I told myself. *Cut them clear off with a train and then run to the nearby house and they'll help. It'll be a close call but it'll be ballsy—they'll stop the bleeding with a tourniquet and then the fingers will be adios. Do it for Jiggs, you little shit. Enough of the minor crap—blow them away with no more hands!*

Not long after this, in the spring of 1994, I stopped at a rest area in North Haven off I-91. I urinated, washed my hands, and cut off part of my left index finger with a Ginsu knife. I had to do it—I had to. I then drove twenty minutes to an ER with my bleeding hand resting in the pocket of the stained T-shirt. (Surgeons at the hospital would later reattach my finger.) I was listening to "One" by U2 as I pulled into the emergency area, and I thought it might be a good funeral song for me. I walked into the reception area and said, "Hello, I was wondering if you could help a man who almost lost his finger?"

"Where is he?" the nurse said.

"Oh," I said, "it's me."

"And where did this happen?" she said, growing concerned as she saw the blood.

"In a rest area about twenty minutes ago—I tried to cut it off." She looked beyond me and made a motion and soon I was lying on a mattress.

Later, in the ER, I asked to see the chaplain, a Father Timothy Shea. He knew me from previous visits, and he prayed with me and asked me to tell him about the significance of the act. He was a short, stocky priest with malodorous breath, and he patted my arm periodically as I spoke.

"I think of it as a talisman—a reminder," I said.

"Of what?" he asked.

I told him that I wanted to die, that I was tired of struggling, and that I almost slit my throat in the rest area before taking it out on the finger. I told him about the train tracks, and that I needed to do something that would remind me how my family would feel if I ended my life. To keep me safe.

He shook his head and said, "My God, young man, what have you done that's so horrible?"

"I've done nothing," I said, and he raised his very bushy left eyebrow.

"I don't quite get it," he said.

"I'll be thirty soon," I said, my voice rising. "And I haven't done a fucking thing in my life."

"Listen," he suggested with a smile, "I'm fifty-six and I haven't accomplished much."

"No!" I shouted, suddenly greatly fed up with this stupid man. "You don't get it—*I've done absolutely nothing!*"

Then I cursed under my breath and struggled until a pretty nurse gave me something calming that made me fall very quickly, far and deep. I tried to tell the priest it wasn't his fault—certainly, it wasn't his fault, certainly, I didn't mean to insult his God or mine or his starched white collar or his breath, but my eyes rapidly fell and I was gone.

THAT NIGHT I HAD AN INTENSE, FRENZIED DREAM THAT SEEMED to whip past me so quickly it jarred my psyche permanently. It was set in an institution that charged $75 million a day. (The price was spelled out in hot-pink neon at the hospital's entrance. Some places had pools and pastoral grounds—these guys had rides, neon, and money.) Everything else was gold and brilliantly shiny except the patients. There were tons of bloated and familiar drooling people and a bevy of bored teenagers who were lost and fragmented. They had shaved, tattooed heads and cigarette-burned faces and foreheads, cuts over their arms, wrists, and bellies. There were extravagantly huge Disney-like scenes and rides—one was equipped with a massive sea with crimson waves, and patients were wading knee-deep into it and scooping the water and *whoosh,* suddenly it was gone.

The patients had hyperdeveloped bodies (huge buttocks, massive breasts, and donkey penises) and vacuous minds. There

was a giant ski slope with translucent snow and they went flying down the mountain wildly. Incredibly, no one ever fell. John Lennon's son, Sean, was there dancing on the slope, and so was Maddy. While this terrible, driving industrial music thumped, she was jumping around and stripping off her clothes and holding her buttocks, which had an awful red rash.

There were so many patients screwing and crying—lots of frighteningly manipulative and histrionic young women pulling out their hair. This one ride had a "Crazy Meter"—you'd sprint at a camera ten yards away, and it immediately assessed your name, your diagnosis, recommended dose of medication, and your risk of self-harm or AWOL risk. I remember thinking, *How the fuck do you get out of a place like this?* Everyone injected with frenzy, drunk on mania, madness, and cackling laughter. They were crying, giggling, dancing, fucking, screaming, grasping with that incessant thumping music.

I woke stunned, shocked from the dream, and after the surgery to reattach the nerves of my finger, an ambulance was called to transfer me back to the Holland Building at the Institute. A few days later I was supposed to go visit a halfway house right down the street on Maple Avenue, but I felt sweaty and scared, and my breathing was shallow. I paced nervously around the unit rubbing my eyes; I couldn't leave them alone. That dream had made me extra cognizant of eyeballs, sockets, all parts of vision. I suddenly felt as if I couldn't catch my breath—every thought felt as if it was flying at me way too fast. I pulled some tacks off the bulletin board in the art room and found a quiet corner where I scraped myself some crow's-feet on the outside of my eyes and then rubbed the blood into my cheeks like it was Oil of Olay moisturizer. I was still only twenty-nine years old, so I didn't have many wrinkles around my eyes, but I thought bloody red wrinkles would look hip, like a tattoo or something.

From there I started to fantasize about ripping my eyes out and chucking them across the carpet. Stomping on them. I was enraged at my eyes—I suddenly had no use for them. First it was the fingers, then the hands, sometimes the ears, and now the goddamned eyes. I stuck my index and middle finger into my left socket and tried to gouge it out, to dig out the whole damn thing. After two or three minutes, the only thing I had was a terrible headache. Eventually, I gave up, and a nurse found me and cleaned my minor scrapes. When I later met with Dr. Collander, he said, "Why are you so afraid of the world that you'd blind yourself to never view it again?"

"I don't know—"

"What do you think is going to happen to you out there?" he said quietly, patting my shoulder. "There's no one waiting to suck you up into the sky, David. That's just not going to happen—you know that now, right?"

"I don't know what I know anymore, Dr. Collander," I said, and he nodded. "I know I don't trust my mind much. I know that."

A few days later we started talking about a hospital in Kansas and I thought, *Sure, what the hell?* I was tired of the psychiatric scene in Hartford and scared of the real world. Maybe Kansas would be different for me, more hopeful. *Sure,* I thought, *why the hell not Kansas?*

10

FLIRTING WITH HOPE
IN KANSAS

AFTER THE INCIDENT WITH MY FINGER AND THEN WITH MY
eyes, my doctors, my parents, and I agreed I should go to
the Menninger Clinic in Topeka. Everyone felt a growing sense
of hopelessness—or at least that's how it seemed to me. I know
I felt heaviness in my chest, a growling, gradual panic emerging
whenever I looked inward. So I didn't do too much of that. I was
just dazed, fat, and nearing my thirtieth birthday. Dr. Collander
said this clinic was known for turning folks around and was considered by some to be the best in the country.

I learned through my father that I'd spent $415,000 of my

million-dollar insurance policy at the Institute and in Chicago. This insurance was something he picked up right after I graduated from Skidmore, just in case anything went wrong. Like an afterthought. "We never could have afforded any of this, David," he told me years later. "There wouldn't have been any private places, any facilities. Just state hospitals."

Talk of money confused and confounded me—the real world was observing from a distance with its calculators and taxes. My mental health meandering could only go on for so long—the real world hovered with its clanging coins. My time was limited, and if I didn't get better, I'd either have to kill myself or go to a state hospital—and no one wanted to go there. Except for the six months after the Big Cut, I always just signed myself into hospitals. I knew I needed help. I was also ambivalent about getting better, didn't know how to do it or even if I wanted to. But as I told Maddy—I wasn't ready to give it up.

My cutting was nearly always nonsuicidal; most self-injury is. According to the Cleveland Clinic's website, "Even though there is the possibility that a self-inflicted injury might result in life-threatening damage, SI is not considered to be suicidal behavior." That said, a substantial portion of suicide victims have had a history of SI earlier in their lives. Although the majority of cutters are female adolescents, it's reported that the gender split is growing closer to even. Still, in my own hospitalization for cutting, I was almost always the sole male on the unit. The Cleveland Clinic website goes on to say that "the behavior occurs more often in those who have a history of physical, emotional, or sexual abuse; people who have coexisting problems of substance abuse, obsessive-compulsive disorder, or eating disorders. Also, it occurs in individuals who lack skills to express their emotions and lack a good social-support network." Though adolescents and young adults make up the majority of the cases, SI has been found in the very young and senior citizens as well.

I WAS DETERMINED TO GIVE THIS NEW FANCY MENNINGER'S PLACE a shot. If you climbed up the large hill a mile beyond the city of Topeka, you could see the wooded grounds of the clinic. There were 515 acres of cottonwood, oak, hickory, and green ash and forty white-brick two-story buildings. There was a huge, open expanse of green lawn, hiking trails throughout the property, and a partially damaged clock tower that had been ripped into by a tornado some years ago. The tower sagged a bit to the left, as if it were sinking slowly from each of the depleted folks who had walked beneath it over the years.

"It's crucial that you remember these shades and colors," my mother said when we first arrived, taking my hand and leading me past the flowers lining the sidewalks. There were a few asymmetrical sunflowers tipping awkwardly above the violet tulips, daisies, and roses. "When you're in there"—she nodded toward the hospital—"don't forget that these are out here waiting for you." There was a huge, maybe twenty-foot abstract sculpture on the grounds called *The Vital Balance*. My parents and I stroked it as we walked through a brief tour.

"Do you think I'll ever get better, Mom?" I asked her. My dad was moving slower, behind us, with his hands clasped behind his back—just like Granpa Fitz used to walk.

"Oh," she said, speaking slowly, carefully, "you're getting

stronger each hour—start with the days at the beginning. Be thankful for simple breaths; even when you feel awful. Go with that and try to be nice to yourself, okay?"

"Sure," I said. "I'll try."

"I have faith in you, David," she said. "Remember that God hovers around those who ache."

I wanted to confess all the awful thoughts I'd had at the Institute and tell her that no one in the world had stood by me more than she had. I wanted her to know how incredibly thankful I was for that, but it slouched away. The thought, I mean; it slipped and slouched away.

My initial days at the hospital were frustrating. I banged heads with a few nurses on the first unit, something that had rarely occurred in other hospitalizations. And so I worried that I'd never get a fair shot—that the staff already had it in for me. This little taste of paranoia didn't bode well for the whole stay. I also kept harassing Dr. Collander on the phone back in Hartford, calling his office and complaining about the treatment in Kansas. How I missed him terribly, how I'd made a massive mistake by leaving his care.

A few weeks later, I was discharged from that environment to a halfway house on the grounds. I felt that expanding fierce panic push into my chest again. This had happened whenever too much time had gotten between me and cutting. The anxiety built and then exploded, and I could feel what was coming. The idea of bleeding dominated my skull, and I started planning for the next event. It felt to me like a sworn duty, my solemn task to perform, and nothing could prevent it. When I didn't have that focus, I felt lost and overly anxious.

In those days, I was always in one of three places: dreaming and planning self-harm; recuperating from an incident and feeling sated for a short period; or anxious and stirred up, feeling lost and without a center. This triptych of despair was extremely difficult to penetrate. My head had almost no room for a therapist to venture into and guide me out of the muck.

I fell into a lockdown zone emotionally that night in Kansas and headed downtown to Hyper Walmart in Topeka (the largest store I'd ever seen in my life). I bought razors and returned to the grounds beside *The Vital Balance* statue and cut my left wrists and forearm. I stood there in the darkness and left my mark with a smear across the statue's base. I was furious with myself and thought, *More perfectly clichéd mentally ill images for David and his fantasies and ridiculous home movies. More stupid, sad, suckered, silly statues!*

I realized then that I could no longer get the enormous endorphin release I'd gotten from cutting in the past. I cursed myself, and an echo of Dr. Presley's voice rang out in my head. "Be wary. Don't let yourself turn into another *professional*, David."

Before long I waved down a security guard, and he called an ambulance and I was given several stitches at a local ER. I was delivered to the Hope Unit the next morning. "It's time for you to do some real work on yourself," a nurse manager said to me when I arrived. "We don't want coercion, we want proactive cooperation."

ON MY FIRST DAY AT THE HOPE UNIT, A YOUNG WOMAN WITH A nearly perfectly oval face and bubble lips appointed herself my personal liaison. Her name was Page and we became friends quickly. She was five feet tall and a little chubby with short, curly auburn hair; she was from New Mexico. Her fair complexion was marked by stray pockets of acne. Her eyes were striking, a funky mix of brown with some blackish-gray specks.

A week later, on Independence Day, Page and I strolled onto the cool grass after dark with others from the unit and watched fireworks exploding high above Topeka. Aides rolled out black rubber mats from the gymnasium, and the rather tragic young women and I stretched out on our backs and took in the show.

I closed my eyes and thought about the Independence Days I'd experienced—most were amazing. Summers at the Cape watching the colors over Hyannis with Molly or that one time in Missouri when we shot bottle rockets at rival preteens across a silver pond at twilight. Bounding down gargantuan sand dunes with my cousins in Provincetown as a seven-year-old boy or going for ice cream at Mad Martha's with Emily in Oak Bluffs while explosions danced around us. *I am relatively lucky,* I told myself, looking at the other patients.

A few hours earlier, I had watched the nine- and ten-year-olds from the day school next door as they chased loads of quick, darting rabbits around the grounds, kicking up a minor dust storm in the steamy dusk of fading peach with streaks of silver. Sometimes I'd get wonderful moments like that. Little emotional snapshots or spurts of pulsing life, where the images or colors or frenetic ribbons of fireworks would show me that I wasn't so blunted and alone. I remember thinking, *This is very minute but it's important. Dr. Collander would say it's crucial. Don't forget it. Go back to the journal and write it down.*

That's what I did every night. I made a list of good things in my journal. The fireworks and their crooked, dizzy fingers of red, white, and blue blurring in my eyes; the fleeing bunnies with their ruffled miniature tan coats; fireflies glowing and then disappearing beyond the outstretched fingers of the kids; and a stray fawn I spotted down by the hiking trails. And even Page—I'd probably include her, too.

I thought I might tell her the next morning that she'd made my list of goodness, but I wasn't sure what she'd think.

PAGE AND A FEW OTHERS HAD TOLD ME WHISPERS ABOUT PAMELA, a thirty-two-year-old blind woman with long blond hair who had been in a cult as a child and was reportedly forced to eat pieces of a baby during a ritual sacrifice. She was the oldest woman on the unit, and her memories of the sacrifice were so disturbing that as a teen she ripped out her eyes and swallowed them. The unit also had a handful of other women who had been in cults, and who spoke vaguely of brainwashing, and the feelings of losing their selves and how difficult reentering reality was.

One day I sat on the porch with Pamela, and it was not unlike a blind date of two folks who'd dwelt in their own darknesses and were now about to swap war stories. Several of the women had said to me, "You should really listen to her story—it's truly something." I thought, *Did she really pull her eyes out—did she have the balls to do what I couldn't?* The other women had talked about her story in the same way viewing a rare rhinoceros might be interesting to a fan of nearly extinct wildlife. I felt guilty about my voyeurism and the last thing that ran through my mind before she sat with me was *David, you little slime.*

Even before she started talking to me, I wanted to walk away—to say, "Pamela, I don't want to put you through anything taxing just so I can hear an unusually weird tale."

Her blond hair was tied back in a ponytail that afternoon, which gave her an efficient, professorial air. She wore wraparound black sunglasses and spoke very quietly, in a subdued tone.

"Do you believe in God? A serene power floating above us?" she asked me.

"I think I'm beginning to, I'm really trying," I said. "Things seem overwhelmingly sad if you don't."

"Yes," she said. "I agree. And why do you mutilate yourself, David?"

"I don't know," I said. "Maybe because I'm numb or feel dead?"

"Are you asking me or telling me this?" she said quickly.

"I like to feel the razor slice through me, to turn myself inside out," I said. She made a small sound of approval and took a drag on her cigarette.

"I think you and I are similar," she said.

I exhaled. "Huh," I said, watching her brush her hair. She looked pretty fit, maybe 145 pounds. I'd heard she liked to work out on the exercise bicycle at the gym across the grounds. As I sat with her, I thought, *I could stick out my tongue at her, give her the finger, and she'd never know.* I was sure she could read my thoughts when she said, "You've noticed I'm without sight? Do you know why?"

I felt nervous, so I shook my head and said, "I don't know for certain."

"I was in a cult for years," she said.

The Moonies were the only cult I'd heard of. Every year the news would report a mass wedding for several thousand brides and grooms in India or Toronto. When a bunch of them approached me on an eighth-grade field trip to Washington, D.C., I noticed that their women didn't seem to be wearing bras. Their gaze felt far away, beyond me. "What was it like?" I asked.

"Heinous," she said. "It's filled with people who seem to care, who say they believe in the essential you. But it's controlled by spiritual sociopaths. People get seduced by evil and do terrible things." She tilted her head up and said, "You must know that?"

"Yes," I said.

"One day," she said, itching the very tip of her nose, "they brought the young children into a room and sacrificed an infant before us. They took a baby's life because they felt like it."

I watched her face contort then, tears rolling down her checks. "Jesus!" I whispered. *I believe this lady. I believe this stuff,* I thought.

She sniffled and said, "Oh, no, David. That wasn't Jesus!"

"Okay," I said, sweating suddenly.

She made a fist and punched her thigh multiple times and said, "I'm not done, David. The story isn't complete."

"Okay," I said. "Of course."

Max, who was staff on the unit, saw her strike herself and opened the porch door and said, "Pamela, no punching yourself or you can't smoke."

"Fine!" she barked. "Just fine. Let me finish telling David about my life."

"Everything okay, David?" Max asked.

"He's fine. He's a grown man!" Pamela said, sternly.

"I'm okay," I said. "Thanks." She waited to hear the door shut before continuing.

"They killed the baby before our eyes and made the children consume pieces," she said. "Cooked it."

"Okay," I said again, watching her closely as my head filled with images of an infant on a spit, turning slowly over a fire. *Can this really be true?* I thought, my hands growing damp. *Do people*

get away with this shit? Wouldn't it have been covered by the na-
tional news? Is she exaggerating? What does a baby taste like?

"I'm not done, dammit," she said. "I grew up and moved on
with my life, left the group and tried to live decently. Tried to
move beyond it."

"Of course," I said.

"But in my teens," she said, "I started seeing the scene at night.
Crazy memories flooded me." She reached up to touch her dark,
wide wraparound glasses, which covered any possible views of her
eyes. It was as if she were checking to see if the glasses were still
there. "But my memories weren't nightmares; I don't think they
were any kind of dream. It was real and terrible and one night, I
couldn't take it, so I reached in and ripped my eyes right out."

This was so disturbing and strange that I lost focus at that
moment and can't say with 100 percent certainty how the rest of
it went. I did, however, become scared for myself, for the woman,
for all of us on the unit. And so horribly sad. My mind raced with
images of the woman eating a tiny finger, biting into a roasted
thigh. A part of me is pretty sure she then stated, "I swallowed
my eyeballs, sucked them down my throat, so I wouldn't have to
remember what I saw. I had to stop my eyes from delivering the
terror to me." By this time, she was coughing and crying and I
quickly grew fascinated with two roses that rested in a skinny
vase next to the ashtray. The vase was cinnamon colored, and on
the base of it, someone had written, "This is for Hope."

I don't recall anything else she said. Instead, I became focused
on the fragrant flowers. Short-stemmed and lightly touched with
a pink blush—just the two of them with the thorns removed.
They seemed to expand and bloom before my eyes, stretching,
reaching out. It felt very important to me at that moment to
stroke the rose petals, to make contact.

I realized I should have grasped Pamela's hand, patted it, and said something like "Jesus, I'm so sorry," or "You've been through a great ordeal." I know that now. And I did *feel* that, did want to do that, but instead I ran my fingers along the satiny tips of the flowers.

Somewhere in there, as she wept and sniffled, I bummed a cigarette from her. I'm not a smoker—never was really. But she gave me a single Marlboro Light, trusting me, as she went to speak with a nurse. My hands shook and my breath felt tight and I quickly lit the cigarette and crushed it into my left forearm. It was a new sensation; it sizzled and burned. Then I threw it in the ashtray, watched the blister form, and exhaled slowly.

"I'm very sorry," I said out loud to the empty screened-in porch and returned my attention to the flowers.

Looking back, I'm ashamed of my selfishness and my voyeuristic curiosity, how I took her terrible hurt and didn't acknowledge it, didn't respect it. I apologized later that day, but she never spoke to me again in any significant way. I can't blame her—I had behaved in a despicable manner.

One of my buddies at Menninger was a twenty-year-old named Lillian, who had more scars on her arms than anyone I'd ever met. (I felt both relieved and hurt to meet someone who enjoyed cutting and bleeding more than me.) She had dramatic tales to go with each scar and constantly scratched herself until she bled and inserted little staples and tacks underneath wounds. "It's not that I want to die especially," she explained one day. "It's that I have huge gaps inside my body—no heart, guts—just holes that need filling. So I fill 'em with staples, tacks, pins, and razors." She said she also swallowed Triple A batteries once so that the acid would "burn her soul."

Another time she snuck a lighter into her room and sat in the shower with her favorite sweater on, this oversize cream-and-purple Benetton thing that I loved. She lit herself up and screamed when the sweater caught and the alarm sounded and the staff went rushing in to assist her. She wept as they doused her in water and towels. For a few hours, I and the other fifteen women on the unit were taken to another ward. Sometime later, we came back, and then Lillian returned to the aired-out Hope Unit with restraints on her arms and bandages on her shoulders. She wasn't badly wounded and later confessed, "I had done the burning business before—same as cutting. But to go up in flames, to perish that way, to swallow up my emptiness in streaks of yellow, violet, and blue, that kinda appealed to me. It made me ache terribly."

She was a sweet, sick, and intense girl, and we mused about one day getting an apartment in Santa Fe with Page and a few others on the unit. We had big plans, grand schemes for re-entering the world. We'd leave behind the silliness of the Clinic and explode into the stratosphere with our talents that would amaze, shock, and cause wonderment and adoration. When I first saw Lillian's wounds, a part of me thought, *Huh, new talent coming up behind you now. She's got the intensity you used to have, David. You're slipping, you're fucking slipping.*

MY MOTHER AND MY OLDER SISTER, LAURA, FLEW OUT TO KANSAS for my thirtieth birthday a month after the incident with Pamela. I had a day pass and could leave campus and, at first, we walked through the small museum on the grounds. There was a three-room gallery displaying how the mentally ill had been treated before empathic hospitals like Menninger arrived. There were etchings of haunted, empty-eyed faces staring back from behind bars and long letters from the forgotten as well as an assortment of cages and pens that were used to hold people, to bind, tie, or shock them.

The museum was small and tight and suddenly felt like a wet quilt draped over my head so that I rushed outside into the crisp air.

Beyond the main building was a huge, open stretch of grass that led to *The Vital Balance*, the statue I'd smeared with my blood some months before. It was named after one of Karl Menninger's famous books. His father had founded the clinic with the help of his brother. It was an immense sculpture, part sphere, part column, made from two tons of black metal. When I pushed, leaned, and tugged on it, my sister said, "Be careful, it's quite *vital* that you not tip that metaphor over."

I don't know why I found that so amusing—just silly, stupid wordplay. But it made me grin and feel light. *Forget about what happened in the past*, I told myself. And so I ran over to my sister and mom and said, "It's *vital* that we get the hell out of this institution!" So, the three of us, smiling, hustled to the car and repeated that phrase all day. ("Doctor, it's *vital* that we get this troubled man a hot dog before sunset!" and, "Nurse, it's *vital* that I not hear another reference to Toto for the rest of my stay in Kansas!") We were stressed and anxious, but that word gave us a purpose, a mission. A *vital* path to some temporary relief. It truly helped us escape my sickness for a while.

We drove to an inn a few miles away that was run by the clinic. Lorraine, an ex-patient wearing a sparkling black-and-red scarf and a large name tag, checked us in.

"You're a patient on the Hope Unit," she said. "I've seen you at the cafeteria. How's it going there?"

"They treat me kindly," I said and then added, "Not too much blood loss so far."

My mother and sister turned and looked at me. "We don't need that kind of comment," my sister said with a grimace.

"It's *vital* that I keep the bloody self-mutilation jokes to myself," I said. They both shook their heads and started walking up the stairs.

"Helen Keller stayed here decades ago during a visit," Lorraine added as a general comment, and then, directly to my mom and Laura, "The two of you will be staying in Heaven."

"What?" my mother said, annoyed.

"Your room." Lorraine smiled, pointing to the top of the stairs. "It's called 'Heaven.'"

LATER, WE FOUND WHAT I THINK WAS A CATHOLIC AUTUMN FAIR outside of Topeka that was raising money for a neighborhood girl named Lulu who had leukemia and extensive hospital bills. A poster of the girl was hanging over the fence. Her auburn hair was covered with a tiny ebony hat. Her eyes were odd—two mismatching hues of blue. One was an icy color and the other, an inky, darker blue. It gave her a slightly off-kilter look, like a dazed puppy. People were selling paintings, crafts and homemade dolls, jewelry, tie-dyed shirts, and corn dogs. They had a stagecoach with a miniature pony, and for five bucks they dressed you in a top hat, a black leather vest, and a curly gray beard and took photographs.

"Give it a shot, David," Laura said. "Throw the hat on for Lulu."

"I don't think I will," I said. "I doubt her real name is Lulu."

"Come on—give it a chance," she repeated. "It's *vital* that you help out Lulu."

"Jump up, fella," the man collecting money said. "It's for a good cause and it is her damn name!"

"Yes, sir," I said, paying the man and then trying to climb aboard. The leather vest wasn't big enough for me, and the top hat was stained with sweat. The fake beard drooped to my navel. I squeezed myself into position behind the pony and smiled for the camera.

"You can give me more teeth than that, son," the man said before mercifully snapping the photo.

At the end of the craft booths and food court, there was a Ferris wheel with Bible quotes printed on the outside of some of the cars. (One read, "Proverbs 17:22—A merry heart does good like medicine; but a broken spirit dries the bones."). Next was the other big draw, a smaller multicolored carousel. There were also compact bumper cars for young kids. I sat and watched my mother and sister entering the line for the Ferris wheel.

Beyond the rides and crafts was a road that led to an open field of flowers. A large rainbow sign stood in front of it, reading, "Free Sunflower Maze—Offer Up a Prayer and Walk Through!" I walked up the road into this brilliant, pulsing garden of yellow. I felt very alive and light just then. My body had felt heavy and depressed over the past four months, but on that day with my mother and sister, I felt almost normal.

The golden flowers were gawky and awkward, lined up like undisciplined soldiers. Some stalks were as high as seven feet and they leaned toward me as if they wanted to share a secret. Their centers were brown, yellow, and a few were maroon. They looked as if they were pondering the folks who marched past, ob-

serving them, bobbing back and forth in the breeze. I reached up
to the petals, stroking them. One child in back of me was crying
because a honeybee had stung him as he reached out. I heard his
mother's voice, soothing, coaxing, bringing him back to the fair
to find some ice. The sun was strong, and I was a little winded
but continued on.

The scene reminded me of being an eleven-year-old boy on
the Cape, riding on the back of a bike with my buddy, William.
We flew past drooping willows that stretched into the trail in
the summer, and we pretended their branches and leaves were
the hands and mouths of sexually ravenous teenage girls. They
wanted to take our photograph and touch our bodies. They
wanted to live our lives, to see through our eyes. We were rock
stars. For one summer, some overgrown willows, Hershey's
kisses, a ripe libido-packed imagination, and root beer was all it
took to entertain us. "Thank you, girls," William said each time
in a deep voice as he reached out. "But we must hustle to our
next concert at the Boston Garden."

"We truly appreciate your support, though," I assured them,
slapping the hands of the leaves as we zipped past. "May God
bless and keep every last one of you."

I turned in the maze and looked around. I stood there surrounded by nothing but the nuzzling flowers. They teetered and
drooped in the autumn light. I heard the buzz of the festival
voices, children laughing, mothers calling, and the tinny music
coming from the carousel. I was alone and it felt good. It was
okay.

I had been taking a movement class at the hospital, and the
leader, Georgette, had been coaxing us to *let go* and imagine a
healthy self taking over our bodies. She insisted that we embrace the idea. "Shake your body like no one is watching you,"

Georgette said every Tuesday morning. She played pop songs and said things like "Boogie down to ante up your self-esteem!"

I had thought it was all ridiculous, but suddenly I reached out my hands and let my head fall back. I spun around with my eyes wide open, slowly at first. I was obese, but still I twirled and moved without too much difficulty. It felt positive, natural. I spun more rapidly, feeling the colors overwhelm me—yellows and maroons and the crystalline blue sky with the dashes of white cirrus clouds. Then I spun even quicker, dancing a little. I twirled and twisted, feeling light-headed, alive. I kept my hands out for balance.

I thought of William and the two of us laughing on our bikes, racing, moving beneath the trees. I thought of diving into the Atlantic, swimming out and scraping the rough bottom with my chest. I twirled and shook and felt myself grow dizzy and stumbled, but I continued on. I saw images of my high school and college peers disappearing from my life, of slicing myself; burning myself with the cigarette after talking with Pamela. I thought of college girlfriends who were happily married, and how I used to lick their bellies. I thought about my illness and shame, about my recalcitrant recovery and moving back home to Connecticut. Would they ever let me come home again? Overwhelmed, I wept a little and stumbled, falling hard into the dirt. I sat and cried for a minute, trying to catch my breath. I turned my head when I heard a child's voice.

"Why is the guy crying?" a small blond boy said.

"I guess he doesn't like the flowers," a woman said, quickly pivoting and taking the boy's hand. "Let's go back, Trevor. Give this gentleman some space."

I struggled to stand, straightening my hair, and said, "No, ma'am. Wait! You have to understand—I truly do love the flowers. They're striking."

She walked back around the bend with the boy gingerly, cautiously, and took a slow measure of me. "I'm glad you like them," she said. "They're the pride of the church."

I reached out to the boy and said, "How is your hand—you got stung, right?"

"Oh, it's better," the boy said. He looked about eight, holding on to his mother's hand. "I put some ice on it."

"Great, just great," I said, dusting off my pants. "Sometimes ice is the best thing for a nasty sting."

The boy looked puzzled at this, and his mother quickly said, "We should probably leave now—have a good day!"

"Yes," I said. "Of course. Good day." I watched them walk away and then said a little too loudly, "I won't be in the hospital forever, you know."

"What?" she said, turning and walking back around the flowers to study me. She was an attractive woman, a little heavy, in her thirties, with brunette curls, substantial breasts. A hardworking lady, I imagined. Perhaps she hadn't been kissed in years. *Knock it off, David!* I thought.

"I'm at the Menninger Clinic but I'm improving," I said, rambling. "Going to start living a normal life soon . . . yeah . . . that clinic is considered to be the best hospital in the country, you know? I read that in *US News & World Report* last month."

"That's great," she said, smiling slightly. "I hope they let you return home soon."

"Yes, to Connecticut," I said. "It's the Nutmeg State, did you know that?"

She laughed. "Well, now, I didn't know that. And it looks like you've become well acquainted with our state flower."

"Yeah, I think they're fantastic," I said, looking around me. "The sunflowers have lifted me today."

She nodded and said, "They're too bulky for me. I like simple things—like a daisy. You'd be hard pressed to improve on the simplicity of that flower."

"Ah," I countered, feeling suddenly buoyant. Absurdly so. I reached out my hand and brought a bright stalk to my face. "But you must appreciate the beauty of this awkward and gangly sunflower. It's quirky and odd, yes. But so big and bounding, like the best things in the world." I brushed some sweat from my eyes and said, "In a weird way, they're like Saint Bernards. Big and goofy but so lovable. I mean look at the color of these things."

"Sunflowers like Saint Bernards, huh?" she grinned. "Now, I've never heard *that* comment before. You may just have a little Saint Bernard in you, young man. At least the possibility for it."

I smiled, placing my hands together in a praying motion, bowed toward her and Trevor and said, "Thanks. That's kind."

"You're not going to get hurt by that, are you?" she said with a smile. "That I just compared you to a big pooch. You won't go tell the shrinks that a cross woman at a church fair called you a large canine."

"Absolutely not," I said. "I'm a brand-new dog."

"Listen," the woman said. "My name is Yolanda." She released her hand from her son's and came toward me, her sneakers kicking up some dirt. "It would really make my day if I could tell my friends that this afternoon I saved a man from despondency." She took a breath and said, "That I saved him from despair."

"Of course," I said, uncomfortable, shaking a little. "Definitely— it's true. At least, for today, you know."

She moved over and embraced me, causing me to flinch momentarily. But she held on until I relaxed. "That's it," she whispered. "That's why I came today to this place." I felt myself growing teary and partially aroused. *How was it possible to feel so good? When was the last time a nonfamily, nonpsychiatric person embraced me? Why is she doing this for me?* "You're going to come back into the world, young man. Don't stop trying."

"Are you some sort of saint in disguise?" I asked, holding her shoulders and giving them a tentative squeeze. "Why are you being so gracious?"

She laughed and reached for Trevor's hand. "I could ask the same of you."

I patted my chest. "David," I said.

She grinned and did the same. "Me, Yolanda."

"Trevor," the boy laughed, watching his mother closely.

"The two of you together are more effective than Prozac or shock," I said, saying it before I could stop myself. "Thanks."

"Tell me you believe in God now, David," she said, holding my stare. "That you'll let him guide you through terrible times and sweet."

I shrugged. "I don't know, Yolanda," I said. "I feel like I've done enough time with terrible—"

"Of course," she said.

"I hope he can give me some version of sweet," I said, my voice shaking. "I'd be ready."

She pointed toward the singsong music of the carnival, the voices, and we watched the Ferris wheel over the stalks of yellow. "Did you see the sign outside this maze? Did you read it?"

"I don't remember," I said.

"It said all you have to do is pray—that's the sole charge for enjoyment," she said. "I'm not a proselytizer, truly. But . . . would you pray with Trevor and me? Would you do that?"

Suddenly I felt closed in, vulnerable.

"I've no idea," I stuttered. "Not big on conspicuous prayer."

"This wouldn't be conspicuous, son," she said. "It's us three."

Then she turned to Trevor and said, "Help us pray, son. Would you like that?"

"Let's kneel," the boy said, very seriously. "It's important."

"Well—," I said and the three of us knelt down in the dirt. I felt unsteady, fat, and stupid on the one knee, but I listened. I listened. The seemingly shy eight-year-old kid said a sweet and rambling blessing, mentioning God, flowers, angels, lost people and how today was, really, a very nice day, and that, truly, this sad man before them was, really, a very good man without direction. There was shitloads of praising—I heard that word frequently. Mostly, I tried not to tip over and wished that my family could see me. I had a feeling it would make them hopeful. Make them smile. I knew it would make my mother grin and feel bright.

Then we stood and Yolanda wrote her address on a wrinkled grocery receipt. She kissed my cheek, patted my shoulder, and said, "Take care of you, my friend." Trevor delivered a very low high-five on his way out and I watched them walk around the bend of the maze and disappear. Just like that. It reminded me of James Earl Jones dissolving into the cornfield in that movie *Field of Dreams*. It felt like a magic trick, a mini-miracle.

Others walked around me at that point, cooing and fawning over the flowers. I spun around one last time, fighting a huge grin, and returned to the carnival. I had been gone thirty minutes. I saw Laura and Mom trying on earrings in one of the booths. I saw the Ferris wheel with the Bible quote attached and I didn't know what to think. The carousel was filled with parents and their children. One boy had a Kansas City Chiefs football helmet on, and it was way too big for him, completely covering his eyes. He couldn't see a thing, and he cried, reaching out his hands until his mother grabbed him. I noticed this and walked over to my family.

"Well," my mother said. "Where have you been?"

"I don't feel so much like a nut," I said, and they turned. "It's delicious. I think I had a minor epiphany in a batch of flowers."

"Really?" Laura asked. "What does that mean?"

"Sound delusional?" I said.

My sister shrugged. "It depends on what the epiphany was about—did you see something odd?"

I kissed their cheeks. "I saw endless lines of yellows," I said. "It reminded me of a quirky, hidden hope. It made me think those times weren't gone. That I had a shot."

"There was absolutely no blood?" my sister said.

"Not a drop," I said, winking at her. "I feel *vital*."

IT DOESN'T SOUND RIGHT, I KNOW, THAT I FOLLOWED UP THE JOY of the sunflower experience with what happened next, but I wasn't completely able to hold on to the goodness. It felt foreign to me, as if I had to wreck and dismiss it. As if it were filled with porcupine quills that had to be jammed into my heart and destroyed.

I didn't cut myself again, but I fell into old ways. I was afraid of anything life-giving, and I didn't want to make that commitment toward health.

I developed a routine of sorts. I rose at dawn, took deep breaths, and meditated as I stared out my window at the frozen grass. Through the colder temperatures, the damn rabbits continued to entertain. They stopped on a dime, they held still on the frosted lawns as the orangey-peach dawns broke open. I studied their miniature hearts thumping rapidly behind their white and tan fur. I loved those moments of watching the thumping. It seemed beautiful.

I fell into the habit of blessing myself with my waste. Every morning I pissed into a plastic cup and doused my head three times and then smeared myself with feces across my face. "In the name of the Father and the Son," I prayed, a rather enraged, sarcastic, seriously lapsed Catholic boy doing his thing. My forehead, chin, nose, and cheeks were covered. I stared into the mirror and whispered, "This is not a problem as long as I'm not ingesting this crap," and then I giggled, unnerved at my word choice until I lay on the bathroom floor, feeling the sharp cold of the institutional tile against my naked body. I studied the pockmarked ceiling from my vantage point and wondered how many patients had done this exact thing. "You are nothing new," I hissed.

Then, lying flat on the cold floor with waste on my face in the middle of fucking nowhere, I tried to be reasonable. "Certainly it appears," I whispered to no one, "I'm having difficulty coping with the world, but does it count if I'm so aware of it? Is one delusional if one knows he's delusional?"

This scatological nonsense lasted about two weeks. In an odd way it gave me some structure and comfort--I felt as if it were my duty to follow the procedure as long as I could. I could not fail at these tasks. The whole process took about fifteen minutes. Every morning.

Study the rabbits.

Piss.

Crap.

Smear.

Ponder.

Shower.

When I felt properly blessed or overwhelmingly confused or just plain sick of the odor, I took a long, hot shower and scrubbed myself thoroughly until I mostly reeked of Irish Spring. Mostly.

Then I got dressed and attended a full day of groups. It was the usual stuff—group therapy, breathing, movement, art, and music. Sometimes a pear-shaped, balding Catholic chaplain came by on Sunday nights and asked Page and me if we wanted communion. She usually took it, but I declined. "I don't feel ready for that type of thing, Father," I said. "I haven't been very . . . clean."

"Are you sure, young man?" he asked. "Jesus works with everyone. You don't have to be perfect."

"Thank you," I said and smiled. "But not today."

I had a withered, gentle, but prescient psychiatrist in Topeka with a mop of shiny white hair who looked a bit like that popcorn guy Orville Redenbacher. He'd fold his long legs and carefully jot down my responses on his yellow legal pad. After a month, he ceased writing, frowned and said, "I believe there's no getting around it. You're emotionally constipated."

"Yes," I said. "That seems accurate."

"I can't seem to reach you, though. There's a barrier between us."

"Did you ever work with Helen Keller or George Orwell?" I asked suddenly, and he chuckled.

"You're angry with me so you're calling me an old-timer?"

"No," I said. "Well, maybe a little. But I also am interested to know what they were like, what things overtook them and carried them to this hospital in Kansas?"

"Oh, I don't know," he said.

"They were here at this clinic, right?"

He nodded and said, "I'm sure what swept them up is nothing too spectacular. When you get down to the soul of a person, what you find is the same ouch, more grief, more tears."

"Did they smear themselves with their feces and baptize their souls with urine?" I asked.

"Is that what you do before breakfast?" he said, watching me closely as he placed the notebook on the table. "Is that what you've been doing?"

"That is what I do sometimes."

"Listen, my boy," he said. "I know you're gagging with pain and madness and feeling stuck. But you must remember that you're not that much different from my next patient who'll walk through that door in eleven minutes."

"Okay," I said.

"It's crucial to remember that," he said, gently pointing my way. "Maybe she doesn't bathe in human waste at dawn, but she feels like it. People are so similar and yet we pretend to be so far away from one another. We forget how close we are."

"Why do we forget?" I said, my voice shaking.

He leaned forward. "We forget because it is too excruciating sometimes to consider that the next patient bathes in it, too. That they feel as you do."

"Could I write that down?" I asked, my hand shaking suddenly.

"You're mocking again, right?" he said, and I shook my head vigorously.

"I'm serious," I said, my throat tightening. "I need to hear that again about our similarities. I want to write it down so I can remember. I need to."

He reached forward and gave me a piece of paper and a pen. Then he rose up slowly, stretching out his long frame. He walked over and patted my shoulder firmly. I looked at his splotchy hand on my sweatshirt, made a mental note that he'd never touched me before this. He was continuing, "It will be a lot better than you think, David. Do you hear me?"

"I hope," I said.

"It might not happen here at this hospital, but you'll rebuild yourself," he said. "I will pray for you—for gentleness to return to your heart."

I wept for the remaining minutes and said, "I may have just lost my single room for a while."

"Yes," he smiled and waited for me to stand. "I do believe that you just lost that luxury. But I think you were ready to give that up."

He walked me to the door, opened it and signaled to a young, heavyset adolescent with a shaved head and a tiny orange bear tattoo above her left ear who was waiting by the window. She grinned at me and said hello to the doctor and followed him into his office. I turned and observed as the doctor closed the door. Then I sat down in the room and waited for a staff to take me back to the unit. I practiced long, deep breathing, watched my fingers tap nervously on my thighs. I studied the early winter rays melting a few icicles—they dripped and thawed slowly, minutely.

Eventually.

11

LOST AND ADRIFT
EVERYWHERE

I LEFT KANSAS AND THE MENNINGER CLINIC AFTER FIVE MONTHS
because I missed my family and my home, and because the
friends I made at the hospital were moving on, being discharged.
In addition to the trip my mother and sister made to Topeka, my
parents had visited a few other times, and though I cried and carried on, they refused to let me return to Guilford.

"It would be unfair to your little sister and to us," my dad said
to me at a KFC in downtown Topeka. "And to yourself. You're an
adult, son; you need to join the world in whatever way you can.

We're not going to spend every night worrying if you're in the bathroom killing yourself."

"Please," I begged.

"You've got to enter life eventually," he said, "even if it's a sheltered group home or something. But it's not going to happen at our house anymore."

With that route blocked, I started obsessing about getting back to the East Coast. I convinced myself that maybe if I returned there, my life would improve automatically. So, with a social worker's assistance, I found a small place called Pine Manor Inn just outside of Montpelier, Vermont. I spent six months there just because it was closer to home than Kansas and I liked the brochures of the place. The sketches on the cover looked rustic and rugged. I picked the inn the same way I had chosen Skidmore—I simply thought it looked cool. I was so stuck then, so turned around in my head, that I just thought a new place would make everything better for me. And, in a corner of my mind, I thought they would probably let me cut myself there for a while. And so I did and ended up hospitalized several times.

I had become a stuck, sick, lost, obese professional mental patient who wanted to avoid facing himself. I left Vermont after six months—too damn cold and depressing up there—and returned as close to home as I could.

I came to Branford, Connecticut, the next town over from my folks, and tried living at a two-bedroom apartment with a fellow depressive who didn't like to flush. I was on disability and Medicare and also attended a day treatment program about a half mile behind a Super Stop & Shop grocery store. I remember being there when the O. J. Simpson verdict came on a television. It was 1995 and people oohed and aahed and then went back outside to smoke, and it was back to business. I ate a lot and came and went every day from the treatment center. I saw my family pretty frequently—we'd get together for dinner or they'd have me over for the day. But I was never allowed to be alone in the house.

I kept hurting myself at my apartment; burning had become the new kick ever since that one time with Pamela at Kansas. I detested smoke, but I learned to enjoy the smell of my skin being singed. My burnt flesh smelled faintly of freezer burn, of danger and dead hair. I decided that ashtrays, generally, maintained good attitudes toward the whole smoking process. They didn't pull away but simply stood their ground. Ashtrays, in a sense, had balls, and I wanted to be as impressive and manly as one of them.

I'd go to St. Raphael's for treatment of the burns, but they didn't keep me there long. I spent maybe five days on the same unit I had been admitted to in 1989. The nurses and technicians were empathetic, kind—they'd seen my type before. One who gets caught up in the system and grows fat and remains stuck in a type of psychiatric amber. Around this time, I learned I had about $200,000 left on my million-dollar policy. Feeling desperate in my emptiness, I contacted my SAFE (Self Abuse Finally Ends) buddies from Chicago, who had relocated to a place called Wild Creek in Illinois.

Hoping I could recapture some healthy fire and hope, I flew there for a month-long program. The tiny hospital was as lovely as any I'd seen—like a hunting club with a duck pond, woods, and elegant walkways. It was run by the same women who had inspired me at the SAFE Program three years earlier. My attitude was simple—*it'll be a new place, a new chance for substantial changes*. I always went with excitement and verve, ready to start fresh.

One day a redheaded woman stepped out of a white stretch Lincoln limo at the front of the hospital. She had a single shock of white running along the right side of her head. She had fancy leather luggage and heels, and was about thirty-seven years old. She had a sort of a Bonnie Raitt thing going on but without the guitar. She was from Tuscaloosa, Alabama, and her name was Jasmine. "The trunk of my car back home is chock full of blades," she told me on her first day. "Nearly every pharmacy I pass, I run in and purchase sharps—something to use later. I chuck them into my trunk and drive on. Folks collect shot glasses, buttons, and stuffed bunnies—for me, it's about the razors."

At the "Getting to Know You" meeting the next morning, she rolled up her sleeves and displayed her recent wounds, whispering fiercely, "I believe what my doctor tells me, and he says I ache more than anyone he's ever met—so deal with that shit, people."

I knew by then that self-injurers could be a weirdly competitive bunch. I had picked up the no-one's-more-screwed-than-me attitude early on, and I viewed other people's scars, burns, and hurts as commendable traits. They were positive, noble things that told me this person had been there and knew how I felt. I was bumping against something I had realized with Maddy years before—for the most part, I didn't desire true help. I didn't want anyone to know my secret. The only thing that fully belonged to me was my blood. That was who I was—*I had my illness and nothing else.*

And so I became a devoted fan of my scabs, blisters, and marks and felt the same about what others had accomplished. Whoever had the worst damage held the trophy in my eyes. The scars were medals earned in emotional battles. *"Lord and Master of the Sufferers"*—I joked around once with other patients, but each of us knew there was tiny truth in the line. Each of us was gifted at hurting, and no one wanted to be seen as the worst at it—or the best. A good portion of the time, my head was so turned around I couldn't remember what I was shooting for. Was it less pain or more? Relief or punishment? Death or life?

I had to struggle to control this competitiveness. The thinking inside my skull at times was, *If you're going to be a bleeder, well then, be the best damn one you can. Take pride in what you do—reach for the stars!*

Each new clinic was another opportunity for me to distinguish myself, but it got overly stale, petrified, for me after Kansas. Yet I continued on. The illusory romance of self-injury lasted just moments, and then shame raced in, and I realized, sadly, that there were no awards for hurting or anything as insanely stupid as that.

The only thing waiting for me and the actively bloody and burned was hundreds of state-run and privately owned white-and-red-brick hospital units with worn-out, tan-colored carpets that were bursting at the seams with yelping, frail young women and men pondering their medication cups and sketching their own versions of engorged wild rats with wings in art therapy. For me, what remained were questions I'd been running from for years. *What would it mean to leave the behavior behind? Who would you become? Who are you now, for Christ's sake—what's left inside anymore, David? Are you afraid you don't exist without a sharp in your hand? Stop, okay? Stop!*

But I couldn't do it. I couldn't look. I couldn't stop.

DR. COLLANDER DID WHAT HE COULD, BUT FINALLY IT WAS UP TO me to say I wanted to see a new psychologist when I returned in 1998. It was difficult to admit that our therapy had run its course; that we were over and had grown stagnant. I know I had, at least. Dr. Collander saved me from chaos and swirling madness in the early nineties, but our relationship had become enabling recently. We had almost too much history—and I was overmedicated. Not a lot got through to me.

I had started living in New Haven at a residential living center for those with mental illness in 1997. It was no longer common for a patient to be in long-term hospital care; the new thinking was to get patients out into the community with shorter stays in hospitals and mental health facilities. A social worker had recommended this place, and I didn't care anymore where I was. I just wanted to sleep and hurt myself every once in a while.

I WAS PUSHING 400 POUNDS AND UNABLE TO WALK MORE THAN 75 yards without losing my breath. The official name of the place was the Foundation, plus my personal, unimaginative nickname, The Haunted House. The two-story red-brick building was a former funeral parlor, and it was right between some Yale University apartments and a church parking lot. It sat diagonally across from a defeated-looking Shell station and an addict-filled Popeyes, with the thriving university just down the block.

The residents ranged in age from eighteen to seventy-two, with histories of multiple hospitalizations and, I think it's fair to say, a basic difficulty in adjusting to the world. Some of us were motley, mouths drooling from excessive medication. Others had difficulty keeping quiet during the voluntary groups that were part of the "Resident and Recovery Enrichment Program," which included horticulture, art, music, and discussion of current events.

I quickly discovered that non sequiturs, psychotic rambling, and inspired verbal expositions were a madly popular form of communication around the building. Random, paranoid comments whipped through the air about venomous snipers on the rooftops and about female cops with teeth in their vaginas waiting to castrate rebellious clients. It wasn't an unusual request for one resident to ask another to please stop coveting his thoughts.

My first group meeting at the house was called by a large African American staff person who told me and six other men how important it was to scrub our crotches with Dial soap every day. We had been rounded up and brought into a windowless office just above the kitchen.

"There've been numerous complaints about malodorous males from guests and some female clients," he explained. "We've gone ahead and purchased soap and deodorant—please, take your pick and get to scrubbing." With that he offered a collection of Dial and Right Guard deodorant products in a Rite-Aid plastic bag and we passed it around sheepishly.

It was dangerous to live in that insular world that felt so distant. The only thing I did when I first arrived was wallow. The staff was incredibly kind and patient and tried to cheer me up, but my daily cycle was simple: sleep, medication, therapy, eat, medication, *World News Tonight*, *Wheel of Fortune*, *Jeopardy*, medication, and more sleep. A damp, well-worn couch in the main room was where I planted myself. I wasn't interested in a woman or a book or an autumn afternoon with rag sweaters and a football game at the Yale Bowl. I just wanted the spongy couch with the miniature pheasants scampering across the fabric.

I remember lifting my face off the couch and gazing out the first-floor window into the real world zipping past seven feet away. There were honking city buses, cherry-red trolleys, tricked-out Lexuses blasting hip-hop, and untouchable Yalies with their ripe buttocks. There were homeless men in bug-eyed sunglasses and dirty dreadlocks, heaving themselves against broken grocery carts with chattering cans and bottles. Everyone moving right by, not even glancing over. Leaving me and the others far behind.

I HADN'T GIVEN UP ON CUTTING—I KIND OF WENT BACK AND forth from bleeding to burning, mixing it up every now and then like soup and salad one night, franks and beans the next. I say that flippantly, but my attitude was similar and careless, almost carefree. Some cynical slashes here, some ironic burns over there. It felt comfortably routine. I had the stock answer ready for social workers who asked me why I continued the onslaught.

"It eases me, relieves the turmoil and stress," I said.

Maybe that was accurate back in the early nineties, but it didn't ease anything by the time I lived at the Foundation. It actually embarrassed me and made my self-loathing fester. I usually skulked around and seethed at my reflection in the mirror with a literal scowl in those days.

I wasn't cutting myself dangerously then. Every move I made with the blade was controlled, calculated. I knew the right pressure to put on my arms and chest, when to drag the blade across the skin and watch the blood spill over the virgin wound. I wasn't interested in drawing a lot of blood anymore, just enough to paint the walls. A few stitches at most, if that. By the end, it was mostly razor scrapes. Something *had* to emerge, though. I *needed* to see it. The compulsion was odd and unusually fierce. Although it no longer gave me a high, I felt an artistic side of me was being stroked, sated. I made little crucifixes, stars, and perpendicular lines and enjoyed decorating the walls of my room with crimson flares.

Once I carried some foot-high hollow white plaster figures up to my bedroom. They were of a boy and a girl, and I waited for the right time to strike. They looked so very young, so untouched, something akin to frozen innocence. Later that week, I slapped some blood onto their faces and legs one early morning as I marked myself up. I watched the figures transform into something cinematic, darkly ironic and pretty in my eyes. I wanted to take photos of each of them, make a sweeping collage for later. I felt moved by my art. The video rolled on in my head—now it was MTV *Live from New Haven*. The show was the same old crap with a new location, but the filming simply would not stop.

The show had to go on.

For the first time, I even wanted to slice off my useless dick. Psychiatrists had been querying me about that topic right from the beginning, and my response was always a "no way." *I think I'll hang on to that, thanks.* But now my thoughts grew so jumbled and harried that I obsessed about slicing my penis. I wanted to throw it out the window like Lorena Bobbitt and stomp on it until it learned its lesson, which I never quite understood. (*How,* exactly, was it supposed to learn the lesson? I wasn't sure, but I liked the idea of banishing the damn thing for its lack of successful contact with women. It would know better next time.) I figured it would crawl back after cold nights alone and creep up my thigh and jump into position.

I progressed from there to thinking that if I cut off my left ear and cooked it up in a skillet, then swallowed it with chocolate

Yoo-hoo, I would be given a type of redemption, a way back to a better life. Maybe this personal communion service could *fix* me. (I know that sounds like some joke, especially with the Yoo-hoo, but it's truth.)

Cutting off my ear was too painful, so I took little strips of flesh instead. One night, with Counting Crows singing "Black and Blue" around me, I ingested a few tiny pieces and said the Hail Mary. I continued on the path for the elimination of the ear, usually the left one. One patient at the hospital later joked about van Gogh with me and I laughed along, whispering to myself, *I am less than nothing, I am my body, I am my Christ, I am less than nothing . . .*

I was a depressed, ill man, but I chatted and made jokes with my family in between the outbursts. I'd head out for tea with my mother and visit with my brother Dennis. I saw Woody Allen movies at the Criterion Cinema with Julie, and later discussed them over scrambled eggs and juice in a diner. I was a highly functioning loon. A Jekyll and Hyde in one fashion. Even when I was stuck inside the act of injuring, I was quite close to the surface, the bone of reality. Yes, I got lost a bit in the heat of it, but I could still talk about the Middle East ten minutes later with the EMTs or a staff member as they patched me up.

What does that mean? I wondered. *Do a majority of bipolar II patients or depression with psychotic features patients feel close to the pulse of reality like me? Am I just a well-disguised performance artist that no one could get a handle on? Why did I have to become the bleeding behemoth?*

Later, I asked my doctors if I could've avoided the anguish, the blood, the electricity, the hospitals. Does being so close to the bone mean I was never actually sick?

They shook their heads. "You can't look back on psychotic events or a prolonged illness with a clear, unfettered, and rational head years later and make pronouncements on how it exactly occurred or decide you were never ill," my psychiatrist Dr. Krav explained. "That's just not the truth. I suppose you can try to pinpoint precisely why you acted in irrational, self-destructive ways back then. But it's unfair to you, David—it'll drive you nuts. It was unfair then, when you were bonkers, and it's unfair to you now when you're slowly questioning more, examining your behaviors. You might not like to hear this, but a quiet, healthy part of you is emerging through these questions. It's the start of something. Your soul is growing tired of the drama finally."

"Yeah," I said, pushing him, "but--"

"Look," Dr. Krav said gently. "You were sick and somehow, some way, bubbles began rising to the surface. Healthy percolation began down deep. It's not huge, but it's something to note."

"Okay," I said.

"But any expert who talks specifics in your case," he said, "who tells you they know exactly why and how you fell apart is as crazy as you once were. You are an amalgam of blurred boundaries—you're not any one diagnosis. You're one rather extraordinary mutt."

"Okay," I said.

"Ask yourself a simple question to decipher whether something you've done is delusional or not," he said. "Would nine out of ten people be secretly smearing themselves with feces in the middle of Kansas? Would nine out of ten folks still be injuring themselves and painting the walls of their room with blood repeatedly at forty years old?"

"I see your point," I said.

"I'm thrilled that you're on the way back to health, David," he said. "But making yourself bleed with razors repeatedly or burning with cigarettes is not what normal folks do—it's not a fail-safe test for delusional behavior, but it's a pretty good one."

Dr. Krav suggested once that my acting out was a desperate attempt to be good at anything in the midst of the confusing pain twirling in my skull. It was a way to be a unique performance artist. Even though I was at the bottom of the totem pole in the world, at least I was an unusual one. I had that going for me. And maybe that identity, of a self-injurer and psychotic fellow dreaming of drowning in his blood, dreaming of giving the most spectacular, one-night-only mutilation show on a stage in front of the lights and people, shows how much I desired to be the best in my small, warped corner of the world.

When my hospitalizations first began, experts started suggesting diagnoses. They couldn't agree on what exactly I had. Some doctors thought I might be mildly schizophrenic, then schizoaffective, then perhaps a borderline personality with a thousand personality disorders. They said maybe it was schizotypal depression or psychotic depression. Eventually, Dr. Laney and Dr. Krav got together and said I had bipolar II with hypomania, an anxiety disorder, and an avoidant personality. That one kind of stuck.

THE PSYCHOLOGIST WHO SAVED ME DIDN'T IMPRESS ME RIGHT OFF. He looked more like an aloof poet than a therapist. Or maybe, if he added a black beret, he would have looked like a rebellious architect. Dr. Laney was a former English teacher with silver hair that swept to the right side of his head, black spectacles, and a white goatee that became a beard in winter. He was pretty directive, even a little pushy, but miles more nuanced than the Freudian gangster, and much more pragmatic than Dr. Collander. (All three had worked together at the Institute of Living decades ago.) Dr. Laney also wore a lot of ocher and caramel linen shirts buttoned up—that's what struck me when I first saw him. "You're kind of boring, but I like your shirts," I said. He was by far the best-dressed doctor I'd ever worked with. And, as the song goes, I've worked with a few.

When we started, I asked him about his therapeutic influences. He made a curious face and said, "A little bit of everything, I guess."

"Is your style too Freudian?" I asked.

"Did Dr. Presley scare you away from Mr. Freud with all his sexual questions?" he said.

"I don't know," I said "I just wonder what you'll use."

"There's going to be a lot of plaid and bright colors in our work this year," he said, and then smiled. "Look, with me, you'll get the kitchen sink," he said. "Anything that works, sir. From Freud, Erikson, Rabelais to maybe even Oprah, along with a pinch of Mark Twain."

"Mark Twain?" I said. "You know, I don't remember much of Huck Finn—is that okay?"

"You know by and by?" he said, closing his eyes for a moment. "He was big on by and by."

"What does that mean?" I said. "It sounds hokey." *The guy is fucking nuts*, I thought.

"I use it to mean good therapy doesn't waste your time," he said. "I won't waste your time. On the other hand, it means healing *takes* significant time. By and by—this'll take some months, years. A wise man, Twain."

"Okay," I said.

"We'll shoot for simple dividends, David," he said. "Incremental moves—rocking, crawling, stumbling, walking, maybe even jogging down the road. The whole spectrum." He sat forward and said, "Ideally, I hope life can improve a lot for you, mentally . . ."

"How about sexually?" I said.

"Well," he shrugged. "Eventually, I hope. Yes. By and by, you know? If you're feeling stronger, who knows what we can work on? But to begin, let's just shoot for honesty."

I nodded and said, "You mentioned Rabelais earlier—"

"Ah," he said, scratching his beard. "A real scribe," he said. "François Rabelais, famous writer sitting in between the Middle Ages and the Renaissance. I just included him because we have to chuckle, we must keep our eyes open and be aware."

"Of?"

"Of the world, of the giants and dwarfs among us," he said. "We can't lose sight of simple humor, or of satire, or our whole body turns brittle. Gargantua and Pantagruel—have you heard of that?"

"I don't remember," I said, and he nodded.

"Don't panic," he said, "there'll be no tests—but I just want to get that mind of yours awake. Inside the pain is a hungry English major waiting to write stories again. To read them. We need to look for signs of life inside David."

"Except for your obscure references," I said, mumbling, "it sounds painless."

"Oh, it's not," he said. "We need to find you in there, and it'll ache. Plus, as little bullshit as possible, okay?"

"Fine," I said.

"Are you a swimmer?" he said.

I shrugged. "I'm not sure I'd float anymore."

"Then we start in the kiddie pool," he said, clapping his

hands. "Dipping your toes in, getting just a mere hint of what awaits at sea."

"Ahoy," I said, and he raised his eyebrow, walked to the bookshelf, where he grabbed a green leather notebook. He handed it to me with a pen.

"I want you to write some basic goals," he said. "Significant improvements you want to reach."

I thought for several minutes and then wrote: "I want to feel alive," and "I want to read a book and enjoy it, to comprehend," and "I want to be in the world without freaking out."

I gave it back to Dr. Laney, and he studied them for a moment. "Good," he said. "We need to be reaching, always pushing. Muscles of the body atrophy and grow slack if you don't use them. Your brain is no different. Yours has been smothered in medicine and sickness, and it needs exercise desperately. You've spent a long period in the bowels of analysis." He stopped and stretched into the air with his hands, "I've got a very bad back, but you were listening, right?"

"You said I've spent too long in the bowels of therapy—"

"No," he said, standing up suddenly and leaning against his desk. "I'm sorry, David—my vertebrae truly hassle . . . I said I think too many shrinks have repeatedly dug into your childhood without remembering that now is the most important thing. You don't want to be in stasis."

"You mean like Dr. Collander?" I said. "You think he was way off course?"

"God, no, I don't," he said, stretching his hands more. *All his bending and twisting made me uncomfortable. Why couldn't he sit still like the others?* "I gather that he saved your life when you had your first break," he said. "He was a great voice of warmth and wisdom. But later on you were away at other hospitals—Menninger's, Vermont, Chicago. In a way I don't think he had a fair second shot with you, so it wouldn't be right to say."

"I loved the guy," I said quietly. "His voice was so comforting to me when I'd call him. A balm, really."

"Yes," he said, nodding.

"Something's up, though," I said, rubbing my arms. "I want to slice myself right now or burn," I said. "Plus, I . . . just want to say I doubt I'll ever leave the group home."

Dr. Laney studied me for a moment before speaking. "That's odd how you phrased that," he said. "But let's not use the word *ever*, okay. I'm simply discussing going for a daily stroll. Speaking to family more often, heading out to eat with them." He shrugged with his hands out. "Maybe volunteering at the soup kitchen eventually. At one point, we'll even get you to a gym." Returning to his chair, he crossed his legs and looked straight at me. "Perhaps the self-destruction comes because you're thinking about confronting it, changing it. The behavior, I mean."

"Yeah," I said.

"We are going to take our time and not panic, okay?" he said slowly.

"Yes," I said. "I think my panic might be protection for my little shop of hells."

"Good," he said. "That shows you've been listening to doctors."

I smirked. "I always listen to my doctors," I said, and then, "You're looking at one malleable motherfucker."

"Oh, my new friend," he said, "how wrong you are. To get to this point in your life and to still be around and alive?" He shook his head. "'Malleable' isn't the word that comes to mind. Try 'strong.'"

"Right," I said, feeling uncomfortable, anxious. "I'm really antsy."

"Okay, then," he said, "let's discuss a calming action—what's something, a signal or movement, that eases you?"

"I don't know," I said. "Miming jump shots, I guess. Just pretend shooting. When I did drugs at Skidmore, especially cocaine, I mimed jump shots for hours. In someone's apartment, in my own room . . . There was no ball, of course." I signaled with my hands, pushing it toward the ceiling, a flowing motion.

"Huh," he said, a little slowly. "And that helped?"

I nodded, watching his reaction. "You're not a big sports fan, I take it?"

He grimaced. "I am an uncoordinated, unmitigated disaster on sports fields," he said. "Even my pretend jump shots never go in."

"You look perfectly capable, if not nerdy," I said.

"Exactly," he said. "It took me two hours this weekend to properly hang a basketball net for my son's . . . rim."

"Say 'hoop,'" I said. "It's hipper."

He pointed to me then, smiling.

"What?" I said.

"You see how this might work?" he said. "I help you become healthy . . ."

"And I widen your experience, show you how to hit a jump shot?" I said.

"Oh," he said, "I'll never hit a jump shot. I've tried—it hits nothing. Not even the backstop."

"Backboard," I said, shaking my head. "Okay, what the hell—I'll assist you in your quest." I made a timid face and said, "So what is it that you do know about sports?"

He held his hands out to his side. "I know who the Philadelphia Phillies are because that's where I grew up. But I don't know players' names or grasp much else."

"How about March Madness?" I said. "Are you familiar with the term?"

"Hockey?" he said, and I shook my head with a slight grin.

"Will I get a discount by helping you?" I said. "I mean, can it be a quid pro quo?"

He grinned. "Well, as of now, no way," he said. "But perhaps if you turn me into a rabid sports nut, someone my son can throw the ball with . . ."

"You'll need several hundred treatments of shock to get started," I said.

"Light me up, Doc," he said. "Anything for the team."

I looked at him for a moment and then studied the snow-covered courtyard out his window, a floor-to-ceiling beauty. There were two dead flies at the bottom of the wide pane. For a half a second, I saw myself outside in the whiteness, blood dripping off of my cuts, red goo into frozen water. *Come on, David— knock that shit off!* Then I said, "You know, I think we may have something good here."

IN THE BEGINNING, WHEN I COULD ONLY SHUFFLE FROM THE group home to Dr. Laney's office, I had to stop twice each way and rest on the benches outside the Yale Law School. Across the street was the Grove Street Cemetery, where they offered tours for history buffs, usually senior citizens working their way from headstone to crypt, sometimes taking notes as the tour guide spoke. The imposing gate out front was inscribed with the words "The Dead Shall Be Raised."

Dr. Laney talked regularly of finding hope inside my veins.

"Wherever hope is now, it feels overwhelmed," I said, looking out the window.

"In the middle of your intense anxiety, cellulite, and crap, I know you believe you're worthy of better things," he said. "Look at your family members—they would have dropped you long ago if you weren't worth it. They would have stopped believing in you and given up."

"But I'm family," I said. "Don't they keep me no matter what? I'll just be forever the freaky brother David."

"Oh, bullshit," he said. "You can't fool me. Somewhere in there lies faith about yourself . . . that dreaded word hope. The concept of redemption is forever present somewhere in most lapsed Catholics—no matter how they try to run."

"Whoa now," I said, with a slight smile. "That's pretty presumptuous."

"True," he said, grinning. "But it's coming from the horse's mouth, one sanctified true believer at your service." He stood up and stretched his back by reaching over his knees. "But be honest, wouldn't it be fantastic to feel alive again, to hold a girl's hand?" he said. "To kiss her? To have a few friends that can't be categorized in the DSM-IV?"

"God, yes," I smiled. "That'd be an achievement."

Dr. Laney nodded and glanced at the clock. "We've got some time here, and I'm going to change the dance card if you don't mind. Instead of listening to you go on about the latest pair of breasts on Elm Street, I say we shoot for the rotten core. Let's try to work on the delusion of a black liquid that exists inside you."

I looked at him warily. "You mean why do I feel that way?"

"Not exactly," he said. "You've shared that already . . . What I mean is, how can we drain away the feeling?"

"Without slicing, you mean?" I said, and he smiled slightly.

"That would be the goal, David," he said, scratching his cheek. "To convince you that it's a large painful mass of feelings. Not something to cut into with a blade but to take apart, deconstruct, defuse with words."

"Okay," I said. "Truly, a part of me knows that—I've read it and discussed it and written it many times."

"Yeah?" he said.

"But then I return to the Foundation, and I'm lying on the bed, and I see my reflection in the mirror and feel viscerally disgusted," I said, "and I want to rip, rip, rip into my guts. Fucking tear in and find the blackness!"

He pointed at my mouth. "You clench your teeth hard when you say that, you know, you bite down hard."

"I can feel it," I said, holding my jaw. "It's a low growl."

"Much of your rage should be directed at the world," he said. "Maybe at the Pricks or the characters around the Foundation. And some for Andy growing up—but you throw every bit at yourself and bite down."

I was silent for a moment, not fully listening. "Are you always going to be around to assist me for the long haul, Doctor?"

His eyes, which were focused outside for a second, snapped back to mine quickly. Almost like a dog hearing a strange whistle, a quick turn of the head. "That's an unusual question—why do you ask?"

"I don't know . . . maybe sadness, doubts about us—how long you'll stick around. Even melancholia. That's what depression used to be called, right?"

"Still is preferred by a few," said Dr. Laney. "Centuries ago many contended that a black substance caused the pain of depression. It was standard medical belief."

"Odd," I said.

"Yes," he said. "But what we'll do is slowly drain your abscess, okay?"

"That's tricky, I think," I said. "It doesn't sound easy for me to undertake."

"No shit," he said. "What's easy to do nowadays, anyway? You're a wily personality, David. Kind of a tricky son of a bitch," he said and then, "First, though, let me say you are a new friend, and I feel affection for you—I like you."

I grimaced. "But not with the same gusto as Judd Hirsh and Timothy Hutton?"

He rolled his eyes. "Skip the therapeutic films, okay?" he said. "Your mind is twisted with anguish, you've got a horrid case of manic depression and a compulsion to damage yourself to no end. It's serious business. You and I have to give ourselves respect— and intellectual weight. And we must respect boundaries. I am your solid friend, just one in a professional capacity."

"Rabelais might skewer that," I said, feeling suddenly brave.

He waved a dismissive hand. "No sneaking your way out of today's session, sir," he said. "Your voice nearly broke earlier when you asked if I care for you. That was real, right?"

"Of course," I said, my mouth dry.

"You deserve a nickname that describes what you do," he said.

"Heroic fighter for freedom?" I said.

"No," he said. "Let's try something more like 'Duplicitous Dave.'"

"Huh," I said.

"Do you know why I say that?" he said.

"I know I can be a sneaky motherfucker out in the world," I said. "On grounds of hospitals, in a rented hotel room, in Topeka . . ."

He nodded and said, "But I believe you are a blessed man beneath the self-loathing, weight, and inner blackness," he said.

"Listen," I said. "I'm nearly forty, women are repelled by me, and I'm surrounded at most suppers with nonlinear conversation."

"Perhaps that's true," he said, "but you have the power to correct your delusions," he said. "Many at the Foundation are not able to do that."

"Yeah," I mumbled.

"You've got to become more cognizant of when you're fooling yourself and others with lies."

"How's that?" I said, shifting in my seat.

"Watch how this works," he said, standing up and stretching his arms toward the ceiling. He walked over by the bookshelf and grabbed one small barbell with his left hand and started doing curls slowly as he leaned against the wall. I watched the veins in his hands grow more pronounced. "You purchase the razors or cigars a week before you injure, right?"

"Sometimes," I said and then, "Yes."

"In between that week and the self-injury, every time you see staff, every time with family, every time you meet me and stay silent, you've lied." He leaned forward and said gently, "You've got to see this, David."

"I'm trying," I said.

"You don't buy blades or lighters in fits of blinding rage," he said. "You buy them with a plan. Now, perhaps you get nuts for a few minutes or enter a small dream state while you burn or cut, but it's very preventable." He stopped speaking for a moment. "The catch for the whole deal is the word 'honesty'—with that component, healing will eventually win out. It will filter through your . . . emotional abscess." He took his spectacles off and rubbed his eyes before placing them back on. "Telephone me." he said. "Leave me messages whenever you want on this office number. Write a book about the damn thing, even. It's time to start calling yourself on the duplicitousness."

I took a breath and said, "You're saying I hold part of the blackness ransom?"

"Definitely," he said. "You know it, too. You're a rigid middle-aged man, trapped in a seriously fucked-up game, and you don't know why you're still playing it."

"Yeah," I said, sighing. "I know. I know you're right."

"But it's wearing you down into *nada*," he said. "It's like you know this but you don't . . . you won't think your actions through. It's turning you into a numbed, lost man."

I felt my whole body fill up then. "My insides are rotting," I said quietly and then tried to stop the tears, swallowing them. I stared down at my sneakers and breathed slowly, carefully until I had control. *Easy, David, easy.* "I think I'm . . . crumbling. Passing away in slow-mo."

"Yes," he said. "There are many dramatic ways of looking at it—but let's not allow ourselves to go there at this point."

I nodded, watching him.

"Perhaps it's not as horrible as it sounds because you can make . . . tangible adjustments on those feelings," he said. "You can have a life and leave blackness, okay?"

"How?" I said.

He sat forward in his chair, pulling at his left sock. "If you work with me on this, David, you'll . . . progress—honesty and some meds every day will get you there. Not hundreds of pills that have you stumbling around like some numbed-out beach ball, but an amount that assists you—and makes life doable. You have it inside of you, friend. You hold the keys, the codes." He smiled slightly and said, "Whatever metaphor you wish to use."

We sat there silently for one long minute. I watched a black-bird dart through the lawn outside Laney's window, and I adjusted my elbow on the chair.

"I don't know if I'm up to it, Doctor," I said. "Honestly, a life without crutches doesn't sound doable."

"Oh, nonsense," he said. "That's horseshit. We'll work on it constantly, hungrily," he said. "There'll be slipups, but we'll get you back on your feet."

As he scribbled a note, I said, "What will I do with myself if I'm not destroying myself?" I picked at my arms and continued: "Sounds crazy, you know . . . I'm just . . . I'm worried, kinda panicked. A girl asked me that eight years ago in Vermont, and I couldn't do anything with it then. I swallowed it and ignored it somehow."

He nodded and said, "Your truth and words will now unravel the sticky, ugly ooze. Good-bye to the blackness."

"Are you sure?" I said.

"It's truly time, David," Dr. Laney said. "We'll strip it down and honesty will bulldoze it. And I'll be here three days a week—I will be here for the long term. And all you've got to remember is—"

"Just tell the truth," I said quietly, and he nodded.

"Remember, now, we go from rocking to crawling to the pool and then the ocean," he said evenly, measured. "Be straight with yourself, stop the lying. We'll get you out among the living before too long."

"Yeah," I said.

"You'll be swimming eventually," he said, smiling slightly. "One day you'll be in the sea with us miserable sharks."

I walked home feeling scared, timid. Alone.

❖

I didn't have a lot of friends by this point—most everyone had fallen away. Maybe they'd call twice a year or send a Christmas card to the Foundation. "Keep working hard, we miss you"— that type of thing. Their message seemed to say, *We're here but we're not equipped to take you on just yet.* My only buddy was Benjamin. He was living at the Foundation when I moved in, but soon after that he moved into a condo that his wealthy aunt bought for him.

Ben was 5 feet 9 inches, about 285 pounds with a scruffy reddish beard and long, bright red hair that fell to his shoulders. He was kind and loyal but, like each of us, troubled. He had schizophrenia, rampant paranoia, and he drank excessively on his medications and smoked Black & Mild cigars like a fiend. His disease was especially ragged and prickly and didn't let its sufferers up for air. Ben always had the shadow of great internal struggle hovering around him.

"Dave, Dave," he said to me once, calling me at the Foundation when he first lived alone. "I fear my whole being is burning in the fiery tar pits of hell." He took a breath and continued. "I know what awaits me in the afterlife," he said. "Excruciating torture and soul murder."

"Try, Benjamin," I said. "Try hard to not obsess about such things."

"That's like me telling you not to obsess about the blades and blood," he replied. He had me there.

Another time he phoned me insisting that Armageddon had commenced outside his curtains. "It's occurring," he whispered, "the non-Christian world is being sucked into the ground right now, so fucking far, fast, and deep. The archangels will be slaughtering villagers and they may take me."

How do you properly chat with someone like that? What do you have to offer except "I'm sorry, man, that's terrible." I told him I had experienced a similar fear of being sucked up into the sky when I was in bad shape at the Institute some years before.

He usually nodded at things I said and replied, "Yes, yes, but how do I get back to the world—can you help me return to the simplicity of a five-year-old kid?"

For me, this wasn't direct communication, but it was something.

A bunch of his buddies and I would gather at his condo and watch movies on the weekends. We'd begin with something animated by Walt Disney followed by some porn followed by something of a religious nature. Maybe the rapture.

I could have suggested something else, but it felt like enough for me at the time—just to be included. We were an odd group: David, the anxious bipolar self-mutilator and the three or four schizophrenics. We joked about the amazing breasts, asses, and absurd penises we watched in the porno. This prompted Benjamin to speak about the lovely, bejeweled box at the center of the earth.

"The vagina is a magical, mythical region that I've never completely visited for very long," he said. "I feel cursed, so very cursed about that fact." Sometimes he went off about Satan and fiery pits. ("They're actually flaming pools of feces," Ben insisted. "My pastor told me that personally.")

Most of our conversations were quite touching once we got beyond the porn and the archangels. Benjamin frequently lamented his first love, in third grade, with an auburn-haired girl who had a gap-toothed, charmed smile. They played together every afternoon with his pooch until something came between them. I think his dog bit the girl or she moved far away without telling him. It was heartbreaking stuff. He had also lost his mother years before, and though he kept in close contact with his dad, he didn't have the kind of support I had with my family. I think he felt very lost and alone.

If it weren't for times when I talked with my family and my doctors, I would've forgotten what normal conversation was. I yearned for linear sentences, anything that made sense. Encountering that was like nectar to me. I started to venture outside the group home just to engage in mini-conversations. It motivated me, in a weird way, like a wandering mutt chewing on any scraps of food he could find. The tiniest conversations became so sweet and important to my ears. Anything helped: little conversations with the man at Gourmet Heaven about his lemons, or saying hello to the East Indian selling newspapers up the street as he spoke of some horrible double murder across town. Perhaps he also discussed the soup kitchen down the street and how they served delicious flapjacks on Saturday mornings. I didn't contribute a lot, but it was a real live chat, with rational, sane answers. I said things like "Yeah, you're right," and, "Now you're talking, man," or, "Are you kidding me?" It was good practice for the world, and I enjoyed it.

Benjamin and I began going to the movies at the Milford Post Mall, or we ate at a quiet diner somewhere in Cheshire or Bethany. Once in a while he'd bring along his buddy Raymond. We'd go at odd hours when no one was around. One time, I heard that Raymond started hollering at the movies when *Die Hard 3* was showing. When a teenage usher approached him, he screamed, "You son of a bitch! You've got the gall to be playing the wrong movie."

"What?" the boy stammered.

"That ain't Bruce Willis up there," he screamed. "You're show-ing us a copy with messages."

"Sir? What are you talking about?"

"I'm talking about truth, man," he said and stormed away.

The gatherings at Ben's place wore on me, probably because my own recovery was gradually taking place. Part of the time I wished a camera was recording it so I could share it with my doctor or my sisters. I wanted somebody other than me to ap-preciate the magical, ironic, nonsensical gems that surrounded me each month.

One important thing to know about Benjamin is that he re-mains my friend—even though I don't see him anymore. He of-fered me company when I didn't know how to acquire any. Plus, when I was truly screwed up and would land in the hospital once every three months and my family was too tired and no one felt like visiting, Ben would show up. Faithfully. He never let me down in that sense, never. He'd bring a pizza or a chicken sand-wich from Burger King and he'd just pull out the food and a Diet Coke and say, "Those fucking impulses got you again, didn't they?" and we'd leave it at that. We just cursed our worlds and ate the food together. That was enough then.

Another decent thing about Ben is that he sensed that I was growing away from the clan. "You don't have what we have, man," he said. "You've learning to live with your bipolar and your com-pulsions to bleed and burn—it seems like you've partly defeated them. But us, me, even Raymond—we've got this freaking shit for life. It don't let up. It sounds bad and maybe defeatist to you, but it's the truth. Our schizophrenia runs us into the ground every day."

And so Benjamin, in own inimitable way, taught me about

moving on, about reaching higher and shooting for the next level and accepting those who can't move as quickly. Or at all. He never voiced it, but he told me when I should go. That I should try and enter the real world without them. We met for a final dinner and had a burger together after three months apart. One of us joked, "This kinda feels like a last supper."

Ben said I should shoot for exciting things, join life, and have a lot of sex. He released me from any guilt in his own way.

"You'll do fine, Dave," he said. "You'll meet a girl out there, and have a good life and we'll be cool, too. We'll just hang out with some beer on Friday and Saturday nights at the condo forever—listening to tunes, watching movies. It's just the way it is, the way it's going to be."

12

JUST BREATHE

Dr. LANEY TOLD ME TO BECOME ULTRAAWARE OF EVERY muscle in my body. To breathe like it was my last gasp. *To imagine fresh, bouncing sunbeams dancing off my cheeks in the mornings.* When he told me that stuff, I thought he was a closet hippie or a frustrated New Ager.

Despite those misgivings, I grew tremendously fond of him. He suggested that I walk to the Yale bookstore and study people's faces and watch their interactions. He told me to just observe folks and have a soda—a diet soda. That's the kind of assignment he gave me—little goals. Shower twice a day, walk around the block, smell the fresh flowers outside Gourmet Heaven.

"I can't do it," I said. "People will gawk at the psycho—they'll want to vomit."

"Let them vomit," he said, with a wave of his hand. "You're a good man who wants to rebuild his life, right?"

"I guess," I said.

"So screw them," Dr. Laney said. "You've got substantial work to do, and people are more concerned with themselves anyway. Too busy obsessing about cramps in their colon or why that beautiful Asian woman in the black turtleneck at Clark's Diner never looks their way."

For several years, he had me read out loud weekly from the "Talk of the Town" in the *New Yorker*. He had them neatly stacked up in his waiting room, and I would read a paragraph about a new Indian sculpture exhibit at the Met. Then he would ask me what the piece was about, and I was usually stumped. I had no idea. For a long time, I couldn't wrap my mind around what I'd just read. Couldn't retain basic stuff. My brain hadn't been working for a year, and my voice was barely a whisper as I read to him in those days; he even had to shut the air conditioner off so he could hear me.

There were no short stories or novels that I could truly absorb; the only task I *could* do was return to my journals and scribble. I could always write. Even though a lot of it was nihilistic drivel, it centered me. I kept ten or so notebooks in my bureau and began jotting down my thoughts.

> *Had an okay session. We discussed images of stabbing a knife or screwdriver into my black-teardrops tattoo repeatedly, hoping it would reach the oil, that the blackness would be tapped. I wondered aloud if that was*

delusional because I FEEL so clear and levelheaded oth-
erwise—he said yes which kind of shamed me . . . I'm in
a sick of everything mood: sick of being fat and ugly and
useless and hairy. I'm sick of the sick fucks around in this
nut shack, of having no friends, no girls, no fucking life.
My life is feces and now I feel like doing it again; like
driving a spear into my heart deep, deep, deeper until
the substance is found. . . . I feel like cutting, clawing,
scraping, smearing and breaking down the walls. I feel
like turning myself inside out, until I implode with my
black shit fuck loser prick asshole cunt . . . I'm left with
a scintillating thought, catchy, smarmy, bullshit line . . .
I yearn to burn.

Certainly not prizewinning prose but it helped me and gave me a way to shape my hurts, to act out with the pen instead of cigarettes or razors. What I didn't realize was the progress that seemed to come from out of nowhere. I'd thought I was still moving in slow motion, but others said they'd noticed differences and improvements in me. I used to fear the throbbing life outside my room and looked at it warily, cynically. But I started to study the Yalies with more interest and walked over to the campus bookstore more often. *What is she studying? I wonder what that fellow writes about? I wonder if he's any good?* Some people said I looked healthier and more stable. I had even become able to watch the local and national news and feel a passion for the stories. It was incremental, but it was growth.

A part of me resented the compliments I got from doctors and staff, and I recognized that accepting them made me complicit in getting better. At that point in my life I was comfortable with sickness and blood—it's what I knew backward and forward—and a part of me wanted to hang on to that, damn it. Giving that up was extremely unsettling—I'd adjusted my mind and body to being a mental patient forever, and when people spoke about healing, it confused me and made me angry. It was an anxiety that bubbled up in my belly, but I also had to acknowledge another part that liked the compliments, the idea of growth. Change. I thought, *This isn't so horrible at all—is it, David?*

ONE SUMMER ANDY CAME TO ST. RAPHAEL'S WHILE I WAS AN INpatient and showed me his beautiful adopted baby with a smile on his face. He was home from Africa where he taught history at an English-language prep school. A year later, Andy was weeping in the psych ER of that same hospital. Andy was leaning his forehead against mine, and a few of his tears were dripping onto my blistered thigh, where I had cigarette burns all over my legs, forearms, and hands. It was the closest moment of intimacy we'd ever shared. He patted my cheek and said, "Why do you do this? Do you save this behavior just for me when I come home?"

"I'll be okay," I said numbly. "I'm fine, Andy—it's all coincidence."

"I don't know what to say, what to do for you. Is your doctor helping you to get answers?" he asked, tears falling.

I looked up at my brother, who seemed a combination of manic, nervous, and jittery.

"It's a complex thing, Andy," I said. "I don't know what else to do but burn—I'm stuck in a repeating pattern."

He was nodding his head at me, rushing me along as if he couldn't wait to speak.

"Jesus," he said. "Jesus." He had a frown and his beard was

thinner than when I'd seen him last. The deep grooves in his skin were tanned, nearly leather. Still, he looked handsome and fit with his defined arms and chest. He was getting my attention by tapping me on my shoulder. He was perspiring profusely.

"I think I may know what you feel like," he whispered to me.

"Huh?" I said.

"On the plane back from Africa," he said, his dark brown eyes staring right into mine. "I was flipping out, thinking that Colonel Gadhafi was going to hijack the plane and torture my ass. I freaked out, I felt crazy, I lost it—I almost needed to be subdued on the plane."

"What does subdued mean?" I said, watching his face closely.

"I don't know," he said. "Medication of some kind. What I'm saying is I felt maybe like what you felt over the years."

"Are you all right now?" I asked, and he nodded.

"I saw a shrink in Maryland. He said it could have been an acute psychotic break that was brought on by psychic stress," he said, his eyes darting around. "So much damn crap happening with jobs and instability in the Sierra Leone region," he continued. "I'm telling you I was out of my head, really screwed. Truly—just bonkers for a short while." Then he stopped and said, "No offense."

"No," I said. "Of course not."

"Lately, I've been feeling very afraid for my family. Afraid of this Gadhafi figure in Libya," he said, frowning. "He looks like a freaking corpse. His face is hollow and looks eaten away, nightmarish when I see him on CNN. You've seen him, right?"

"He's an odd duck," I said.

"He's always on CNN," Andy said. "I was terrified I'd be dragged away and tortured for answers or something."

"Are you okay?"

"I hope," he said, looking down at my legs. "I hope I'll be okay—this stuff better not flare up again."

"What were you being tortured for?" I said, trying to take in this information as a nurse came into the room and took my blood pressure. Andy said hello to the nurse, whose name tag said Meghan, and she asked me how I was feeling. It was like we had run into one another at the neighborhood grocery during the holidays. I smiled, held my hand up for a moment until she finished, thanked her, and continued with Andy. "I mean, in the images that were in your head, what secret were you keeping that Gadhafi wanted?"

"What?" he said.

"The secret—what did Gadhafi want from you?" I said.

"Oh, God, I wish I knew," he said. "The thing is, it's, you know, I don't have anything to hand over to him, to give away. No secrets for him to torture me for."

"Right," I said. "I'm glad you're okay, you know?"

He shook his head and frowned. "You don't think something . . . like that would return to attack again?"

I shook my head and said, "I don't know, Andy. I can ask Dr. Laney when I see him on Monday."

Right at that exact moment in the treatment room at St. Raphael's, we knocked against something profound: a shot at closeness, truth, or breaching a divide in the most primitive way. *Would he stop pitying me? Would he be straight with me? Would I give him another chance? Is the distance and lack of time we've spent together too much between us? Was there even a relationship there to build upon?* But I was covered in blisters and numb, and he was nervous and rushed and left five days later with his family to fly back to Africa. It never went any further than that.

As far as I know, he's never had any trouble again. No more mini-freakouts. No more bonkers.

Andy and I have basically the same relationship today that we always had. We are civil and cordial, not very close, though we embrace each other when we meet. He's forty-eight years old and lives in Tanzania with his American wife and two adopted African boys.

He's a good and reverent person now—truly, he is. A solid, practicing Catholic. We see each other maybe once a year when he's home in the summer, or if a grandmother passes away during the year, he brings his kids and wife. He was involved with World Vision and Catholic Relief Services for years doing important work. He teaches currently and is quite a giving and capable person. By now, he's apologized for his behavior several times, though we remain stiff with each other. We just seem incapable of . . . getting anywhere.

WHEN ANDY AND I WERE KIDS, WE DID LAUGH AND PLAY SOME-times, of course. What I would like to do now is remind him about those times and use them to erase our bad history. At the Cape, we used to have underwater contests with my dad and Laura. I was probably seven, and Andy must have been nine or ten, and we'd hold our breaths and see how many times we could swim through my father's legs without touching.

I insisted on making my belly scrape the sand when I dove down—if I didn't feel the chafing of the rough surface against me, I popped up for air and started the whole process again. When I surfaced, my eyes would sting from the salt water, and my breath would arrive sweetly in my lungs. If we glided back and forth three times or more successfully and didn't bump into my father, we'd get a couple dollars that we could use to buy wax lips and Hershey's candy bars at Thelma's Gift Shop. Thelma was a kind, overweight Italian lady with a slight mustache. There was an adult greeting card section at her store that was apparently too risqué for children. Andy and Laura always ignored the cardboard sign that read *FOR MATURE EYES!* with black Magic Marker and slipped beneath the maroon tasseled rope (just like a movie theater) and absorbed the messages.

"Stay away—read the sign, Sonny," Thelma always said to me (and *only* me!) whenever I approached the area.

There was another time that was almost sweet. When I was in third grade, Andy and I went sledding behind our house. It was an icy January afternoon; the air was bitter and froze my nostril hair. The slope was very steep, and the sky was hurtling fat flakes down on us that gray-white Saturday. We decided to climb up the slick terrain for one final run. We each had a Montgomery Ward sled we had gotten for Christmas that year. The neighborhood kids had just hustled home after a few runs because of the frigid temperatures.

We climbed back up the severe grade by walking sideways, plunging our feet into the crispy ice and snow for traction. Andy turned to me and said, "I think we can go faster if you jump on my back, and we go down together on mine for this run—it'll be wicked." So I released my sled and let it descend by itself—we both watched it career alone into a snowbank at the base of the hill. Then I climbed onto Andy's back, and we took off, flying down the run, giggling and yelling together.

He screamed out in a tone I didn't usually hear, "Holy shit, holy shit!" I gripped his shoulders, and my eyes burned in the cold wind, and my mouth was wide open eating massive flakes, and we approached a large mound of white and WHOOSH! We were airborne for maybe a second, but it was a pretty amazing second. Every time I think of that ride, which is not infrequently, that second becomes an hour, a day, maybe a week in my mind. I stretch that thing out like some saltwater taffy we might've bought from the shelves of Thelma's Gift Shop.

After that second and a half, we teetered sideways and flew into the trunk of a gnarled pine tree. I got a deep slice just above my left eyebrow, and Andy's scalp got walloped, and we both needed stitches. "We better tell Mom about this, or she'll flip out," he said, and so we ran toward the house and then on to visit the local ER and then on to the rest of our lives. We left that precious moment and the cheap sleds behind in the snow. And perhaps I learned an early lesson—*folks pay attention when you bleed*.

That day was one of the sweetest times for me, especially when I look back. It was a moment filled with so much possibility, especially when we were floating above the snow. Just before we knocked our heads. I'd like to tell Andy that we were utterly free for that millisecond. Giggling, laughing. I'd tell him how much I want to take that laughter, that no-holds-barred-screw-the-world type of moment, and wipe away our bad times, just wipe them out and leave the two of us sailing through the air on that ass-freezing winter day, with no one else around except the chubby flakes, gnarled pine trees, and some scattered crows picking at scraps.

We'd be alone, coasting around the neighborhood on our cheap little Montgomery Ward sled, looking down on the crap that needs erasing. We'd soar, climb, and coast into the past and the future, erasing the heinous squabbles, wounds, and bruises. Perhaps, then, everything might just fall away and disappear for the two of us. Every one of his punches—the mocking, the bickering, the bruises. Even my bratty, pouting faces. Then while we were at it, we'd take care of my years of illness. Slicing myself on a hospital fountain of porcelain in 1990—gone! An upscale Hartford hotel room with sharp implements and enough bloody wounds to last until morning—gone! Buying fat cigars to burn the fuck out of me in 2001 in some ancient graveyard near Yale—completely disappeared! A decade in a troubled group home—absolutely gone!

If that could happen, if there was some way to do that, maybe I'd go back with the sled to Andy's life and help him erase his horrors, too; his tears and shames that accrued over the decades. Maybe we'd find the root of his rage or at least we'd help him out as much as possible. Clear out the pain and the events that rocked our lives. Just pack that crap away and stuff it into some rocket and blow it off the face of the earth. Just leave the two of us laughing like two harmless, sweet children enjoying a bitterly cold winter afternoon.

THOUGH I CONTINUED TO BURN OR CUT MYSELF, I WAS NEVER able to achieve that dreamy, deep fugue I experienced during the Boston incident and the one Big Night in 1990. During my ten years at the group home, I ended up being hospitalized between twelve and fifteen times. I had become a razor-blade junkie who was constantly chasing that high. The addiction isolated me far from every person in the world, but especially from those I loved.

Dr. Collander once told me that most nonlethal self-injurers burn out of the habit by the time they are thirty years old. They move on and grow up. They find a passion, a mate, a life. I hung on until I was forty-one years old, like a freak of nature. And as I neared the end of my troubles, I clung to them even more desperately because giving up the habit meant giving up who I was.

When the Foundation cut off my allowance, I took my CDs to Cutler's Record Shop to get cash for blades. After several more trips to the hospital, the home took away my music. When the tunes disappeared, I started trading my books; parting with Freud was easy, but John Cheever and Kate Chopin were painful. I traipsed down to the Book Trader Café on Chapel Street with the *Essential Book of Poetry* beneath my arm.

"You sure you want to unload this tome?" the cashier said. "It seems like a keeper."

"You know how the economy is," I mumbled weakly, ashamed and unable to make eye contact. *I have sunk to a new low,* I thought, but I quickly pocketed the six dollars and hustled over to the Rite-Aid. Then I waited for the precise time to mark myself up.

I was pathetic, frightened, and didn't know how to stop.

I HAD BEEN TAKING CLOZARIL, WHICH WAS TOUTED AS A MIRACLE drug for schizophrenics but was also used to treat some bipolar and refractory depression patients, for more than a decade. Among its side effects was substantial weight gain. But once the Clozaril was decreased, I was able to start losing pounds and working out at a gym. This didn't stop my mother and me from taking our weekly treks to Celtica, an Irish shop near College Street, for tea and scones.

She usually brought me a new book of poetry or talked about her work as a minister. We even talked about the word "hope," but in small doses so I wouldn't pull back. On one particular day, as my mother's hands quivered slightly from newly diagnosed Parkinson's, I was filled with an energy that could only be called manic or overly wordy or, I don't know . . . I don't know how to explain it. I erupted with a quasi-confession, my sneakers tapping nervously beneath the table.

"I've been obsessing some . . . writing and stuff about God," I said. "And I hope there's a spirit, a guide that shapes . . . you've used the term grace before, right?"

She nodded, surprised.

"Whichever is the appropriate . . . term," I said, embarrassed to be speaking of such things. But lately, my voice hadn't been sounding quite so awful to my ears. "I hope he or she isn't pissed off for everything I've . . . done or the way I acted," I stammered. "I hope she can direct me in returning . . . kind of. That she can prop me up until I put the blades and lighters down and walk clear of the mess."

After a few spilled tears from her, I spoke about the doctor in Kansas with whom I worked. How he kept on reminding me of the phrase "weller than well." "He told me Karl Menninger wrote a book with that title years ago," I said.

"And what does it mean?" she said.

"I think," I said, "it's a concept that a person can have a life, then break down and lose it completely, receive therapy, and then return to the world stronger than he or she was to begin with. That the healing can transcend the original life at times."

"Okay," she said.

I took a breath and said, "Stronger than before, the malaise and crap set in and almost destroyed him." My heart felt like it wanted to bounce out of my throat.

"Are you okay?" my mother said, "If it's too hard, you don't have to tell me all this now."

"No," I said, wiping the corners of my dry mouth with my sleeve. "I want to." Then I took a breath and a sip of tea. "It's like my nearly destroyed pieces," I continued, "can be fortified with some epoxy from other seared folks . . . scared souls. They can be built up, patched together, and can make me more alive . . . than before."

"Yes," my mother said, gripping my hand. "It sounds possible, good. Now listen, David. You've got to hang on just a bit more, okay? Don't lose desire yet."

"Yeah," I said to her, my voice quiet, shaking. "We . . . I . . . almost feel inside my chest, a turning . . . a newer version. A different . . . me. It feels like it'll be good, a relief, and then other times, I think it's going to crush everything I've worked on." I stopped for a moment to catch my breath. "Like an evil mist, you know," I said, "lurking around an island in some silly fairy tale."

My mother nodded and said, "I've never heard you talk so directly about something positive."

"Who knows how lasting the stuff is," I said, watching some Yalies holding hands at another table. The girl had a squash-colored scarf she kept fingering, and I felt a need to touch it, to stroke the softness. "What was I saying?"

"About the new feelings," she said.

"Yes, okay," I said. "Dr. Laney said that old doctor was bull's-eye but I wasn't ready to hear it." I wiped my lips again. "Said something like no one is entirely alone with their . . . hang-ups, difficulties. Crosses . . . whatever the right word is. That, basically, everybody smarts, hurts in places. The whole R.E.M. thing."

"What R.E.M. thing?" she said.

"It's just a band with a song, a good song called 'Everybody Hurts,'" I said. "A sweet video, too. The point is, everyone has the burdens, open wounds." I grimaced a little as I looked down. "Just not as obvious as mine."

"Right," my mother said.

"I know that's disgustingly basic, clichéd, and ugly," I said. "Probably taken out of a childhood psychiatric textbook, and it doesn't sound like an answer to my problems. No deep revelation or anything . . ."

"Who cares how it sounds, David?" my mother said. "The important thing is it rings true."

As she was leaving, I cried quietly for a brief moment when she embraced me. I don't think she noticed, or maybe she knew I didn't want to show her tears just yet. Too much unsteadiness bubbling inside and seeping through. Things were truly percolating, and I held tight to her for a few seconds and stuffed the tears back down my throat. *No sobbing, no sobbing, damn you, David!* I walked away for ten yards and then turned back. She waved to me, and I smiled, coughed, and started back to the Foundation.

A few nights later, Laura took me to Gourmet Heaven. She was struggling with a third occurrence of breast cancer by that point and wore a white-and-pink-polka-dotted bandanna to cover her head, which was bald from the chemo. We sipped decaf tea and cocoa, and she talked about her frustrations with the illness that had dogged her again and again. Her face was thin and pale, but her support shone in her eyes, which were nearly always bright and shining.

"My God," she said. "With our family, it's like a rotating tragedy-of-the-month club, isn't it?"

Dr. Laney had emphasized how important it was for me to start new with my family. He wanted me to spend more time with them, to invest myself more, go out to dinner, take risks. My family had visited over the years, but I had always kept a distance. The gauze veil was there, filtering out any chance of real connection. A lot of the time we spoke of happenings, of life and holidays and graduations, of cousins, but in one way or another, we had given up on me. A decade and a half is an eternity for a family to see their loved one damaged. It's impossible not to get caught up in the complacency and inertia of the illness.

And yet, after the time with my mother, I felt the family's presence more intensely, as if we were girding ourselves up for one unspoken, enormous Irish stampede of momentum that would kick my illness's ass. I know that's melodramatic and simplistic, but just as my descent into anguish felt like a rotten, ugly red tide sweeping me away, I was feeling a new wind pushing me along. Straightening me out a bit, cleaning me up, helping me stand. I started to feel more stable in my moods, not so high and low. Definitely not so low. Parts of me felt that the benign force that had guided me toward help when I hurt myself back in 1990 was now moving me toward a . . . larger thing. Possibly a real life.

WHENEVER MY FAMILY DROPPED ME OFF AT THE FOUNDATION after a pass, I walked alongside their car to the traffic light, waited for it to turn green, and watched them disappear down the street. From there, two more sets of stoplights carried my family farther, where they took a quick right and disappeared around the Episcopal church. Their brakes would pump-pump-pump, glowing red. Once in a while, they honked before leaving. I walked down the dark street, following them, hoping they'd turn around and carry me home. It could be raining or sleeting, the sidewalk could be slick, or one time, there was a raging taxi fire at the traffic circle fifty yards across the street. It didn't deter me, I still followed them, watching them disappear and thought, *I'll be done with this shit someday. I'll be in that car, I'll be driving. I'll be headed home.* Then, finally, each time, I accepted that for one more night, or week, or year, I would be sleeping in the fucking haunted house.

I approached the wide pine-green doors and punched in a four-digit code. Back then, it was 1, 3, 6, 9, and the door would buzz open, and I was sucked inside. Is it too nauseatingly dramatic to call it a netherworld, a trapdoor that led to frantic madness and worse despair?

Probably, but I'll say it anyway.

The tricky part about describing my time at the New Haven Foundation and its characters is that good people—interesting, creative, and talented people—were overshadowed by the more acute psychotic bullies dominating the place. Yes, there was camaraderie, warmth, and understanding of one another's wounds. But there were also folks who stomped into the main room and informed us that they'd just defecated on the back stairs or had done pot and crack down the street. (Granted, one might argue that I was just as disturbing to folks with my repeated incidents of self-injury.)

The noise inside the place made it a struggle to feel connected to the outside world. It felt so damn raw and harsh walking back through the door, back into the world of frequent chaos after being with the partially normal. After I started growing, truly stretching beyond the psychiatric realm, returning to the Foundation hit me like heavy jet lag. The therapeutic milieu wore me down and sent me to bed. It was a parallel world that shook, rocked, and swiveled me.

One place of peace inside the group home was art therapy, which was held in a finished, low-ceilinged basement on Saturday mornings. I'm exactly six feet and I had to bend over in one section down there. It sometimes felt like I was going to be crushed, like that subterranean world of despair and malaise had grown so heavy that the building was caving in on us. A crooked billiard table was set against the wall, and clients' artwork hung on a clothesline. Wild, abstract paintings, delicate still lifes of fruit and crucifixes, lonely figures surrounded by black-eyed Susans and bursting purple daisies dangled from wall to wall. With the hues and shapes being crafted on those mornings, the room transformed itself into a beautiful refuge, a safe nook of color.

TOWARD THE END OF MY TIME AT THE GROUP HOME, I LIVED IN Apartment 10 with Gregory. I was already feeling hopeful and stronger. I discovered that Gregory was a fantastic resource for challenging, linear, intelligent conversation, and for humor.

The first time we met, he was out in the courtyard, chastising a psychotic named Jerry for threatening to blow up a colony of ants with cinnamon, cloves, raisins, and water. Gregory tried to point out to this fellow that cinnamon, cloves, and raisins would do nothing. There would be no explosion, no fire, just damp . . . raisins and ants. That was the thing about Gregory—he had an excellent sense of the real, even when the world around him was mostly insane. He was like a postmodern comic-book hero for me—a truly decent man sticking up for truth in the face of numbing apathy, illness, and horribly depressing conversation. His superpower was an incredible intelligence and expansive knowledge of world affairs and city government. He also had a deep, deep patience. I was thrilled when I found out I'd be moving into his apartment up on the second floor.

His blood is bluer than blue, from a classic Manhattan Wasp clan of successful investment bankers and lawyers. A deceased mother in the society pages all those years ago—very, very old money. Summer place on Long Island. Gregory was brilliant and handsome, an academic all-star in a J. P. Morgan family. Early on, he went to Hotchkiss for boarding school and then went straight to Harvard. He told me his one dalliance in the counterculture was mistakenly sharing a plate of marijuana brownies with a famous mayor at his own kitchen table one evening.

Editor of a Harvard newspaper, Gregory also started as a guard on the football team. Then he graduated with high honors. He toured China and Germany in the seventies and gave speeches on public policy. He edited a conservative magazine at Dartmouth up in New Hampshire. where he taught for a decade. Politically, he started on the left and then moved to the right, but he shifted some of late. "I've come over to the dark side somewhat," he laughed.

He wrote many books on politics. He has never been about small-time things—not during his peaks of accomplishment, and not now, as he's returning to health.

We laugh frequently when we get together—two souls waxing philosophic, angry, sarcastic, with great melancholy. Obviously, my mind is Little League material in comparison, but he's always humble and treats me with kindness. Nowadays, he still looks like a chipper professor who's overslept for a week or so. He's a recovering alcoholic and a bipolar man. He's sixty-five years old, and his knee is failing, but his mind remains sharp as a tack. Even with his wear and tear, he still looks capable of lecturing graduate students about modern political theory. Presently, he leads two classes at the Foundation. Simply put, he's an amazing person.

I used to practice reading to Gregory frequently, just like I did with Dr. Laney. He'd sit in his leather chair in his room, chomping on a gnarled black pipe, and give me constructive criticism. Sometimes I practiced discussing subjects with him, such as who belongs on the list of the greatest writers in history, my feelings on the death penalty, or why the president needs to step down. He'd play the devil's advocate in our conversations, push me to stretch as much as I could. He assisted me in becoming stronger, healthier, closer to normal. He prepared me for the world.

Gregory is my real-life ghost of Christmas past because he shows me what I might have become. Is that terrible to say about a friend? I love him and respect him, but I've never seen someone tumble further. He has pictures in his room, newspaper clippings. He's shown them to me a few times. Graduations from Harvard, a Polaroid of an Independence Day barbecue with a towheaded son wrapped around his neck. They're both eating hot dogs, grinning in their matching striped polo shirts. I have some of his books, and his inscription to me reads, "To my friend . . ."

On Sunday mornings, Gregory and I walked together to the Kasbah Café on Howe Street and sat there for an hour or two. It's a Moroccan café that opened when we were sharing the apartment. The café is set back in an alley, so many have easily missed it. Only some brave souls have discovered the treat: a verdant garden that opens wide, exploding into lushness during the summer. There is a large fountain, and the garden is lit by many lanterns and bright with multicolored mums and roses. There are laminated movie posters inside, and they have poetry readings and folk music on Thursday nights.

I loved the plants and trees at the café—my favorite was a sinewy banyan tree. It's one of those twisting, gnarled, ropey-muscled beauties. Bird feeders and little trinkets hang from the branches. There's a footbridge with a tiny, gurgling stream in back, and at night, miniature white lights sparkle through the half-acre lot. It's a beautiful spot in the midst of a really crappy street.

Gregory and I drank soda, ate brownies, and talked about women, politics, and memories of victories and defeats. Then, inevitably, the conversation returned to the Foundation. We laughed and said we were the BBOCs, the big bipolars on campus. We discussed who was in the hospital at the place, what new person was sleeping with whom. Or how fascinating that new bloated depressive from Alaska was. We smiled about the discordant Moroccan music at the café—how it ground against our brains.

"Do you have this CD?" was the joke between Gregory and me when we heard a singer over the speakers in the garden. "No." He smiled and rubbed his whiskered chin. "I haven't had the opportunity to purchase it just yet." Sometimes they mixed up the playlist and slipped in John Coltrane or even the Beatles. We heard Moroccan dance music, some African salsa-like tunes, and then, out of the blue, a quick, gentle tenor sliced through everything.

"Blackbird singing in the dead of night . . ."

◆

FOR A LONG TIME, I HAD NIGHTMARES THAT DUNG-EATING SNAKES and rabid crows were pecking away at my guts as I lay on an operating table. I dreamt weekly that clueless, crazed doctors strapped me down and didn't use painkillers. They sliced me open and ignored my polite questions for assistance. "Excuse me," I would say to them, "I realize you're busy with the operation again, but did you notice there are snakes devouring my heart, my guts? How about the birds? Did you pick that up?"

Other times, I dreamed I was running around my childhood basement with my head and upper torso missing—two legs covered in gushing blood, spilling from the waist, tumbling and tripping over myself, moving slowly and oozing pus.

In recent years, I started to fight back in my dreams, but it took forever to pierce the balloon around the dream. I had to be present and real to the bastards in my vision. "Why can't I stop these characters?" I asked Dr. Laney. "Why won't the doctors respond to me? It feels like they're killing me."

"Perhaps it's an awakening, a slow coming-to that's occurring," he said. "But there's another part of you, the part ruled by anxiety, that wants to hold on to the illness, the toxicity."

One night, it was maybe late 2005, the snakes were having a go of it again, like they always did, and I shrieked at the surgeons. This time those motherfuckers heard me, they felt me scream, and they even looked at me with their bleeding, gashed-out eyes. In the dream, they had wheeled me into the operating room, and the snakes were munching on my heart, spleen, ribs, and I started hollering. At first I couldn't articulate it, I felt as if I had a stutter and was tripping over myself. "I . . . I . . . I." Suddenly, I seized the doctors and brought them down to my belly. I gripped their slimy scrubs and yelled, "Look at this, you stupid pricks—don't you understand? I AM ALIVE . . . I AM FUCKING ALIVE!"

When I told Dr. Laney about the dream later that week, he nodded, closed his eyes, and said, "And from there, the new heart throbbed with life."

"Is that a famous quote or is that just a passing Laneyism?" I said.

"Strictly a passing Laneyism," he smiled. "But your journey has been an epic, filled with questions, dead ends, and now, new life maybe."

"What's the lead for my bountiful epic?" I said.

He shook his head. "That's your call, paper boy. What would you say? In journalistic terms, how do you grab the editor with your story, prick his curiosity?"

"I don't know—maybe something about self-injury, the ballooning weight?" I said.

"Come on," he said. "Think, think—something like how did an upper-middle-class white kid with a partially happy childhood grow so screwed and broken?"

"That's good," I said. "Continue."

"How did he grow obsessed with blood and destruction of self?" he said. "Can one pinpoint the birth of the disease, the self-loathing, or is it all about random synapses misfiring?"

"Whoa," I said. "Doc's on a roll."

"Was it just about genetic disposition, a grandmother, some aunts, and an uncle in institutions, screaming and calling out?" he said.

"You really belong back in front of students," I said.

"And then one who died by her own hand," he said. "How does one explain it? Where do once-healthy minds turn and fly to? And finally, finally, the kicker—" He pointed to me and said, "How would you finish that off?"

"I don't know," I said.

"Try," he said. "Something about losing everything . . ."

"Okay, yes," I said. "Maybe . . . how in the world did the former nut get lucky enough to recapture his mind?"

"Right," he said. "Though others won't see years of suffering as a luck thing," he said. "More like intense, hard work and years of frustration."

I was quiet for a moment. "You think this stuff is real for me?" I said, my toes tapping an excited rhythm. "The desire, the dreams—I mean, is it happening?"

"You're experiencing it, you're dreaming it," he said. "You tell me."

ALONG WITH AID FROM GREGORY, FAMILY, AND THE STAFF AT THE Foundation, the support of Dr. Laney was constant and crucial in my healing. Undoubtedly, the most crucial. He helped me find my footing—no, scratch that, he climbed into the morass of sewage where I flailed, gripped my hand like a vise and didn't let go, and pulled me into a standing position. And then he walked me out. He showed me what a strong male intellectual person could be. Eventually, he showed me it was okay to desire things. (What does Bruce sing in "Badlands"? ". . . It ain't no sin to be glad you're alive . . .") To yearn for better and bigger things: women, internal peace, and an apartment away from the hysteria of the Foundation. A life, dreams, large dreams. He taught me how to have those thoughts again. It was like playing tennis with a pro when you are just plain awful or at least extremely rusty. If you practice long enough with the expert, you get better.

I started to get better.

For Christmas I always gave Dr. Laney books; for the first five years we worked together, most of them had a theme of mental illness: Anne Sexton, Sylvia Plath, Susanna Kaysen, William Styron, Kay Jamison. On our sixth Christmas, I gave him a collection of John Ashbery poems.

I'd never seen my psychologist so happy.

"When you shot beyond the psychiatric subset of Christmas gifts, I thought that was the most positive sign in our work," he explained later. "It made me believe that you were going to emerge. I honestly didn't know up to then if you'd ever get . . . very much better. I know I said that I did—but the best I hoped for initially was stabilization of symptoms. Then you surprised me with the Ashbery poems, which have some dare, heft, and frolic to them. The gift was a sign that you were moving toward the lightness, that you were going to be okay."

I think, somewhere down deep, I knew I would be, too.

13

A REDEMPTIVE CHAT

DR. LANEY AND I HAD A PIVOTAL SESSION IN THE SUMMER OF 2005. I, settled into his familiar bulbous navy couch, stared out his floor-to-ceiling window, and admired the Ansel Adams photographs on the wall. I had just returned from a brief hospitalization for mutilating my ear with a razor. Dr. Laney's window overlooked an apartment courtyard, and sometimes we studied tenants in their bathrobes watering their hydrangeas or pruning forsythia and made jokes about their hair or their sex lives. On that early summer day, he asked, "What do you see out there, David? What's going on inside that head? Is it the usual crimson and razors?"

"Of course."

"Why 'of course'?" he asked.

"Familiar territory," I said. "It's my specialty, my thing. The repertoire is very limited."

"Would you like to change that repertoire?" He leaned forward and said, "Let me rephrase that: Isn't it time you stopped this crap?"

"I don't know if I can," I said and shifted underneath his gaze. He rose and walked over to his bookcase and removed a familiar forest-green leather-bound notebook. He had me use this book frequently, and I had written goals in it over the years. When I started with him in 1998, the first entries read, "I want to feel alive," followed by, "I want to read a book and enjoy it, to comprehend," and, "I want to be in the world without freaking out."

"That's not the question." He handed me the book and said, "Let's write a new goal, would you mind? Very ambitious but doable. I want you to write it out that you will change your repertoire radically. How about, 'On this day, with three stitches just removed from my left ear, I vow never to cut or burn myself again.'"

I studied him as he returned to his chair, folding his legs one over the other, attentive, therapeutic-looking. I quickly wrote, "On this day, I vow to never mutilate again." I set the pen down and then looked back out at the courtyard and imagined myself on the grass without my shirt, ripping, cutting, and filleting myself, burning. I closed my eyes and said, "What were we saying?"

"*You* weren't saying anything," he said. "Your mind just retreated into the familiar blood-and-burns territory, right? Let's get frank: What do you fear?"

"I fear that I won't ever have a decent life."

"Would you like to change that?" he said. "I mean, if you

could walk outside now and be free of your thoughts, your depression, what exactly would you say?"

I said, "I'd find a nice Yalie, perhaps a brunette, one with succulent breasts, and ask if I may nibble upon her."

"Okay," he said, smiling slightly and handing me a pen. "Let's jot the goal down. We can't afford to avoid thoughts, to forget anything. That's what the hospitals and their sedation were for, that's what suicide watches and six months inside a cage did. They turned you into an unthinking vegetable."

"Yes," I said.

"Well, let's be clear. Would you like to move away from that stuff and move closer to the succulent, massive . . . what else do you need them to be?"

"Buoyant," I said. "They must be buoyant." And then, "Why are you pressing me today?"

He ignored this and said, "Would you like a pretty woman to recite poems with you and laugh and encourage you? How about being held, would you like that stuff?"

"Yes, goddammit," I said. "Of course—you know this. You've asked me before."

He looked at me quizzically. "Then why don't you start doing it right this second? Enough with the ear, stop burning with cigars, why can't you be honest now—today—and stop?"

"It's just—"

"Please don't give me the old line of how you're not worthy," he said. "Look around; look at the dregs in the world that have girls. Manson still gets letters from women who want to have his baby. There are no shortages of females—the key is to find a good one who is funny, wise, and can talk about writing, art, and silly things like peanut butter and fluff sandwiches."

"Then where are these scores of women today?" I said, annoyed. "I don't see them around—I think you're coddling your investment a bit."

"Fuck you!" he said slowly, seriously. "That's silly! Why can't you succeed? What is so damn appealing about an institutionalized life to you?" He looked at me, and he said gently, "Christ, aren't you tired of blood and blisters? What is it precisely that keeps you from leaving the mutilation behind?"

I looked at him and said, "I don't know, maybe it's all about green bile."

"What the hell is green bile?"

"Did you watch the Oscars a few months ago? Did you see Mrs. Robinson from *The Graduate*?" I said.

"Anne Bancroft," he said. "No, I didn't catch that. Tell me about it."

"It was toward the middle of the show," I said, rambling a little. "She came onstage, and she's elderly now, of course, and was presenting some special award to a cinematographer. She's regal, still classy. All that stuff, a woman of achievement—"

"Get to the bile."

"Okay, okay," I said. "It was her turn to speak, and she didn't know her lines, or she had trouble reading the teleprompter or something. She just withered under the glare of fifty-seven million eyes. It was sheer panic and horror for a few seconds. It was as if she partially turned to jelly, and what I saw on her face is what lurks deep inside me."

"An intense fear of public speaking?" he said.

"Forget it," I said, annoyed.

"Come on," he said. "Push, let's push a little. What do you think people will discover—what do you fear that lies inside that is so damn different and awful?"

"I don't know," I said. "Why are you in my face today?"

He sighed and said, "You're thirty-nine, okay? I don't want you to lose this next decade like you lost your thirties."

"Yeah," I said, "me neither. I guess . . . it's just that I believe no matter how skilled you are, or how supportive my family is, if you ever broke me down to bare essentials, folks would turn away from the horrible scene in disgust. They'd scream, embrace their children, capture it on a cell phone camera, and some anchorman would say decisively the next evening, 'This is what happens to people who have nothing in their heart, nothing in their body whatsoever to offer the universe. These are nothing people, only their green bile is left behind.' That's me—bile."

Dr. Laney sighed, signaled to the clock and said, "We've got to end early today. But I must tell you, most of the world doesn't give a flying Freud about your bile. Most of the world is neither supportive of nor against your suffering, just a kind of benign indifference. But it's time for you to leave."

I looked at him with my mouth open. "Aren't you supposed to leave me with something better than, well, the cold world will go on? I just spilled my fucking guts."

He rose and said, "And why do you feel I should push back harder? Your venomous self-hatred and rants are the only things you listen to, right?"

"Screw you."

"It's time to go, David," he said, rising. "I'll see you on Wednesday."

"Fuck it!" I said and stood up, grabbing my windbreaker.

He opened the door slightly and then shut it quickly and turned back to me. I was right in his face, too close, and so I took a substantial step back.

"I hate to repeat a phrase that you heard eleven years ago," he said.

"Which one?" I said.

"It's not any different than what that old Kansas doctor proclaimed when you covered yourself in excrement," Dr. Laney said slowly. "At one time or another, many believe they're bile or useless, wretched, and immoral creeps. And you know what, maybe some people really are." He took a breath and said, "But the simple fact is *you* are *not*—your mind was once gone, but that's not reality any longer. You are on the way to a life. You'll mess up every once in a while, like you did last week with the ear."

"So—"

"Don't fight this anymore, David," he said, touching my shoulders. "There is nothing left to rail against. You are not the same person you were ten years ago or even five months ago." He paused and said, "Look, once upon a time for a brief period, the mutilation offered a high; it spoke for you early on when you couldn't form words. So you went off the beaten trail a bit, and you bathed in it, went on stratospheric trips. But there's no more reveling or smearing left for you to do. You did your damnedest to drive everyone away with the bloody scenes."

He looked at me with a grin and said, "First you thought you deserved to be covered in shit, then you believed at your core was nothing but an oozing black scum, and now you talk of the green bile. You've suffered through a horrible bout of the crazies and experienced thirty-something hospitalizations. But people, the people you love and who have loved you, are still there, aren't they? Still waiting for you to come home."

"What if I'm really scared?" I said, my voice quivering.

He smiled and said, "You think?"

"Well, I am."

"Of course, of course," he said. "This work is filled with ouch.

It's not a fanciful, crazed psychotic break with blood fests at midnight; some crazy, crimson orgy on protected grounds. Or in some rented hotel room with John Malkovich's echo bouncing around. You were fucking nuts then, but you . . . are . . . not . . . now. Not even close. It's time to step out of this prolonged nightmare, to step out and embrace someone crucial, okay?"

My voice broke and I said, "You?"

"No, foolish man," he laughed softly. "Not me. Well, maybe me, at some point, but mostly it's you. You've got to come back to the world. I tell you, friend, you are not filled with green, black, yellow, or hot pink bile. You are lonely, very stuck, and filled with emotional scars *like everyone* in the world. That means broken folks in the hospitals and outside of them—people like your dad, your mom, your sisters and brothers, your friends, both insane and sane. Your scars are just more obvious to people—they are on the outside."

"I don't know if I have it in me," I said.

"Oh, Christ, you can," he said, smiling. "You have so much inside for this world: love, some writing skills, a fucking heart the size of a 1985 Lincoln Town Car. Come on, you are pulsing, alive, buzzing, and shaking at this moment, right?"

I nodded and said, "Yes."

"You want to step away from the crap, the blood? From all the painful history?" He gestured with both hands. "Step away from it, David." Then he shook my shoulder with his hand and, for a second, patted my cheek. He opened his door and said, "Step."

As if on cue, I started crying a little right then, but quickly bent over and turned it into a cough when I saw the next patient staring at me from the waiting room. I walked out and grabbed a tissue, blew my nose hard. I turned back to look at Dr. Laney, and he met my eye and closed the door. I walked down the hall

and took the elevator to the lobby and put on my 3XL windbreaker and nodded to the doorman behind the desk. It was late
afternoon, and the Yale students were away on break, leaving
New Haven quite empty. I heard throbbing music coming from
the headphones of a passing woman in the lobby. She felt my
stare and looked over for a moment and smiled, then continued
on her way out the door. I took a deep breath, stepped onto the
sidewalk, and then started back to the group home.

I never cut myself again.

WOULDN'T THAT BE THE MOST IMPRESSIVE ENDING FOR MY YEARS
of self-injury? All it took was for the good doctor to build me
up, boost me and break my balls at the same time. But, unfortunately, it didn't end that way, and the mutilation didn't cease.
I struggled with the desire and easy way out that self-injury offered me. I continued to write in my journal, usually gory and
melodramatic stuff, but if you haven't figured it out, that's part of
my gig. It's in my blood, as they say.

Four months later, there were plans for a Halloween celebration at the Foundation. The social worker hung up yellow-and-
violet signs made by patients that read, "Come One, Come All.
Prizes. Food Is Part of This Year's Halloween Bash." It's difficult
for someone on the outside to grasp how pathetic those activities
were for someone who was *almost* well. I was tired of forced fun,
slack faces, drool on the spicy Doritos, and lost people stuffing
their cheeks and dancing poorly to a cheap recording of "Monster
Mash."

I'd had enough of bloated faces—mine included. It had been
three months since I injured myself, so I felt itchy and nervous. I

could tell I was headed down the same old shit plan as I started making quick notations in my head to burn. I had asked Laura for ten dollars on Halloween Eve during our weekly visit at Gourmet Heaven. I felt like a prick as I did it—and I was a prick for doing it—but I waited for her red Mazda to make the turn and disappear down the street before I ran across the street to the Shell station and bought two packs of Merit cigarettes and a Bic lighter.

The next morning I was up early, telling myself, *You don't have to do this—don't be stupid! Call Dr. Laney. Be honest; show him you've been listening.* I left the home around 8:30 a.m., even though my appointment with Laney wasn't until 10:00 a.m. I walked to the wooden bench in front of the Grove Street Cemetery, right across from the Yale Law School. It was sunny, a little cool, and I quickly tore open the cigarettes, lit one up, and plunged it into my forearm. "Take that, you silly fuck," I said out loud when the first butt singed my skin. "You knew this ride was over, but you did it anyway—you are one odd duck." Then I jammed the rest of them onto my arm one by one, my teeth clenched.

I felt oddly sentimental as I watched the students hustling through their day fifty yards away. I wanted to shout at them, to tell them to enjoy their youth. *Celebrate it, people. Don't worry about the freaking grades so much—have a life, for God's sake!* When I finished, I walked across the street to the university and threw the cigarette wrappers in the trash. I took the cherry-red Bic lighter and carefully balanced it on a stone wall. A freebie for a smoker, I guess.

Then I walked toward Dr. Laney's office, feeling loose. He didn't say much when I showed him my arm at the office.

He called the ambulance, shook his head, and said, "You'll

have to wait until you're discharged now to prove you mean business." He was angry, and I was ashamed, embarrassed, but I was certain that my life as an ashtray had ceased.

We waited together in his office for the EMTs. When they arrived, the technicians joked about the Red Sox while quickly dabbing Bacitracin on me. They walked me out through the hallway. People stared, and then glanced away, ducked back into their offices. I wanted to explain that I wasn't really a mess, that this wasn't me. But they'd turned back to their lives, and soon I climbed into the ambulance. A couple embraced inside a café across the street. The girl's breasts strained against her ivory sweater, and the man laughed. They turned and looked my way.

The technician strapping me into the stretcher asked, "You having a tough time, pal?"

"I've been a lot worse," I said.

Then, with the sirens off, we rode to the ER. I studied the streets of New Haven from the stretcher. The burns weren't that serious, so I felt some naïve, bizarre confidence. During that brief chat with Laney and on the ambulance ride, I grasped some basic facts: I'd crisscrossed the country from hospitals to group homes and back for a solid chunk of time. While my peers were having careers and starting families and having lots of sex, I drooled, bled, and fidgeted in plastic pastel chairs reciting to psychiatric interns the crucial differences between healthy anger and aggressiveness.

I had been zapped with electricity and morphed into an overmedicated, obese man. I had watched from nearly unbreakable locked windows as one season twirled, groaned, and shifted into the next. I was tested, analyzed, and probed and yet I emerged only with some basic wisdom about myself: I needed people in my life and people needed me as well. I couldn't pretend I wasn't part of the human race, couldn't hover on the periphery and make sardonic one-liners. I was needed—I had to participate. And, more important—this time I wanted it. Badly.

The ambulance slipped down the almost deserted Grove Street. I looked out the oblong windows in back and watched a stumbling woman holding a crumpled brown bag of whiskey or beer hanging around the entrance to the cemetery. I suppose what she held in her hand doesn't really matter. She had a significant potbelly and a smile on her face and if I wasn't hallucinating, she was waving at me inside the ambulance as we passed. Drunk off her ass with the late morning light shining on her, she had no specific reason to smile. But she did, and I appreciated that.

I STAYED FOR JUST THREE DAYS AT ST. RAPHAEL'S—MY SHORTEST time there. When I was discharged, I told the staff I was finished with cutting and burning and the melodrama—forever. I was done with smeared blood and shit. They wished me luck, yet I could tell they'd heard this before—I was just another gentle, obese, chronically ill fellow with positive intentions.

I headed back to the group home with a new determination, a new grit. Not long after, Dr. Laney said, "When I met you in 1998, your mind was essentially . . . my choice of term would be 'shredded.' Like confetti. But now I think you've got a really good shot—if you push yourself, we can go places."

"How far can we go?" I said, and he smiled.

"We'll see, buddy," he said. "But you can go places."

He told me that my *thaw* had begun, that things—some good—would bubble over. He said it might be uncomfortable for a while, and that I should prepare myself to have some awkward, strong, and difficult emotions rise up and spill. A few months after returning from the hospital, I meet Laura at our café across the street for our weekly chat.

We sat down among the collection of daffodils and tulips and the bright melons and lemons and we drank decaf tea. Laura told me how she was doing but then she noticed my wet eyes and said, "You're looking better," and then, "Are you okay? You're shaking, David." That's when I began to weep for I don't know how long. It felt like an hour or two days or a week. I wasn't sure where it kicked off, but I couldn't stop when it got rolling.

"That's right," Laura said and held my hand as customers stared at me. I'd always been the one who wouldn't weep, who wouldn't do it. Not with Dr. Laney, not with anyone except Dr. Collander back in 1991. And that was just once—nearly fifteen years ago.

I covered my eyes, shielding them from Laura, fearful that the customers might mock or grow sick from my emotive display. I'd believed for way too long that I was a lonely, melodramatic, impotent clown who couldn't defend himself, who couldn't ask for life or hope or something as tacky or tasteless as assistance. Accepting a hand was right up there with uselessness. Asking for help was revealing your cards—it was immoral, desperate, extremely gauche and displayed grand, significant weakness.

But then another voice piped up—was it God, Vince Lombardi, my mother, Dolores Price, Franny Glass, Robert Cormier, or James Taylor, maybe? Or, my fucking goodness gracious, was it me? Was it David, my own voice, defending myself for the first time in years? *I can do this stuff well—I can cry, laugh, sing, sprint, dream, fly, love, flip, hope, skip, dive, fuck, swim, leap, help, shine, color, soar, dance, fight, and write, write, write my life down until it's cohesive, powerful, and unstoppable.* I hesitated, looked at Laura and thought, *Can I truly do life over at forty? Am I capable of joining society, the real world, the deep-ended ocean, as a middle-aged man? Do folks really start this late in the game and find friends, love, a life, or a career? Can I swim with the sharks like Dr. Laney suggested—can I do that?* I pondered the questions as my tears flowed.

The positive spark, the intense epiphany, was majestic, scrumptious, and overpowering, and it lifted me and deposited me into the rays of sunshine in the *Family Circus* comic strip I used to read as a boy. I felt released, flighty, silly, freaking alive, and yet still, still, I cried. I reached down to my sneakers and tried to pull myself together for Laura, but I couldn't. Not yet. There were more tears, snots, and thoughts rushing down to my cheeks, just pouring off me. My brain sped on, up, and out came the thick, heinous blackness. It hurled from me like fumes.

Then I saw the friendly, grinning faces of the tragic girls in every hospital ward I'd ever stayed in, particularly the ones who had helped and prodded me along the way with their lightness, scars, and secrets. Shine, Page, Lillian, Holly, Maddy. Oh, I'm so goddamned sorry, Maddy! The cutters, burners, depressives, bulimics, alcoholics, schizophrenics, the emaciated and drooling mugs of the Foundation, the happy souls with their quirks, psychosis, resilience, and wonderful kindnesses. I saw their non sequiturs, their obsessions, their dreams and their strengths, their warmth. Their unstoppable lives—maybe some would be stuck and sick forever but the decency, the power in each heart was untapped, waiting for someone, anyone, to ask how their life was going. Why doesn't anybody ask them that?

Faces shimmied through my mind's eye. I saw the somber, strict nurses and the helpful, funny ones; the psych technicians who shared pizza with me, who instilled self-respect; I saw the friends, I saw Tony, Gregory, Bill, Grant, and Benjamin. I saw hurting patients who died or nearly evaporated from depression's inertia; those that remain ill today, tomorrow, and forever. I saw them all.

I saw a lineup of doctors who'd helped rescue me from a life as the ultimate *professional*. I spotted Grinder, Shelly, Laney, Krav, and good old Dr. Collander. Even the Freudian gangster himself. I even saw the bloody nights in too many ERs; the blades at Rite-Aid after Rite-Aid; the scabs and the stitches, the Bacitracin and the burns.

But also . . . also, I cried over my parents' embraces, believing in second, fourth, and thirty-seventh chances after my constant failures and screw-ups. Christ, did they give love and never quit! I watched my giggling sisters, brothers, each of them—Laura, Julie, Dennis, and Andy. Oh, my brother Andy and his rigidity, the sapped-out and tapped-out energy that relationship sucked from both of our worlds. I saw Julie on her first day of kindergarten in that yellow coat, then onstage in Manhattan; Dennis smiling and strutting with the gold medals jangling around him. I hear Laura's full-throated, full-throttled laughter, her strength. Three times over.

I saw life, so fat-filled and freaking terrific for a while. I saw snow days in middle school; the white-foamed oceans of my youth; girls in their bouncing bikinis at Bay View Beach, their taut calves and tight bellies. I saw Molly giggling, waving from her blanket on shore with her Coppertone; I saw Emily jogging, tan, thin, and long. And my God, how about the wonderful music, the lifesaving, swinging, bebopping, rockabilly, disco-thumping, house, folk, jazz, and the rest that got me through. I saw Circuit Avenue and the Vineyard summer of silliness, of Huck, smiles, chambermaids, and the stupid, asinine, spastic, riotous shaking and dancing. *"Don't give up, you're not the only one . . ."* I saw the whole deal as I wept. I witnessed every goddamned, motherfucking, screaming horrific joyful hateful ecstatic minute.

I stopped finally, thoroughly spent, and asked Laura: "Where did my life go, sister?" and "Why couldn't I stop years ago and why did I waste so much time?"

"Because you were very, very ill and scared, David," she said, her cheeks wet. "And now you're melting in the most moving way."

"It's embarrassing," I stammered, wiping my eyes and blowing my nose with a tissue. "It feels so good, but I'm so obvious in everything I do, you know? Cutting, burning—stupid literal actions." I held her hand. "But you, you've suffered greatly with cancer, a true disease."

"Oh, stop it," she said, laughing desperately. "Let's not have a battle of the diseases, here. It's just about over, David," she said. "Imagine how wonderful that statement is. How weighty, refreshing, and succinct. The long and ugly ride of depression . . . is . . . almost . . . over."

Ten minutes later, as we finished up and threw away the numerous tissues, the night air hit my face and I felt relieved, lighter. Laura and I bundled up, and I walked her to her car beside the bank. I stood beside her red Mazda 6, thanked and embraced her, and watched her drive away. And then I immediately knew the feeling around me, in me. I could name it. It was a bracing and brilliant type of clarity. The veil, the damp, gauzy veil that had separated me from the rest of the world forever was disappearing. I could feel and see parts of it still hanging around the fringe—but it was leaving. It was going away.

Two days later, I sat at a diner in New Haven with my mother on a frosty but sunshine-filled afternoon, my thaw in full tilt. Weeping was the new mode of communication after my long drought—each day was a mea culpa with rotating family members. I had already cried my eyes out with my sister in a café, with my father at a restaurant, with Dennis and Julie, and now I sat with my dear mother, more loyal to me than anyone in the world. The red vinyl booths made farting noises as I adjusted my substantial body and reached out for her long fingers across the table. I wept again, apologizing for the truculence of the illness, my sedated, zombie-like state for the decades. The other customers stared for a while but then turned back to their pea soups and sandwiches.

My mom patted my hand gently. "I won't hear of it, David," she said. "Don't you understand? You were my beloved, a happy child—my favorite."

"Didn't you ever give up hope?" I said. "Why did it take aeons?"

"David," she said, smiling as her eyes became wet. "We sensed it many months ago, do you remember? Do you recall the afternoon when you mentioned hope at the cafe? But even before that, sweetie, before that, there were signs. I knew you'd return."

As I strolled up Elm Street several months later and passed a women's center and some posters for a few parties, I saw that many of the Yale students were carrying graduation gowns and hats. A Yale University commencement was something I used to dread—the promise, the youth, and the incredible folks rolling into town.

Years rolled through, whole troops of classes would get their diplomas and leave for Manhattan, Minneapolis, Cairo, Bangladesh, and Osaka—anywhere. I combated the feelings of worth-lessness by writing—it was an old friend I'd kept at bay. I had been journaling through the years, most days actually. But the desire for more of a flow to shape into stories called out to me so strongly that I escaped to my desk and wrote dispatches from the battlefield inside and outside that house. As I captured my life on an old word processor, I found that compared to my old sloppy, mad journals, the new writing was more coherent, more structured.

I covered the blood and guts, of course, but I also wrote about people who left the Foundation and did okay in the world. Folks like the schizophrenic woman who didn't speak for a year and a half, and then started working and living in the community as a fund-raising volunteer for the Red Cross; the alcoholic-depressive who sobered up and worked at a soup kitchen and lived across town; the obsessive who works as an electrician on the shoreline and will marry soon.

Even the cute eighteen-year-old girl who lived at the group home for ten months and then went on to graduate from college and start her career in marketing in Boston. Each of them was an independent, proud, and very capable person. Hopeful, possible images suddenly sprang up—no flickering, frilly angels or any-thing. I just found myself more open to writing about the streak of orange in a little girl's sweater or the Yale parking lot across the street and how sometimes on Sunday nights in December after a storm everything became exquisitely silent, still and sheathed in white. I never would have thought of describing a city parking lot as beautiful, but that's what I began to see.

◆

ONE DAY, I RETURNED FROM THE GYM AND TOOK IN THE BRIGHT, pulsing scene of New Haven. I went by an auditorium, a preppy clothing store, a fruit stand, a convenience store. At one time the area was sketchy and a bit run-down, but Yale had invested a great deal of money there, and it became thriving and alive.

There was a large Episcopal church with a rainbow sign that read "Soup Kitchen," and an outdoor café bustled with customers sitting under a bright purple awning. They were young, old, homeless, happy, sick, sad, rich, poor, brave, cowardly, healthy, barely alive, and scared. They were talking, texting, bitching, and smiling all at once. This scene used to depress the hell out of me and keep me inside for weeks. It used to come close to wiping me out, actually. But that day I felt like there was perhaps . . . possibility.

I went inside and volunteered to work at the soup kitchen. That's where I met Alice Mattison, a gifted writer who later taught a fiction course I took in Provincetown. I then found a job counseling peers at the Connecticut Mental Health Center. I began to shave alone for the first time in thirteen years, without a staff person observing. Taking the blade and using it the way it was intended felt, at first, lascivious, a panicked thrill. It was like I was betraying so many old acquaintances. It took a while for everything to turn, but things do take me a while. A year and a half after burning myself on Halloween, I started looking for apartments.

Nothing was easy or complete at that point: seventeen years of destroying selfhood, and my body wasn't going to say goodbye without a fight. Many nights I felt a feverish rush like some staph infection out of control. At those times, I called my family, left messages for Dr. Laney, and wrote in my journals, "There is no blackness inside—there never was. You were sick, it was the sickness." I pressed my pen down so hard, so intently that it often tore the pages. But I kept writing. I was filled with the same drive that I'd once used to destroy myself, and the closeness of those two feelings really scared me. Where once there was a rush of destruction and mayhem, now there was creativity and passion for life.

Initially, I steered clear of shaving aisles in pharmacies. And when I saw someone's razor sitting on a bureau or bathroom sink, I had to exit the room. I didn't want to give my mind the chance of pondering *possibilities*. To this day, I still don't like to be near box cutters. So open, cocky, and taunting. The stuff may be gone from me forever, but still it haunts.

I can still see the tears and hear my parents'g screams that evening at the Institute. The way their bleary eyes studied me when I was rolled out of the trauma room in a wheelchair, oozing and newly sutured. At the time, I thought that trauma affected only young people. That when people grew to be fifty-five or sixty years old, they became tougher, maybe even impenetrable. Silly, right?

I was twenty-four years old, but so insipid and naïve. I know that isn't earth shattering—most everyone is naïve when they're young. When you're not looking, events and disease sweep right through you. They obliterate folks, and before they know it, they're trying to eat parts of their ear in a darkened corner of a group home. I know my decades of drama and illness will linger in my family's minds forever, and the worst part is that it came completely and directly from me.

Sometimes depression and minor mania still get the best of me, and I feel beaten every now and again. Underneath my significant medication and great support, I'm still a bipolar fellow with a disease, but things are so much easier. And, thank God,

I know the buoyancy will return. That night with Laura in the café was the moment when the gauzy stubborn veil finally broke apart. And, after a few months, it disappeared completely. The terror is finally gone. That's the greatest thing about my own experience. I don't want to generalize and step on anyone's toes. I don't want to paint too rosy a picture for mentally ill folks of the world or say something totally unrealistic like the crazies just have to get up and *try* a little harder. But for me, the broken pieces came back together.

It took many years and hard work, but they mend and strengthen in new and important ways. The pieces jell, bond, and jump up and down and feel ten years old again when spring kicks in. They saunter into kitchens and kiss their future wives, they listen to music, and they go to movies with their younger brother named Dennis. They shave in the mornings without a care, and then they dump the used razors in the trash. They walk into an office and sit at a computer and write true tales about a guy surrounded by his family and how sometimes people return from several kinds of death in a pretty fucking incredible way.

EPILOGUE

FIRST NIGHT OUT

I DIDN'T SLEEP MUCH ON THE FIRST NIGHT I MOVED OUT OF THE Foundation. I sat on my bed in my apartment on Orange Street and experienced real live fear. It was eerily quiet; there was no cackling and no banging and no one screaming about the dark bastards crawling around in someone's skull. All I heard were a few slamming doors, flushing toilets, dinging elevators, and jangling keys in the hallway. At 2:15 a.m., I heard my pretty and exuberantly loud wheelchair-bound neighbor having very vociferous and rambunctious sex. The sounds shocked and aroused me—like a shooting blast of cold air after an eternity of smog and humidity. I got out of bed and ran over to my front door and looked through the peephole.

I couldn't see any monsters lurking in the hallway—nothing to be afraid of. I listened to the mating down the hall, my ear pressed tightly against the door. It was the echoing of a young woman living with all the passion she had. I admired that. *I wanted that.* It went on for a good fifteen minutes and afterward I walked over to the television and watched a PBS special with Bill Moyers. At the group home, the television was always showing Yankee baseball reruns or *Titanic.* I never got to watch what I wanted. But now it was 2:46 a.m. on Sunday, August 11, 2007, and my life was entirely mine.

And that was the moment when I felt the remains of the gauze drop away completely and utterly. I was sitting on my uncomfortable wicker couch that night while Bill Moyers discussed crucial things and realized I was free. I closed my eyes and reached up into the air and ripped the remnants down around me. I stood and kicked the air, punched it. I probably didn't *have* to do that, but I'm a dramatic guy, and I was moved and excited. It was early, early morning so I couldn't yell, but my eyes grew wet. *It's gone,* I thought. *The veil is utterly gone.*

Suddenly, I saw my friend and basketball captain from high school chatting with Bill Moyers. Eric had on a blue blazer and cool shirt and snazzy socks and the caption below his face said he was a columnist for Salon.com. His hair was gray-white. I listened to his impressive answers, grabbed a bowl of Honeycomb cereal and said, "Way to go, Eric—you tell 'em!"

When I moved to 66 Orange Street and the veil lifted, everything in my life felt like it needed an exclamation point. I lived as keenly as possible, appreciating the bouncing bosom of a passing lady or the gratitude of a Chapel Street shopkeeper on a Saturday morning in November. Every moment was raw, alive, and succulent. I noticed the salt-and-pepper stubble on a homeless man outside a diner, the cratered texture of cranberry bread at a bakery, the hot pulse of a morning shower, and the wispy thrill of dogwoods in a New Haven park. There were no more brick walls keeping me away from life. The lady down the hall continued her noises every now and again. Being a bachelor who'd been out of the sexual game for years, I welcomed any invitations into that world. Any at all.

DR. LANEY TOLD ME TO JOIN AN INFORMAL WRITING GROUP, TO SIT in a café and think not about how far away people were, but to realize that I was an active, tangible life that added something to the planet. That I could bring responses from people that involved friendship, sex, love, laughter, and intellectual and casual conversation. I learned my physical breath was more than a check mark on a census list; my life represented potential, acts, discoveries, and, eventually, accomplishments. There was no room for nostalgic thoughts of self-injury—no twenty-foot razors and close-ups of tainted, yellow teeth and angry, ranting lips. When those images started now, I could pull down the screen in my mind and shut them off.

Laney and I kept it basic: deep breathing, visual imagery of positive things, working out, and going for walks. Volunteering at the soup kitchen. By reading aloud to him, I had also started to read again for pleasure just before I moved out of the group home—it was as if my pilot light clicked on. I went back to Kate Chopin, Hemingway, Fitzgerald, Updike, and Cheever and added new names: Joy Williams, David Gates, Mary Gaitskill, Harold Brodkey, Alice Mattison, Denis Johnson, and Wally Lamb. It was the sweetest love, the richest taste in the world to have that back for me, to have the hunger again. I also stopped writing about blood. Instead, I wrote positive hopes, goals—I examined my fears and nightmares but without harping. That was a basic rule in our therapy.

Don't harp on the heinous and always be honest to yourself and others.

I embraced writing as Wally Lamb had suggested back in 1992. I wondered if I could write a structured, lengthy story. I thought, what if I put my inner camera down for a while and sat down in a café with a notebook and pen, and wrote good, important tales? Let them pour right from my gut onto the page. I could concentrate on the essential, the real-life stuff, the true, the buried, and the obvious.

What would happen if I wrote down everything that had occurred in a coherent narrative? What if I captured the good and the bad—the people, the botched decisions, the wounded spirits, the wasted months and years? Everything. My simple, confusing, nasty, sickening, beautiful, gory, luscious story. And what if I was able to bring in the others, the mentally ill voices who don't ever get to speak, to shout and be heard? Who don't have the resources that I had, or the family support, or the luck.

I wondered if I could assist others in some tiny way by what I write today. Could I show them how it's been done by someone who felt lower than gnat shit and still returned to the living?

Could it . . . help?

The thought stopped me cold. Maybe I could help.

Cool, I thought. *Cool.*

GREGORY

I still see Gregory once a week at the Kasbah Café, and sometimes I use ridiculously goofy confidence builders that sound desperate now that I'm out of the home and he's still there. ("You're unstoppable and unflappable.") Rather Pollyannaish material that I'd never have accepted when I was sick. But I can't seem to help it, and once you're healthy, you'll say anything to see a person you love emerge from the storm. You're considered sick, then you step through an old green pine door with your suitcase, and suddenly you're considered well. Then, when you turn back to look through the doorway at your sick colleagues, they seem farther away, almost untouchable. Diminished somewhat.

That's what it's like now for me with Gregory.

But I'm confident he'll get himself out one of these days. Maybe move into a new home with his wife. Find a comfortable spot where they can go and hold each other, watching silly shows on television.

SHINE

I tried to find Shine when I first left the institutions and discovered she had died of cancer a few years earlier. When I first got out of the Institute and was living at home in 1992–93, I talked to her frequently, sometimes two or three times a week. I learned she had a plump black cat named Crispy-Crunchy that perched in her grandma's rocking chair near the window. She regularly phoned into a popular radio station and told them her true name was "The Shining Beacon." She spun these grand tales, waxing on about her hordes of boyfriends and romantic escapades to Paris and Milan.

I'd be driving up for therapy with Dr. Collander and I'd hear the disc jockey say something like "Next up we'll talk with The Shining Beacon and catch up on her dalliances." I thought she was the coolest thing in the world. And so gentle—a fragile, melting snowflake that could crumble or disintegrate at any moment. One time I visited her outside of the hospital—she was staying with her mother, and we sat on a rose-colored couch and watched an episode of the *Smurfs* while she told me how boring her life had become.

I ordered her a few funky, expensive hats from J. Peterman and sent them to her apartment in Wallingford. There were fedoras, dusters, and some goofy, over-the-top things you see women wear at the Kentucky Derby. We went to the mall once and she strolled past the shops looking like an emaciated scarecrow with her lace and black leggings and one of my extravagant hats with a dangling rose ribbon. I waddled beside her, still pretty fat. Sometimes teen girls snickered and said things like, "Look at that ridiculous couple—the whale and the wicked witch."

Shine responded with a cackle. "Watch yourselves, wenches," she warned. "Adolescence will crush you, too, my awkward, ugly ones!"

She adored her grandmother, and we once had tea and scones at her Formica kitchen table in Wallingford. I brought Lorna Doones (a favorite snack that my grandmother served to me and my mother and sisters when I was a kid). Later, Shine and I talked shop, about blood, suicide, and death, and finally we came to the conclusion that we didn't really know much of anything. At one point I remember her saying we were too young to think we understood certainties about life. That may sound too easy or simplistic but really, coming from a very troubled young woman, it was an affirmation for me. It's a bit of wisdom that I've stored on the back shelf of my brain ever since. *We know so little—don't make any rash decisions just yet.* She gave me a lasting hope with that nugget.

According to her obituary, bladder cancer got her in the end, and she spent her last years near Boston. Dr. Collander told me just before I left him in 1998 that he heard Shine was spilling from one problem into the next. He described her as having an addictive personality. He said she had started using heroin and was not a person I should be in contact with. "I know it's difficult," he said. "But she may be beyond help and perhaps she would drag you down."

I regret terribly that I didn't help her, didn't ever telephone her. I was halfway across the country for part of those days in Kansas, and when I returned, I landed in Vermont. I guess I probably loved her at the time and was confused about it. After that brief moment of fooling around on the grounds way back when, we both cooled it off and decided to keep it platonic. My appetites were so minimal in those days anyway. I guess we thought it would be best if we just stayed friends. She was a hell of a buddy, I'll tell you that. Quite a gem.

I still miss her like nuts.

I miss each of the hospital girls terribly, the lovely messiness of their troubled faces and funky smiles. Every one of them had obvious and significantly cracked parts, but they allowed a confused fat guy from Connecticut to borrow their grins, jokes, hope, and CD players, and use them to build me up when I was feeling sunken and near dead. They helped me dance when I was so disgusted that I couldn't glance in a mirror without spitting, without giving myself the finger. Their laughter, fears, tears, and touches patched me up better than any nylon sutures ever could. I think that each of my slow improvements was made with those women beside me, inside me. They are the women of David's recuperation; from the crazy-sad ones at the homes and hospitals to my own sisters and mother to female nurses and doctors around the country. They are forever like waking dreams of exuberant flora to me: sometimes in disarray, other times beautifully formed and languishing in the light.

Dr. Presley

Dr. Presley died several years ago—he had a heart attack. I imagined that it probably occurred when he was having sex with twenty-two-year-old triplets, but that's just my own fantasy. I felt truly sad when I heard about it. For all his Freudian digging and assaulting, he loved his patients. Was he unorthodox? A little twisted? Definitely, *but* he was a very warm soul. I saw him a few times in his spotless red Mercedes, snaking through the hospital grounds, taking patients over to his office. This was just before I left Dr. Collander back in 1998. Someone once told me that Presley shuffled *Hustler* magazines to his male clients. I know that's weird and screwed, but if you're a male between sixteen and twenty years old, it probably seemed like the most brilliant therapy in the world. A master plan, if you will.

Dr. Collander

I still send a Christmas card to Dr. Collander every year, and I met with him about two years ago when I told him I was writing a book. Some people have said he'll be disappointed in how he's portrayed and say I don't give him the highest marks, but I'd disagree. I think we both share responsibility for things not working out, but there's only so much a doctor can do to help a patient. For whatever reason, conscious or unconscious, I resisted and re-sisted—I don't see that as a doctor's fault. I know one truth—Dr. C's voice, skill, and guidance gave me shelter and direction when I was utterly and spectacularly rudderless. He saved my life several times. We're human—him, me. Especially me.

WISE MAN WALKING

Dr. Laney recently said, "I think you're learning there are no great secrets in this life. You just take it a step, a day, at a time. You don't eat too much every day, you exercise, you build friendships with girls and guys, and you work and try to be self-sufficient. In between that, if you feel so moved, you write stories that have meaning."

I was overwhelmed with gratitude that day and overcome by how much he helped transform me, saved me from the harsh gray-blackness of the ugly, mad disease. He nodded as tears ran down my face. "It was the both of us, brother—you and me," he said.

Nowadays I'm still on a lot of medication and I see him once every two weeks. He frequently reminds me how far we've trav-eled. "If you build yourself up, good things will come," he used to say. That was his mantra: build the body, the mind, the spirit. Exercise, go to movies, to plays. Even give a church or two a chance. Read and write as much as possible, stop verbally muti-lating yourself for every mistake. Reread the classics. Catch an opera once a decade at Lincoln Center or go figure skating at

Rockefeller Center. And then a hopeful life will come, though maybe not in a flash of light with a drumroll and doves soaring.

But it'll come.

I GOT A SWEET CHRISTMAS CARD A FEW YEARS BACK FROM EMILY, that semiperfect girl who once broke me in two. I had forgiven both her and me long ago for being so young, silly, and naïve, for falling out of love. For being . . . regular humans. For being normal and abnormal. She's gone on to a successful career, marriage, children—I'm pleased for her. She's done well, flourished. Maybe I'll run into her at some bookstore down the road, and we can have some decaf tea.

Then there's summer lover Molly, who has been a faithful writer to me; each October and Christmas I get a kind card. Or I call her on her birthday. She has five children now. It's incredible and curious, how lives fray and fall away and then move together much later. She's had awful challenges and has emerged as pretty and strong as ever. I saw her several summers back when she came over with her three-year-old son at the Cape. I gave her a polished stone that said HOPE. She laughed, and said, "Good Lord, you're finally rising back into the world." What a smile she had that afternoon.

OLD BLUE EYES

If I had to choose just one family member to write about, to represent my whole family and how important they all are to me, I think Dennis is the best choice. Dennis lived right down the street from me for almost two years on Orange Street after I got out of the group home. He remains the most even-keeled fellow I've ever met in my life, always offering me support in his own unique way. He still works at keeping my father's dealership clean and tidy, and when I asked him last Christmas Eve how he retained such a placid mood throughout life, he stroked his chin.

"Well, I'll tell you what I know now, okay?" he said as I drove him out to my folks' house in Guilford. "You have to concentrate on things in front of you, okay? Some of the things we take for granted can be taken from us." He gestured like a preacher in the passenger seat, his hands bumping against the dash. "I'm extremely comfortable in my skin as a Williams syndrome person." Then he blessed himself and spoke loudly. "I believe in God," he said, "and I think he helps all us Williams people by giving us a music gene and we can dance nasty and to the beat when we get together at the yearly conventions."

I asked Dennis for a few more thoughts. We listened to the radio, one of his passions. I took Route One because of the traffic on the Q Bridge, and we slipped beneath it quietly. There were barbed wire fences surrounding the gargantuan Getty, Exxon, and Hess oil tanks. Intimidating, hulking things covered in winter light. There was a lone plum cottage, maybe the harbormaster's, resting on the edge of the frozen Sound, dwarfed by the ships. Off to the side were some beat-up pickup trucks with flat tires. The cottage was odd-looking, out of place. Like something beautiful placed next to the beasts, the drudgery and the ideal.

There was a dive bar with an orange neon sign that blinked, "We Sell the Coldest Beer in the Nation" and a few used-car outfits caked in snow. In the twilight of that evening, everything seemed so alive, fresh, and artful; every tree, condo, spare tire, or crushed Diet 7UP seemed ready for a close-up. I wanted to take a bunch of snapshots and save them for later and write about them, tell their stories. Not the old, twisted, ghosted, and distanced paparazzi shots in my head, but real, true images of what lay before me.

I saw an abandoned, crumbling building with fractured glass and a big "No Trespassing" sign. Click. Dirty snow with ground-up cigars and black ashes with one curly yellow ribbon twisting out of it. Click. A middle-aged woman putting her dress on in a dimly lit condo in East Haven as she watched TV. Click. The stores looking brilliant and hungry for dollars— huge, eighty- to one-hundred-foot signs stretching into the night sky advertising Casual Male XL, Home Goods, CVS, McDermott Chevrolet, Wendy's, Chili's, Shell gas, China Buffet. The hungry, gnawing capitalism at work that had seemed so garish and frightening to me two decades ago when I had my first breakdown. Just then the stuff looked nearly harmless, a simple fact, like someone's neon dreams in motion. It's not like I had been transformed into Ayn Rand or anything, but I appreciated the colors, the dreams involved.

When we merged back onto I-95 beyond East Haven, most of the bright lights had been left in our wake, so I asked Dennis to tell me about his favorite moments in life.

"Oh, there have been many," he said. "When Laura married Paul, when Andy married Mary, when Julie got married to Rajiv, when you left the damn hospitals for good, when Laura didn't have any more cancer, and I'd have to say each of the Special Olympic medals I've won."

"Yes, sir."

"Fucking A," he said, and I laughed. "That's right," he continued. "I won every freaking event I've ever entered. I'm a champion."

"Well," I corrected him, "maybe not every event—but a good portion of them."

"Details, David. Minor details," Dennis laughed and then we were both quiet in the rushing darkness as we flew down the highway, listening to some new pop song on the radio. I looked over at Dennis, and he was mouthing the words, always moving forward. A steady rhythm.

Rocking.

AMY

When I made the final leap away from institutional life, I landed just beyond my anguished, psychically devoured peers and discovered a sweet, sexy girl with blue-gray eyes, Batman Band-Aids, and a sizable sunflower pin at a Bridgeport zoo. She was waiting for me beside the Amur tigers' cages, and for seven delightful hours we strolled, admiring bison, meercats, and aggressive turquoise peacocks. This was April 2009, and in the following weeks and months, Amy made me feel *present, alive,* for the first time in decades.

It had been a year and a half since I left the group home. She was doing a bit of late-blooming herself, having just lost seventy-five pounds over nine months. She was brand new to the world in a way, not dissimilar to me. She was a graphic designer in Hartford with a great job and a streak of stubborn charm, a creative and witty red-blond beauty who loves to photograph flowers. She had gone on e-Harmony after many misgivings, and I had been on the dating site for four months and was ready to give up. The women I had gone out with were mediocre and distant, and they kept their hearts to themselves, wouldn't reveal much of anything.

Amy and I had first connected via e-mail, and she didn't want to talk on the phone; so in an odd way, it was an old-fashioned/ newfangled romance. We wrote twice a day. I got up early and stayed up late to check for messages. Amy snuck to an Internet café at lunch to look for my notes and wrote me back. She admitted later to spending hours on each e-mail, making sure she answered every question and responded to every thought with just the right touch of not-too-witty charm. I was still getting comfortable with computers, so the site timed out on me a few times after I had written several novellas. Eventually Amy explained the whole copy and paste angle of Word that I hadn't grasped at the local community college. We were like kids with long-distance romantic pen pals. After the first week of e-mails Amy suggested the tiger cage at the Beardsley Zoo as the perfect meeting spot, but we couldn't meet until the following week.

I begged her to phone me, but she stood fast, saying she wanted the first time she heard my voice to be in person and not tainted by a crappy cell phone. At the zoo, we sat down together on a bench beside a few peacocks and ate tuna sandwiches so we wouldn't have to worry about our breath. Then, after kissing me some, and running her hand up my arms, she asked a question that appeared so simple but held the weight of the world.

"What's this?" she said, pointing to the scars.

"I used to cut myself," I said.

Then she asked if I did it anymore, and I said no. After a more thorough reviewing process a few days later (she consulted with a shrink to find out just how fucked a fellow I was), we were on our way. She later said what helped her believe in me was her own triumph over dark times in her past. And that a person's history doesn't always define his future.

How do you argue with a girl like that?

Our courtship was like revisiting parts of my adulthood that I never got to live: we made love everywhere, played laser tag with pissed-off ten-year-old boys, and saw violent movies—she adores explosions, sci-fi, and comic-book flicks. We studied a few waterfalls, left our prints on the ribbed sand flats at low tide on the Cape, and mused about our future together, along with a few admissions: hidden scars, vices, fears, slights and hurts. I even took to calling her Sunny, my dream girl.

Four and a half months later, I led Amy blindfolded up the Scargo Tower on Cape Cod. Dennis and Laura had decorated the inner winding staircase of it with sunflowers and hydrangeas and left Champagne on ice at the top. I hit my knee up there and gave her an opal ring (she hates diamonds!) and she agreed.

We set the date for Halloween 2011.

Amy and I moved in together two years ago in a cluster of apartments and condos just off the interstate in Middletown. It was a real challenge at first to share a space with another person again—the first time I'd done it since the group home. I had adored my seventeen months alone on Orange Street, and I bristled initially with the adjustment. But I grew to savor Amy beside me, a new family, a lover, a friend for life. A person who needed me to be strong—a concept that was unfamiliar to me after years of being the sick one.

I was dismayed at first to hear the constant hum of traffic on I-91 from our apartment's front door. But I learned to enjoy the sound, the droning, busy-bee-ness of it. Today I savor the just-another-guy-and-girl feeling of our lives. Surrounded by seminormal people with doubts, desires, and real fire, passion. Folks who cook, love, screech, drink, kick their walls, and weep just like everybody else. People not so different from those I met in Kansas, Chicago, Vermont, and New Haven. Faces that are empty and bereft at times but filled with the desire to push on. Continue the quest. Or at least get up and try again. When I hear the highway outside, I hear the pulse of our own lives keeping time with the worlds. I'm no longer a caged bystander cursing from a window with his collection of rage, stitches, Bacitracin, and Thorazine, but a participant. Someone with a new, pretty girl, a dreamer who believes in me.

Imagine that.

For our first Christmas together she made a poster of a quote that, though a little cheesy, helped me greatly at the old zoo, the first zoo, the group home in New Haven. It's attributed to Mary Anne Radmacher. I used to read it each day before I headed out to see Dr. Laney. It now sits above the guest bed in my office.

Courage does not always roar, sometimes it's the quiet voice at the end of the day saying, "I will try again tomorrow."

MFA

In late May I visited Enders Island off Mystic, Connecticut, the place of my high school retreats thirty years ago, and showed it to Amy. It became home base again for me, the spot where for two years I studied with twenty-seven other students, wonderful poets and writers, from Fairfield University. We received our MFA degrees in January 2011.

When Amy and I were there in May, there were daffodils and tulips lining the walkways. We'd come to Mystic to check out wedding locations—there were a few places on the water that looked promising, rustic inns with their cool wraparound porches. The big chapel on Enders Island has the infamous arm and fingers of one St. Edmund sitting in enclosed glass, but to the right of it is a singular four-foot sculpture three feet off the ground: a carved Virgin with one arm raised toward the sky and one hand resting on her heart as she hovers on cottony clouds. She impressed me, that lady. I had noticed her during a winter residency a year before and I wanted to write about her.

A decade ago I would have been enraged and lusting to smear blood over her. I would've been lost, cynical, cursing, and mourning my whole pathetic life. But then the wooden carving of the Madonna with a gown of summer-sky blue humbled me and touched me. Her auburn hair glowed, her face tilted up. Behind her, though, was where the dazzling stuff lay. Melted glass or some sort of plastic sheet hung behind her body—tiny, one- to two-inch white and red lights make the colors explode in variations of gold, red, melon, Kelly green, lavender, turquoise, pink, oatmeal, and lemon.

Its effect was one of real beauty and elegance, and it brought about in me a rush of hope. I'm not the most faith-filled guy; I'm very cynical at times. But when I saw the inspired art, the sculpture, it moved me. A type of hunger seized me. The nadir of something, a belief, rose. Where had it been—that hope, that faith—for the decades? I figured it got trapped and intimidated by the thumping tambourines of the Charlton Hestons, the Sonny and Chers that were bouncing around in my skull. I nearly drowned numerous times in my crimson fantasies, my shredded psyche taking wild punches at anything that offered a way out.

But it didn't win—I mean, *that's* the really cool, arresting, and serene part. It didn't win. I'm not saying I know who has the exact way, the true path. I only know life can get a thousand times better, and that there's brightness and hope to be soaked up in the world. If you're a fan of slogans, jingoistic catchphrases, I'd say the line for this tale is "Hang the hell in there." Stick the whole ride out, even when everything seems horrific and destroyed. People are out there who can assist, and life, a truly good life, is a real possibility. From a man who thought he was shit, came hope, love, and more.

For those still struggling with mental illness, I have no easy answers. Hang on—try to surround yourself with the best psychiatrist and therapist you can find. For those who self-injure, all I can say is that doing that doesn't get you closer to anyone. It only increases your loneliness. Stop. Ask for help. Seek out counseling. Death is no answer. Try to believe in something: a God, a song, a book, the ocean. Don't ever give up.

People get better.

AFTER A NEW YEAR'S CELEBRATION ON ENDERS ISLAND WITH THE Fairfield writers in January 2010, I made my way onto the crispy earth, right outside the main house and the dorms. The snowy ground glistened. I trampled across the frozen grass, stiff beneath my soles, and found my way to another Virgin. This one was outdoors, a glowing concrete lady with arms outstretched, protecting her sea-swept stone chapel. Floodlights at her base made her shadow appear gigantic, brilliant. It was 1:00 a.m., and the wind hooted and the grass blades crumpled and split in half as I crunched my feet down hard. My cell phone buzzed. It was Amy calling from our deck in Middletown, watching the sky.

She said she was lonely and was freezing her ass off after returning from a party. I told her I didn't sense the cold much, that I felt hyperalive, awakened. She mentioned the glowing, fat fullness above and then she whispered my name. I studied that same moon, the way the whiteness reflected and bounced crazily off the slapping, lapping black sea. I told her I wanted to taste everything, to fall on my knees and crunch the frosted grass, to eat the snow, the ice. To suck, lick, inhale, and breathe in every inch. Amy was giggling then, saying, "Good night, Mr. Hyperbole," and I felt indestructible, superb. What lay before me was a sugary sweet vision, and the precise phrase, the only prayer I could see fit to mumble was "Thank you."

OUR WEDDING WAS WONDERFUL, SIMPLE, JUST A SMALL GROUP OF friends and family at a church in the Connecticut woods. My mother officiated at the ceremony, made up of a little Anne Sexton, a little James Taylor, a few prayers from Amy and her mom. Dennis was the best man, my sisters sang, and my father read some Rilke. Then people danced, though I couldn't get Wally to do his moonwalk. Still, it was an electric night. Amy and I walked back to our rooms from the inn after everyone left and studied the stars. They looked so shiny, so alive.

My years in mental institutions are long gone, thank God. I'm only forty-six years old, and I've still got a good chunk of life to go. My time so far has been maroon, scarlet, and black, very black. But now, there's also chartreuse, indigo, and lime. Today I look at my scarred body the same way an old musician might look at his instrument. Beaten and worn, but it's a good machine. I'm a good thing. It seems funny to say it like that, a little too self-helpy, I know, a little preachy. But when you throw all the pieces together, I'm a good and whole thing.

ACKNOWLEDGMENTS

THE BIGGEST THANK-YOU IS DUE TO MY ENORMOUSLY SKILLED and kind friend/agent/wizard Richard Abate, who has a small scene in the story but is one who's been a massive factor in the making of this book (and my career). Editor Henry Ferris, in his calm, understated way, helped reshift and shape the first seventy pages, making me a lot more insightful and gifted in my prose than I actually am. Thanks for Henry's vision and cool confidence throughout. Thanks to copyeditor Georgia Maas for her expertise. Also to the impressive HarperCollins team: Tavia Kowalchuk, Sharyn Rosenblum, Stephanie Kim, Andrea Molitor, and Lindsey Meyers. For the singular cover design, thanks to artist Adam Johnson. For my incredible sisters, Julie and Laura, and my steady brother, Dennis, along with Rajiv, Paul, Charlie Ketchup, Russ, Helen, Ron, Tracey, and Aragon. For my extended family's support and love over the years. To Michael White, who believed from day one. For Mother Hastings, Aaron Perkus, and everyone else at the Fairfield University MFA program. Thanks to mentors Rachel Basch, Paul Lisicky, Amy Benson, Roya Hakakian, and Sarah Manguso. Also to a talented faculty with wise words along the way: Baron Wormser, Da Chen, Joan Wicker-sham, Joan Connor, Nalini Jones, Kim Bridgford, Eugenia Kim, Al Davis, Bill Patrick, Pete Duvall, and Larry Bloom. Thanks to gifted writers and buddies like Krista Richards Mann, Elizabeth Hilts, Christine Shaffer, Donna Woods Orazio, Ioanna Opidee, Pat O'Connor, Kelly Goodridge, and early reader Jennifer Walsh, and the whole Enders Island clan.

For help along the route, thanks to Alice and Ed Mattison, Tony Walker, Bill Parisi, Doug Yates, Jan Hunt, Sue LaVoie, Karen Bonnitz, Dianne Petrillo, Stacia, Jim, Jerry, Brooke Crum, Judy, Joy Powell, Susan Amster, Leslie Hymen, Melissa Kahn, Gabrielle Danchick, Lynn Haney, Brian Francis Slattery, Bennet Lovett-Graf, Mark Oppenheimer, Peter Novotny, Karen Conterio, Wendy Lader, Phyllis Hare, Edgar, Terry and John, Joseph Rutlin, Thomas Anthony Landino, Richard Kravitz, Chris Mosunic, Jim Shanley, Joe Moore, Jay and Taffy Bowes and Eric Boehlert, Tim Devaney, and Kevin Healy. For Marguerite, Roseann Pandolfi, and Maria Rincon. For everyone at the Foundation who hasn't given up and who didn't give up and is still striving. For Doreen, Valda, Donna, Louis, Pat, Anna Scharf, Tai, Rich, and Sha-hab. Again to Wally Lamb, who sent a letter when I first got into Fairfield, and then again to HarperCollins to help me land this deal. I started believing in real-life guardian angels when I met that man.

IMPORTANT LINKS AND SITES

National Alliance on Mental Illness at nami.org: The nation's largest nonprofit grassroots mental health education, advocacy, and support organization. It has online support and gets you in touch with local chapters. Pursue them—they have great resources.

National Institute of Mental Health (NIMH) at nimh.nih.gov is another great site.

S.A.F.E. Alternatives at www.selfinjury.org is a nationally recognized treatment approach, professional network, and educational resource base, which is committed to helping you and others achieve an end to self-injurious behavior. 800-DON'T-CUT/800-366-8288.

The Depression and Bipolar Support Alliance at dbs alliance.org has incredible amounts of information and support on mood disorders and bipolar disorder.

GLBTQ at www.thetrevorproject.org is the leading national organization providing crisis intervention and suicide prevention to lesbian, gay, bisexual, transgender, and questioning youth.

Clevelandclinic.com is a trusted source of information on self-injury and bipolar disorder and everything else under the sun.

Two helpful Connecticut sites are:
www.ct.gov/dmhaas
connecticut.networkofcare.org/mh

www.selfinjuryfoundation.org
mindlink.org/rights—info and rights of the mentally ill

CRISIS LINE NUMBERS FOR IMMEDIATE HELP— 24-HOUR NATIONAL CRISIS LINES

800-273-TALK: nmha.org (Mental Health America) an important nonprofit resource and support.
800-SUICIDE (784-2433)
TEEN HOTLINE: 877-332-7333
Boys Town National Hotline: 800-448-3000 (TTY 800-448-1833)